REGIONALIZING CULTURE

REGIONALIZING CULTURE

The Political Economy of
Japanese Popular Culture in Asia

Nissim Kadosh Otmazgin

University of Hawai'i Press
Honolulu

18 17 16 15 14 13   6 5 4 3 2 1

Library of Congress Cataloging-in-Publication Data
Otmazgin, Nissim, author.
Regionalizing culture : the political economy of Japanese
popular culture in Asia / Nissim Kadosh Otmazgin.
pages cm
Includes bibliographical references and index.
ISBN 978-0-8248-3694-8 (cloth : alk. paper)
1. Popular culture—Economic aspects—Japan.
2. Popular culture—Economic aspects—East Asia.
3. Popular culture—Economic aspects—Southeast Asia.
4. Cultural industries—Japan. I. Title.
HD9999.C9473J34 2014
306.30952—dc23
2013008549

Designed by Janette Thompson (Jansom)
Printed by Sheridan Books, Inc.

For Michal Alexander

CONTENTS

////////////////////////

PREFACE

////////////////

Why study Japanese popular culture in Asia? The first reason is that cultural industries are the fastest-growing sectors in many of the world's economies, and in Japan and East Asia they have been increasingly gaining the attention of both the government and the public, encouraged by the possibilities for attaining "soft power." Japan's cultural export industry is an enormous business, which has still, I think, not been given appropriate attention.

The following figures provide some indication of the scale of Japan's cultural exports: According to Sugiura Tsutomu's calculations (2008), the export of popular culture merchandise and related royalties, income, and services coming from products such as recorded sound and image (music, anime, movies, video games), books, magazines, paintings, and art and handicrafts has more than tripled from US$8.37 billion in 1996 to nearly US$25.4 billion in 2006. The rate of this export growth is astounding, especially given that during the same period the export of Japan's total merchandise trade (of both culture- and nonculture-related items) has grown by only 68 percent, from US$447 billion in 1996 to US$752 billion in 2006.

The Japanese government, for its part, has been recently embracing Japan's cultural exports, regarded as economically profitable and diplomatically useful. The state's support for the cultural industries includes a wide range of initiatives involving no fewer than thirteen governmental ministries and agencies, all attempting to take part in this rising sector. A recent example is the establishment of the Creative Industries Division in July 2011, within the Ministry of Economy, Trade and Industry (METI), to supervise Japan's "cool" promotion abroad and assist Japanese small and midsize culture-related firms pursue a global strategy.

The second reason has to do with my own fascination with popular culture's ability to connect different people from different places. While traveling in Asia in the late 1990s, I was surprised to see the dramatic changes taking place in the local popular culture and media markets and the massive scale of regional circulation and consumption of commodities such as movies, pop music, animation, comics, video games, television programs, fashion magazines, and their derivative products such as food, toys, and accessories. I thought that buying a pen, a table map, or a shovel was, after all, different from listening to a music CD, watching a television drama, or reading a comic book. The difference is, I think, in the way cultural products comprise images and messages that can strongly arouse feelings of proximity, as well as convey messages that have a higher potential for shaping the "receiver's" aspirations and identity.

Let me give some examples from my own experience. My first image of Japan, as far as I can remember, was of a society populated entirely by sword-wielding samurai. This image was created through watching the American-made drama *Shogun* at the age of nine or ten. Back then, I was fascinated by the way Japan—its culture and its people—were depicted in this drama. Thereafter, this fascination encouraged me to pursue my interest in things I regarded as "Japanese," such as karate, zen, and sushi, which, in turn, brought me to pay special attention to any newspaper article that talked about Japan. I eagerly listened to stories about Japan from my two sisters who visited the country. In my early twenties, when I decided to travel and study abroad, the choice of Japan was clear.

As a student in Japan, I sometimes went out with friends to sing in a karaoke bar, and this experience reinforced my appreciation for popular culture's ability to connect people. While singing karaoke, I noticed that my European, North American, and South American friends were singing almost the same repertoire of songs, mostly American music. This was the music I myself routinely listened to while a teenager (the time when the bulk of my musical taste was shaped). Chinese and Korean friends, however, were less familiar with these songs.

The third reason for my interest in this topic is that I think the study of Japanese popular culture in Asia is relevant to the study of other cases. Through the examination of the Japanese experience, it is possible to draw important conclusions regarding the role of popular culture in cross-nation processes and dynamics and in international relations beyond the boundaries of the region. Looking at the transnational flow and acceptance of popular culture overturns conventional wisdom as to what the driving forces of change are. One's attention is redirected away from the state and highly institutionalized arrangements and is turned instead to the agency involved in the creation and marketing of culture-oriented commodities. This case study, I hope, will not only be useful for analyzing the impact of the Japanese cultural industries in Asia, but also might help explain similar developments in other cases.

The research for this book was made possible by generous financial and logistical support from several institutions. I gratefully acknowledge funding for field research in Asia and some much-needed time and facilities for writing from the COE Program, the Kyoto Foundation, the Hoso Bunka Foundation, the EU's Marie Curie International Reintegration Grant, the Israel Science Foundation, Cornell University's East Asia Program, the Hebrew University of Jerusalem's Faculty of Humanities, the Harry S. Truman Research Institute for the Advancement of Peace, and the Louis Frieberg Center for East Asian Studies (both under the aegis of the Hebrew University of Jerusalem).

Since the earliest conception of my research, I have received instruction, support, friendship, and insightful readings from so many teachers, colleagues, and friends. First, I thank my advisor, Professor Shiraishi Takashi, whose acquaintance I first made after reading his book when I was an undergraduate at the Hebrew University of Jerusalem. He continued to provide guidance during my graduate studies at Kyoto University and has since provided me with wise direction at various key junctions in my research. My deepest sense of appreciation goes to Caroline Hau, who was a vital source of intellectual stimulation and incisive critique along with vital encouragement and support. My sincere gratitude also goes to Ehud Harari for his scrupulous help in drawing scientific and theoretical tools for my research, and to Ben-Ami Shillony, who was always ready to offer new insights and dimensions when looking at my findings. Peter J. Katzenstein read earlier versions of the manuscript and was of enormous help in placing my research within the right theoretical and conceptual frameworks. Without his help, I could never have completed the book as it is. Since we first met in Kyoto, Eyal Ben-Ari has greatly influenced my work, reading large parts of the manuscript, in some cases many times over. Helena

Grinshpun was always patient when listening to my arguments and ideas during our studies in Kyoto and during countless discussions over the past two years in our shared office space in Jerusalem.

This study has also benefited greatly from discussion and learning from many people, all of whom gave me invaluable advice, help, and criticism. Among them are Hamashita Takeshi, Patricio Abinales, Meron Medzini, Mark Selden, Baruch Knei-Paz, Arieh (Lionel) Babitz, Chua Beng-Huat, Mōri Yoshitaka, Aoyagi Hiroshi, Lisa Leung, Mizuno Kosuke, Hayami Yoko, Jean-Marie Bouissou, Marco Pellitteri, Miki Daliot-Bul, and Mikami Takanori. Shin Hyunjoon and Ubonrart Siriyuvasak were of enormous help during my fieldwork in Seoul and Bangkok, introducing me to valuable sources and sharing with me their experience and knowledge.

My colleagues from the Department of East Asian Studies and the Truman Institute at the Hebrew University of Jerusalem were always ready to offer a critical eye along with advice and encouragement. I wish to thank Steven Kaplan, Yuri Pines, Gideon Shelach, Lihi Yariv-Laor, Michal Biran, Orna Naftali, Galia Press-BarNathan, Arie Kacowicz, Avraham Sela, Sigal Ben-Rafael Galanti, Yona Siderer, Shalmit Bejarano, Tsujita Kyōji and Mariko, Noa Oppenheim, Galit Aviman, Yagi Morris, Alon Levkowitz, Yishay Yafe, Noga Efrati, Lena Shillony, Menahem Blondheim, and Ofer Feldman. My thanks also go to the Truman Institute's administrative staff for the supportive and warm environment: Naama Shpeter, Hillary Gordon, Cheryl Cashriel, Miriam Ben-Dor, Kochava Klimuk, Meital Cohen, and to the secretary of the Department of East Asian Studies, Kinneret Levy.

I am grateful to Patricia Crosby at the University of Hawai'i Press for sharing my enthusiasm for this project and for making this book a reality. My gratitude also goes to the production team at UHP and to two anonymous reviewers for their excellent comments on the manuscript. I wish to thank Drew Bryan, who did a wonderful job copy editing the text; Yoshida Chiharu, who carefully read the manuscript and checked the Japanese names; and Ariel Goldstein, who helped me compose the tables and the bibliography.

The encouragement given by colleagues and friends is fully appreciated. My thanks also go to all my fellow students and friends who patiently listened to my presentations and ideas and shared with me their knowledge and thoughts. Among them are Benoît Jacquet, Kati Lindstrom, Jamie and Katharine Ravetz, Assaf Harlap, Dalia Ganor, Ruti

Harari, Avi Lugassi, Doron and Ada Cohen, Yoshida Chiharu, Morita Toshihiko, Azuma Thooru, Azuma Miyuki, Takashima Toshiyuki, Kyogoku Kenichi, Aizawa Nobuhiro, Okamoto Masaaki, Kitamura Yumi, Oka Michitaro, Onimaru Takeshi, Morishita Akiko, Uchida Haruko, Kawano Motoko, Nakanishi Yoshihiro, Nathan Bedenoch, Lim Boon Hock, Suzuki Shinji, Kobayashi Satoru, Chalermpol Chamchan, Wahyu Presetyawan, Achakorn Wongpreedee, Changna Shishir, Matsuura Mikiy, Andi Amri, Belle Asante, Maruyama Akiko (Beatriz), Kusuda Kenta, Endō Tamaki, Hosoda Naomi, Yamaguchi Kiyoko, Miyauchi Haruna, Yoshimura Chie, Matsumoto Mariko, Nasir Uddin, Tsunashima Hiroyuki, Mizutani Yasuhiro, and Murakami Saki.

I would also like to convey my sincere gratitude to all those people, too numerous to name here, who gave up their valuable time to be interviewed by me during my fieldwork research in Tokyo, Hong Kong, Singapore, Shanghai, Bangkok, and Seoul.

Finally, I would like to express my heartfelt thanks to my parents, Miryan and Yitzhak, and my four sisters, Naomi, Ziva, Osnat, and Hagar, for their many years of encouragement and support, and to my life partner, Junko Otmazgin, for the continuous understanding, patience, and assistance, and for sharing with me the love of our two children, Eden and Kfir.

Nissim Kadosh Otmazgin
Jerusalem, December 2012

I acknowledge the following sources, where earlier and substantially different versions of some parts of chapters 2 and 3 appeared as "Cultural Commodities and Regionalization in Southeast Asia," *Contemporary Southeast Asia*, 2005, vol. 27, no. 3, pp. 499–523; and "Contesting Soft Power: Japanese Popular Culture in East and Southeast Asia," *International Relations of the Asia Pacific*, 2008, vol. 8, no. 1, pp. 73–101.

The comments and help I received from all professors, colleagues, and friends were of immense importance, both in pointing out problems in my analytical argument and in helping to overcome some of the pitfalls. Whatever merits this book might have are very much due to them. I am of course solely responsible for the many remaining faults.

A Note to Readers

Romanization follows the Hepburn style; macrons indicate long vowels.

Japanese names follow the practice of surname first except for those authors who regularly publish in English. Japanese words are translated according to the Kenkyusha dictionary system.

Yen-to-dollar exchange rates are calculated according to the Research and Statistics Department of the Bank of Japan (www.stat.go.jp).

INTRODUCTION

////////////////////////////////

Popular Culture and Regionalization

During the past two decades, Japanese popular culture products have been widely disseminated and consumed throughout East Asia.[1] As a visitor to any of the region's big cities can easily observe, Japanese popular culture is widely available as part of a confluence of American, Chinese, Korean, and other popular cultures. Many of the fashion journals sold in Hong Kong are from Japan, whether in the original Japanese or in a translated Cantonese edition. In virtually every big city in East Asia there are shops that specialize in Japanese-style clothing and accessories, updated with the latest fashions from Tokyo. Japanese comic books (manga) are routinely translated into Korean, Thai, Bahasa, and Mandarin, and they dominate East Asia's comic book markets. Japanese animated characters, such as *Hello Kitty, Anpan Man,* and *Poke'mon* are ubiquitous, seen on licensed and unlicensed toys and stationery in the markets of just about every Asian city. Japanese animation (anime), usually dubbed, is the most popular in its genre. *Astro Boy, Sailor Moon,* and *Lupin* are successful examples of animated characters seen in almost every shop that sells anime in Hong Kong, Singapore, or Taipei. In bookshops and kiosks across this region's big cities, it is possible to find translated or original versions of famous Japanese fashion magazines such as *CanCan, JJ, ViVi, COOL, Cutie, Vita, Myojo, Brand,* and *nonno.* Japanese music has also become well established in urban areas and accounts for a share of music markets throughout the region. Live concerts by Japanese musicians draw thousands of fans across East Asia, fueling interest in Japanese contemporary culture. Karaoke bars commonly offer a wide repertory of Japanese songs. Japanese music artists such as Hamasaki Ayumi or Nakashima Mika, and Japanese bands such as SMAP, Wind, AKB48, or L'arc-en-ciel are but a few of the names that are widely known to East Asian youngsters but which remain relatively unknown in Europe, South America, and the Middle East.

In the 1990s and early 2000s, Japanese popular culture occupied a sizable position in the popular culture markets of East Asia. According to a survey conducted in 2006 by *Yomiuri Shinbun* (one of Japan's leading daily newspapers), 25 percent of South Koreans aged eighteen or older prefer anime and comics from Japan over American or locally made animation, compared to 30 percent of adults in Indonesia and Malaysia, 18 percent in Thailand, and 12 percent in Vietnam. For movies, the figures were 10 percent in South Korea, 21 percent in Indonesia, 18 percent in Malaysia, 19 percent in Thailand, and 12 percent in Vietnam.[2] Japanese pop music was estimated to occupy between 15 and 20 percent of the music market in Hong Kong during its peak period from 1996 to 1999, and between 8 and 12 percent in 2003. In Singapore, the share of Japanese music was estimated at 8 to 10 percent of the music market between 1996 and 1998, and about 5 percent in 2003. In Bangkok, estimates for the years 2002 and 2003 were 4 to 6 percent. In Seoul, Japanese music was estimated to have captured between 10 and 12 percent of the music market in the first six months after the market was opened to Japanese cultural products in 2002, and approximately 7 to 9 percent in 2004.[3] Japanese television dramas were also popular in South Korea, before the mounting success of Korean and Chinese dramas in recent years. According to figures released in 2007 by Japan's Ministry of Internal Affairs and Communication, approximately 60 percent of TV programs exported from Japan in 2005 were broadcast within Asia. According to a 2002 survey conducted by Hakuhodō, Japan's second largest advertising company, 10 percent of Bangkok residents polled expressed a preference for Japanese television dramas over other types of TV dramas; this was the same percentage that indicated a preference for American television dramas. The popularity of Japanese TV dramas outstripped that of American dramas in Hong Kong, Singapore, and three Chinese cities: Beijing, Shanghai, and Guangzhou. Japanese television dramas ranked second in popularity among youngsters in Hong Kong, with 65 percent watching Chinese dramas, 22 percent watching Japanese dramas, and 8 percent watching American television dramas.[4]

This book poses two central questions about the variety of Japanese popular culture products found in markets throughout Asia: (1) Why has Japan's popular culture proliferated in urban East Asia? (2) Given this proliferation, how is popular culture likely to affect the dynamics of regional formation in East Asia? My answer to the first question is simple: In order to understand the pervasive presence of Japanese popular culture in East Asia, we need to look at the organizational aspects of cultural production rather than limiting ourselves to identifying distinctive sociocultural features or narratives that are presumed to be embedded in Japanese cultural commodities and resonant with Asian consumers. We can better understand the spread of Japanese popular culture throughout East Asia by looking at the mechanisms assembled by the culture industries in order to commercialize, manufacture, and commodify[5] popular culture.

My answer to the second question is more far-reaching. In this book, I argue that the proliferation of Japanese cultural industries in East Asia provides new insights into the relationship between cultural commodification and the notion of regionalization. By regionalization, I refer to an indirect, bottom-up process that increases proximity between markets, institutions, and communities within geographical and conceptual domains broader than two states. The experience of Japanese cultural industries in East Asia over the past three decades shows that the expansion of cultural industries into new markets, motivated by a desire for more consumers for those industries' products or services, plays an important role in fostering market-driven, consumer-oriented mechanisms that have broad political and social implications for the region. Those mechanisms promote the evolution of regional cultural markets and propagate a regionwide transformation of structural arrangements and policies to commodify and market culture, hence supporting regionalization. The resulting circulation of popular culture contributes to region making not only from an institutional standpoint, that is, the creation of transnational markets and the establishment of collaborative ties between all relevant parties (companies, agents, promoters, distributors, retailers, etc.), but also in terms of the dissemination of lifestyle communalities and concepts that occurs when different people in different places consume the same cultural products.

Popular culture plays a constructive role in pulling people closer together by providing them with shared experiences. The commodifica-

tion, production, marketing, pirating, and consumption of popular culture leads to the construction of new frameworks for delivering images,
ideas, and emotional expressions that can stimulate feelings of proximity
and belonging. The spread of popular culture may help people across
Asia develop a common language made up of the same sounds, images,
and texts available on CDs and DVDs, on TVs and movie screens, in
comic publications, on commercial billboards, or via the Internet. These
commodities and images need not be uniquely Asian as long as they are
shared by wide segments of the Asian population.

Obviously, cultural industries are not the single determinant of
regionalization, nor is popular culture the only conceptual key that
explains regionalization's inner dynamics. The claims I make here, however, are that the politics and economics of regionalization necessitate an
examination of cultural industries, and that the transformation generated by the regionalization process cannot be properly understood until
regional developments in the organization of commodified culture are
better grasped and fully contextualized.

In other words, popular culture is an important aspect of regionalization. Looking at the circulation of popular culture in East Asia advances
our empirical and theoretical understanding of how regionalization
actually works and, more basically, what constitutes a "region." First, it
sheds light on the impact of nonstate forces that have no political center
and—in a market economy—are not controlled by governments. Second,
focusing on popular culture overturns conventional wisdom about the
driving forces and actors behind regionalization. It directs one's attention away from highly institutionalized arrangements, such as security
alliances and free trade agreements (FTAs) and looks instead at agencies
involved in the creation and marketing of cultural commodities.

To support this argument, I develop a three-part explanation. First, I
show that the Japanese domestic market is home to a highly developed
machinery for producing and commercializing popular culture, one with
specific features that differentiate it from the "Hollywood model" of making popular culture. These features have made Japan a major producer
and exporter of popular culture to East Asia and an object of regional
emulation. Second, I explain how the Japanese cultural industries have
become integrated into markets for popular culture throughout urban
East Asia. Not only does the emergence of these markets allow different
people in different places to share the same set of cultural commodities

and thus offer the ability to share lifestyles and ideas about how to live, but it also encourages cooperation among all those involved in commodifying and commercializing culture, including producers, promoters, entrepreneurs, agents, distributors, etc. Lastly, I demonstrate that Japanese cultural industries have been exporting standardized popular culture organizational methods and production formats, which have been gradually adopted by local industries. For many local producers outside Japan, Japanese industries represent a forerunner and a model of how to construct a developed popular culture industry that can offer an alternative to American cultural products. The development of organizational arrangements used for commodifying and commercializing culture in East Asia is thus heavily influenced by the methods and experiences introduced by the Japanese cultural industries. In many fields the Japanese model for organizing popular culture has become the regional standard.

In the following chapters, I show that by creating new markets for Japanese popular culture and by implanting the "Japanese model" of popular culture production, the cultural industries have propagated a transformation of the structural arrangements used for commodifying and commercializing popular culture. Understanding the adaptation of Japanese organizational methods for cultural production in East Asia is important not only because of the images Japanese popular culture reflects or the cultural practices it engenders (such as *cosplay*, whereby fans gather to show off costumes that imitate their favorite anime heroes), but also because such acceptance and adaptation underpin a deeper transformation of cognitive frames, cultural views, and structural arrangements related to "culture."

I would like to make my argument clear: I am not suggesting that the operations of Japanese cultural industries ultimately lead to the formation of a Japanese-dominated regional identity in East Asia, to the homogenization of cultural practices, or to the imposition of Japanese norms and values on local societies. The flow of popular culture in East Asia is multidirectional. A variety of other popular culture confluences, both global (American) and regional (Chinese, Korean), have rapidly intensified in recent years and Japan itself has become an avid importer of popular culture from other parts of East Asia, although there is a conspicuous asymmetry in the import-export ratio, with Japan generally exporting much more popular culture within East Asia than it imports from the region.

In addition, although cultural industries create *platforms* upon which different people in different places in East Asia are exposed to a variety of Japanese popular culture products, and possibly to a new range of images and messages, these cannot be read in any monolithic way. The consumption of popular culture is a highly generic process wherein the images and "meanings" extracted from products tend to diversify and are subject to individual interpretations. Consumers, after all, are active subjects who try to make sense of what they see and hear, rather than passive subjects entirely manipulated by the producers or marketers of cultural commodities.

The intriguing question about the choice of the Japanese case remains: To what extent can Japan be considered a useful case study for exploring the relevance of popular culture production in other parts of East Asia? I believe we can extrapolate from findings in the Japanese context to understand similar developments in East Asia and possibly beyond. The Japanese case exemplifies how popular culture can effect regional formation, both in general by creating shared markets for popular culture, and specifically in terms of how Japan's cultural industries influence the development of local industries, which have conspicuously adopted the Japanese production and marketing model. At the same time, it is important to note that the regional circulation of Japanese popular culture and the expansion of Japan's cultural industries within the region are not Tokyo-sponsored operations aimed at constructing a new regional identity, nor do they manifest any Japanese cultural hegemony in the sense of domination or control. Rather, Japan's cultural "power" shows up as the ability to influence the organizational basis for popular culture in East Asia.

Outline of the Book

The title "Regionalizing Culture: The Political Economy of Japanese Popular Culture in Asia" reflects my effort to grasp the dynamics of popular culture production and dissemination in East Asia by using a big-picture, political-economic approach rather than engaging in detailed content analysis of certain products, images, or genres. The title also hints at the indirect consequences of these processes on region making in East Asia and on the very notion of a "region." On the one hand, many Japanese popular culture products have been regionalized in the sense that they are present in East Asia in a variety and concentration unseen in any other part of the world. On the other hand, these popular culture operations themselves have an impact on the regionalization of East Asia by connecting culture and economy and by creating links between various industries and communities across the region.

In this introduction, I have outlined the phenomenon this research is concerned with, that is, the salient presence of Japanese culture in East Asia. I have introduced the central argument of my study: that cultural industries underpin regionalization in East Asia by creating markets and propagating a regionwide transformation of the structural framework for commodifying and appropriating culture.

In chapter 1, I develop an analytical model that combines a traditional political-economic approach with an approach that considers characteristics specific to the popular culture market. I briefly review theoretical supports offered in the field and underline their advantages and limitations. I then examine the relations between "popular culture," "high culture," and "cultural industries." These terms have a complex history, and their meanings demand clarification. I identify and map associated products, fields, and activities, and I examine the distinctive ways in which cultural industries operate.

In chapter 2, I offer an orientation to understanding East Asian regionalization. I look at the main characteristics of this "region" and show that popular culture is intrinsically significant to the regionalization process in East Asia. The chapter highlights some conspicuous characteristics of East Asian regionalization: namely that it is essentially market-driven and overwhelmingly focuses on urban centers with large populations of middle-class residents and not on nation-states as a whole. After clarifying major concepts related to "regionalism" and "regionalization" in East Asia, the chapter establishes a regional paradigm for analyzing Japanese cultural industries, showing that a dynamic East Asian popular cultural market has already been in the making for the past two decades and has greatly contributed to the regionalization process.

Chapter 3 examines the Japanese cultural industries in their domestic market by looking at (a) how culture is commodified, (b) the size of the domestic market, and (c) Japan's cultural exports portfolio. Here I posit that the structure and size of the domestic market and the experience of Japan's cultural industries at home have fostered the competitiveness of Japanese cultural products abroad. The chapter shows that the Japanese domestic marketplace is home to a highly developed machinery for producing and commercializing popular culture. This chapter also analyzes the Japanese government's growing involvement in the country's cultural exports over the past two decades and the importance attributed to this topic in Japanese public discourse. The chapter shows how the development of cultural industries has modified government policy regarding popular culture, and it notes that the development of cultural industries has now become an item on the Japanese government's economic and diplomatic agendas.

Chapter 4 describes the creation of a regional market for Japanese popular culture. It examines the expansion of Japanese music and television companies into East Asia since the end of the 1980s and provides a quantitative analysis of the market share of Japanese music and television programs in the region. The chapter shows how Japanese music and television companies have become actively involved in local cultural scenes and demonstrates that Japanese music and television have carved out a sizable position in East Asia's markets. Chapter 4 also examines the role of piracy in enhancing the dissemination of Japanese cultural commodities in East Asia, underlining its role as an efficient distributor of popular culture.

Chapter 5 investigates the impact of Japanese cultural industries on local cultural industries in East Asia. It discusses their influence on local cultural production and appreciation for Japanese products. It argues that the importance of Japanese cultural industries lies not only in the carving out of transnational market share, but also in regionwide dissemination of cultural production formats and the resulting organizational transformations. The chapter starts by examining the transfer of Japanese cultural formats to the culture markets of East Asia and their adaptation by local cultural industries, especially in Korea. The chapter ends with a summary of in-depth interviews with sixty-eight cultural industry insiders in East Asia and examines why there is a high appreciation for Japanese cultural products and production formats. It shows that high product quality and the power of Japanese branding are the main reasons for the success of Japanese popular culture products in the East Asian market.

Chapter 6 summarizes the book's main findings and explores its implications. It then discusses the impact of the expansion of Japanese cultural industries on the regionalization process in East Asia and offers wider analytical and theoretical insights into the relations between popular culture and regional formation.

Empirical Research

Although there is much anecdotal evidence about the popularity of Japanese culture in East Asia, there is no comprehensive source of empirical information. Providers of official statistics in Japan and in the rest of East Asia have not mapped out the cultural industries sector, so relevant information is either unavailable or is listed in a series of overlapping categories, such as art, entertainment, leisure, culture, media, sport, etc. Most existing studies on Japanese popular culture abroad focus on specific examples and emphasize textual representations and the reaction of audiences to cultural exposure (for example, Craig and King 2002; Allen and Sakamoto 2006; Allison 2006; Inoue 2010; Ishii 2001; Iwabuchi 2004; Martinez 1998; Moeran 2000; Mōri 2004; Mitsui and Hosokawa 1998; and Treat 1996). Moreover, while there are many works dealing with Western-based cultural industries (Beck 2003; Hartley 2005; Hesmondhalgh 2002; Holt and Perren 2009), there are very few in English or Japanese that comprehensively analyze the mechanisms and capabilities of Japanese cultural industries.

In recent years a growing number of scholars have turned their attention to the production side of culture and media (Mayer, Banks, and Caldwell 2009; Caldwell 2008; and Ross 2004) and to related labor conditions (Caves 2002; Christopherson and van Jaarsveld 2005; Baker and Hesmondhalgh 2010), but their work has focused on the Euro-American experience. Notable exceptions are Hamano (2003) and Nakamura (2003, 2004), who examine the structure of Japanese cultural industries in the domestic market, and Berry, Liscutin, and Mackintosh (2009), who look at how popular and media culture shape Northeast Asia from a cultural studies approach that focuses on "creative industries" and their growing importance in an era of globalization.

Given the lack of hard data on this topic, the empirical side of this study has two central aims. The first is to evaluate the degree of popularity and the variety of Japanese popular culture products in local markets, both in quantitative and qualitative terms. The second is to examine the impact of Japan's cultural industries on the local cultural industries of East Asia. The latter task makes it possible to demonstrate that in addition to content export and the carving out of market share, the externalization of cultural production formats is also a factor in the overall impact of Japanese cultural industries in East Asia.

The research focuses on East Asia's nine biggest markets for Japanese cultural exports: Hong Kong, Taiwan, South Korea, Singapore, Indonesia, Malaysia, mainland China, Thailand, and the Philippines. It is based on data taken from export records, market surveys, and case studies of Japanese music and television companies' activities in these markets. It also includes approximately eleven months of fieldwork in Hong Kong, Singapore, Shanghai, Bangkok, and Seoul between April 2004 and June 2006, and again in June 2010 and October 2011.

In the course of my research I employed a variety of methods, including in-depth interviews, fieldwork, data analysis, and reading of empirical material in English, Japanese, and other languages. First, I conducted in-depth interviews with sources in the cultural industries, in Japan and other locations in East Asia.[6] The interviewees were all directly or indirectly engaged in producing, promoting, marketing, regulating, or studying popular culture in East Asia, especially Japanese popular culture. They included sixty-eight individuals from major music and television companies in Hong Kong, Singapore, Shanghai, Bangkok, and Seoul, as well as government officials, officials from affiliated organizations, academics, media specialists, promoters, and workers from media-related organizations. I asked them questions regarding (1) local cultural markets, especially regarding music, television, and piracy; (2) the popularity, appreciation for, and demand for Japanese popular culture products in comparison to other popular culture products in the market—both domestically produced and imported; (3) cooperation with Japanese culture companies' personnel, agents, and promoters; and (4) their opinions on various aspects of contemporary culture, society, and politics in East Asia.

Next, I conducted a survey of 172 shops selling mostly music, movies, television programs, and animation series in Hong Kong, Singapore, Shanghai, Bangkok, and Seoul, from April 2004 to May 2005. The survey examined the number of titles of Japanese cultural products offered at each store relative to American and locally manufactured products. During the survey, the shops' managers and workers were also asked about the popularity of Japanese music, television programs, animation, and movies, and about the general preferences of consumers who visited the shops.

Third, I conducted a survey of primary sources in Japanese, English, and other languages about the export, presence, and consumption of Japanese popular culture in East Asia. These materials included white papers, think tank reports, advertising companies' estimates, cultural preference surveys of consumers, government statistics and data, and other related publications.

A fourth tool of investigation was consultation and exchange of information with researchers, journalists, and other specialists in Japan, East Asia, and elsewhere, as well as a review of literature related to cultural commodification, industrialization, and regionalization. This background literature will be introduced throughout the book, but I would like to mention here a few studies that were particularly helpful: the works of Hesmondhalgh (2002), Hartley (2005), Castells (1996, 2000a), and Cottle (2003) regarding how cultural and information industries operate; the works of Iwabuchi (2002) and Allison (2006) on Japanese popular culture outside of Japan; the works of Borrus, Ernst, and Haggard (2000), Ernst (2006), and Hatch and Yamamura (1996) on the Japanese automobile and electronics industries in East Asia; and the studies of Katzenstein (2005), Katzenstein and Shiraishi (1997, 2006), and Pempel (2005) on the regionalization process in East Asia.

CHAPTER 1

////////////////////

The Political Economy
of Popular Culture

This book is about the political economy of Japanese popular culture within East Asia. By "political economy," I mean the relationship between economic matters (such as the workings of markets) and political affairs (such as the decisions of government agencies). I use the term "popular culture" to refer to commercial cultural commodities, such as television dramas, music, and animation, and their derivative products (such as games, foods, magazines, toys, accessories, or stationery) and spin-offs (such as DVDs and video-on-demand). By "East Asia," I refer to urban areas of both Northeast and Southeast Asia.

The focus of this book is on the character, dynamics, and wider implications of the recent emergence of regional production, marketing, and consumption systems that support popular culture in East Asia. It seeks to understand the cultural economics underlying this field and the processes of regionwide sharing of cultural formulas and styles. Specifically, I have looked at the operations and strategies of Japanese cultural industries, which organize the commodification, manufacturing, and marketing of Japanese popular culture in East Asia, and their responses to the changing political and economic environment of this region over the past three decades. In addition to focusing on Japanese cultural industries, the book explores the production and exploitation of "culture" in the context of regional circulation of cultural commodities and images; it seeks to investigate a regional economy of popular culture.

What is "political economy" and how does it relate to popular culture? For much of the twentieth century, political economy was viewed as both a field of study that examines relationships between economics and politics and as a synthesis of economics-related methodological approaches applied to the analysis of political behaviors and institutions (Weingast and Wittman 2006, 3; Gilpin 2001, 3). George Kurian (2002, 265–266) defines three major traditions of political economy: classical political economy as expounded by François Quesnay, Adam Smith, David Ricardo, and other physiocrats who believed in a "natural order" of economic life; the Marxist interpretation, which emphasizes economic explanations for political decisions; and the modern tradition, which primarily addresses questions arising from the intersection of economic and political affairs and uses statistical modeling techniques to explain politicoeconomic phenomena.

The terms "critical political economy" and "political economics of communication and culture" are relatively new concepts associated with cultural and media studies. The first term relates to the "Frankfurt School," especially to the works of Theodor Adorno and Max Horkheimer. Adorno and Horkheimer used this term to signal their disgust with the commercialization of artisanship. According to their view, when art is devalued by being repackaged into a mass-consumption commodity, it loses its tradition, spirituality, and other "high" moral assets (Adorno 1991; Adorno and Horkheimer 1973). The second term is used more frequently in media and communication studies, especially in reference to print and broadcast media. This term implies a focus on ownership and control of media-related industries, interconnections between media conglomerates and smaller companies, and links between the private sector and government (Golding and Murdock 2000; McQuail 1994; Mosco 1996; Napoli 2009).

The study of popular culture from a political economic approach is relatively new. So far, it has been the object of little cross-level or cross-disciplinary academic research, and its terminology is yet to be fully defined. In East Asia, the majority of studies on Japanese popular culture outside Japan have been rooted in anthropology or cultural studies and have taken an ethnographic and interpretive approach, with a focus on case studies and a strong tendency to prioritize analysis of textual content and images used in popular culture (for example, Craig 2000; Allen and Sakamoto 2006; Allison 2006; Berry, Liscutin, and Mackintosh

2009; Craig 2000; Desser 2003; Inoue 2010; Ishii 2001; Iwabuchi 2004; Martinez 1998; Mitsui and Hosokawa 1998; Mōri 2004; Soderberg and Reader 2000; Treat 1996). These studies provide substantial testimony for the proliferation of popular culture confluences and contain rich information and valuable analyses related to the practice and "meaning" of popular culture. But because their focus is mainly on the consumption of popular culture and on the images it reflects, the production and distribution networks that put popular cultural products into circulation tend to be overlooked or referred to only in passing (Otmazgin 2008b).

At the same time, the fields of political science and economics have paid little attention to the study of popular culture—especially that of East Asia. Because they do not regard "cultural industries" as a viable object of analysis, these disciplines largely ignore this sector or label it unimportant. Very few studies have examined the impact of cultural industries on regionalization in general or the impact of Japanese cultural industries on the regionalization process in East Asia in particular. Notable exceptions include Katzenstein (2005) and Leheny (2006). In his book *A World of Regions* (2005, 150–156, 162–167), Peter J. Katzenstein indicates possible reciprocity between Japanese popular culture and regionalization in East Asia. David Leheny's study (2006) focuses on the discourse generated by Japan's cultural presence in other parts of Asia and its relevance to soft power theory. These works provide a good starting point for exploring Japan's popular culture in the context of the region. Neither, however, identifies the industrial clusters that facilitate the circulation of popular culture, as they are more concerned with citing specific cultural products or practices to support their arguments.

The wider literature on the production of cultural commodities provides some theoretical and methodological support to the study of popular culture,[1] despite a Euro-American-centric tilt and disagreements between political economists and cultural studies scholars over the nature of the relationship between economy and culture. To attempt to disentangle or unitize two overarching theoretical traditions—political economy and cultural studies—or to explore their definitions in any depth, would be far beyond the scope of this book.[2] It may be useful, though, to address those of their analytical foci that touch directly upon the production or distribution of cultural products in order to develop a framework that might make it possible to transcend some of the limitations imposed by any one discipline.

Broadly speaking, political economists tend to see the production of culture as the result of capitalized manufacture of cultural commodities, while cultural and media studies scholars view any production as something embedded in a particular socioeconomic context, to the extent that contemporary economic relations have been "culturalized."[3] Nicholas Garnham (1995, 2005), one of the most ardent supporters of the political economic approach, insists that we cannot understand the practices and manifestations of culture without analyzing its political economic foundations because certain core structural characteristics of the capitalist mode of production—such as the market, available material resources, necessary technology, etc.—shape the terrain upon which cultural practice takes place. Garnham identifies the *production* process as the primary focus of any analysis of culture, because this process determines the range of consumption options and the wider social effects of those choices. Similarly, Andrew Calabrese (2004, 9–10) argues that production and consumption of culture are parts of a single linear process that is "contained" by the economy. Under this logic, the production of culture is equivalent to any other pursuit of material means and culture should therefore be treated like any other rationally and industrially produced commodity.

Cultural studies scholars disagree. They argue that what matters is the *culture of production* rather than the *production of culture* (cf. du Gay and Pryke 2000; Negus and Pickering 2004). According to their view, economic organizations are embedded in a particular sociocultural context and exposed to various cultural discourses so that any form of production is cultural production. For them, the development of an economy is the result of cultural beliefs, behaviors, perceptions, symbols, values etc., and not the other way around. Cultural studies scholar Lawrence Grossberg (1995, 76) epitomizes this view: "Certainly economic practices and relations determine the distribution of practices and commodities (although not entirely by themselves), but do they determine which meanings circulate and which do not? I doubt it. Those articulations are much more complex and difficult to describe. The fact that certain institutions (and individuals) would like to control how people interpret text or what they do with it does not mean that 'intention' actually determines what people do and think, that is, the effects of practices. Are the real effects determined? Of course, but in very complex ways, across a multiplicity of planes and dimensions, of codes and structures, as the result of a particular struggle to articulate particular sorts of practices to particular sorts of effects."

There are others, however, who find a middle path that bridges these two extreme approaches. Economist Robert E. Babe (2009, 4–9) offers a dialectical middle ground. He agrees with economic historian Harold Adams Innis, who says that throughout human history, culture and cultural artifacts have supported and were simultaneously supported by their surrounding society's predominant mode of economic and political organization. In this sense, culture and political economy have long been mutually supportive. Babe goes on to claim that political economy and media and cultural studies were fully integrated during their formative years until the poststructuralist turn taken by cultural studies in the 1960s and 1970s caused them to split into hostile camps. He further posits that political economy and cultural studies can be reintegrated on the basis of cultural materialism. Another notable middle-ground approach is offered by media studies scholars Bilton and Cummings (2010), Caves (2002), Baker and Hesmondhalgh (2010), and Cottle (2003). For them, research in the field should look at *workplace practices* in the media industries, using an ethnographic approach that puts workers in those industries at the center of the analysis. According to Simon Cottle (2003, 4), "attending to how these producers practically manage and 'mediate' a complex of forces (economic, political, regulatory, technological, professional, cultural, normative) that variously facilitate, condition and constrain their forms of media output reveals further levels of insight and understanding."

An Integrative Approach to the Study of Popular Culture

Building on the work of Castells (2000a) on the information society and McQuail (1994) on media industries, and considering the theoretical traditions discussed earlier, I favor an integrative political economic approach to the study of popular culture, one that defines the fields and strategies it uses and underlines both their advantages and limitations.

The political economic approach to the study of popular culture focuses on analyzing cultural industries by using economic models and other analytical and intellectual tools used for analyzing manufacturing industries in general. This approach concentrates on the economic and industrial aspects of the story, explores questions related to the interaction of politics and economics, and provides a better view of the big picture by articulating the relations between cultural industries, the market, and government.

Several key features distinguish the political economic approach from earlier ethnographic and interpretive studies. The political economic approach essentially relates to popular culture as it would to any other industrially produced commodity, in the sense that it consciously ignores messages, meanings, and narratives in favor of viewing popular culture in economic terms such as monetary value. This approach to analyzing a television drama, for example, pays little attention to the social and cultural messages the drama reflects in favor of analyzing information regarding the cost and organization of production, distribution routes, number of broadcast hours, economic value generated, and the "product's" broader commercial potential.

To understand the economic system that enables production and distribution of popular culture commodities, we also need to look at newly emerging *organizational arrangements* (both formal and informal) related to the commodification, manufacturing, and marketing of popular culture. These arrangements are important because they form part of the financial, transnational, and commercial infrastructure that underpins previously studied subjects such as audience reception or text analysis. The political economic approach looks not only at production processes, but at the production and distribution system as a whole in order to identify participating companies, networks, and agents and to examine their strategies, their responses to macroeconomic conditions that cause fluctuations in consumption of cultural commodities, and available distribution and marketing routes. All these factors influence the organization and operations of cultural industries and the ability of the sector as a whole to provide popular culture to consumers.

Another key feature of the political economic approach is its focus on *technology*. Technology is imperative to all stages of commodifying and marketing culture and is therefore an integral part of the analysis. Technology in popular culture might mean the application of knowledge to create a product (for example a television program or a pop music album), reproduce copies of it (for instance, in the form of a DVD or CD), deliver it to consumers (through satellite TV, Internet, or trade), or enable consumption of it (by providing a TV set, sound system, or DVD player, etc.).

As chapters 2 and 4 further discuss, the dissemination of widely accessible technological tools for reproducing and consuming cultural content has vitalized regional circulation of popular culture in East Asia. The broad dissemination of TV sets, sound systems, personal computers, and DVD players has enabled people to consume cultural content on a daily basis. These technologies have also spurred cheap reproduction of cultural commodities and are especially important to the lucrative pirating operations of East Asia, which are based on cheap manufacturing and the ready transfer of products to new audiences. Today, anyone with a recording device can burn pirated CDs, VCDs, or DVDs containing movies, television programs, or music for distribution to waiting consumers, and anyone with a computer or smartphone and Internet access can download and distribute cultural content online.

In addition, the political economic approach looks at how cultural industries are affected by government regulation, especially at the national level. State regulation can come in various forms, including restrictions, sanctions, initiatives, and subsidies, which may aim to restrict, regulate, or support the production or marketing of popular culture. Although many of the processes examined in this book are transnational in nature, national governments remain important in that they can stimulate or stifle the production and circulation of cultural commodities. Even studies on the production of Internet-based media, considered the most vibrant and resilient media of our time, have shown that state policy continues to shape the work of cultural industries well into the age of globalization (Christopherson and van Jaarsveld 2005). In recent years, East Asian governments have realized that their previous attempts to direct the flow of popular culture were ineffective (Otmazgin 2005, 514), but that has not stopped them from continuing to try to intervene in determining which popular culture commodities citizens should consume or which products local cultural industries should offer. Some countries try to steer the market by imposing quotas for domestic production or limiting the operations of foreign companies. Such tactics are especially common in Malaysia and China, where mass media is subject to tighter government control.

Like other methods, the political economic approach considers the characteristics of specific popular culture markets and the distinctive ways in which cultural industries operate. The approach recognizes that the people, companies, and networks that run cultural industries make their decisions in the context of specific sets of conditions, constraints, and institutions, which obviously have an impact on the outcomes. Although the end goal of cultural industries remains the generation of profits, their work is affected by specific economic and structural conditions. This is why a specifically applied understanding of the popular culture market is needed.

Moreover, while it is true that popular culture can be commodified and commercialized like any other commodity, it is still distinguished by special qualities. This is because popular culture commodities—more than most other commodities—are likely to provide context that helps people fulfill a wide range of social and personal purposes and encourages the development of new aspirations. Consider, for example, the role of Hollywood movies and television in introducing "the American way of life," how the Beatles and the rest of British pop culture affected youth's relationship with authority, or the impact of Japanese anime on Asian youngsters' fascination with Japan. After all, using a pencil, a chair, or a frying pan does not affect the consumer in the same way that watching a movie, reading a comic book, or listening to music does. The difference lies in how popular culture products reflect messages and narratives that have greater potential to shape people's images and identities (Story 1999, 128). Thus, the industries that organize and handle popular culture not only construct mechanisms for commodifying and marketing popular culture but also unintentionally generate value in terms of feelings, identification, and perceptions. These unintended consequences are likely to have broader, more long-term effects on the lives of consumers than the immediate profit-seeking operations.

Finally, the political economic approach acknowledges its own methodological limitations, especially when it comes to analyzing the process of consumption. Although I agree with the view that economic organization and economic logic provide a solid explanation for the production and distribution of popular culture commodities, I do not think that cultural industries are able to determine the exact meanings that might be attached to products or to anticipate the interpretations that consumers will give to cultural commodities. Consumption is a highly selective process that includes the individualization of positions, the redefinition of values, and the fragmentation of messages (Castells 2000b, 7; Tomlinson 1997, 181). "Meanings" are therefore constantly being contested, redefined, and diversified, and they cannot be read in any monolithic way.

This does not mean that a political economic approach should stay away from audience research or from examining the process of consumption. It does mean that it is impossible to interpret the meaning or articulation of cultural commodities by looking only at the production side. A political economy approach that looks only at production offers little support for determining how capitalistically and rationally produced popular culture products eventually shape the identities of consumers in certain communities.

When it comes to consumer reception, specific ethnographic studies are more useful than studies that look only at production. The case of Japanese fashion in Busan, South Korea's second largest city, is an example that comes to mind. During a visit in 2005, I got the feeling that Busan was a more "Japanese" city than Seoul in terms of young people's fashion, because I saw more young people dressed according to Tokyo's fashion codes (even if the clothes themselves were made in Korea or China) and a wider selection of Japanese fashion magazines on display in local bookstores (which may not be surprising since Busan is just across the Korea Strait from Japan). In this case, it may be possible for a researcher to obtain sufficient data regarding the circulation of Japanese popular culture in Busan to establish the degree and nature of Japan's cultural presence, but this will not be sufficient for determining the nature of the impact that Japanese popular culture has on consumers' identities, since consumers are free to develop their own interpretations of whatever popular cultures they choose to consume.

A political economic approach to the study of popular culture and related industries has an important role to play. This approach, however, needs to be modified to account for the peculiarities and complexities that distinguish popular culture "commodities" from other commodities. It is necessary to consider not only the mechanical reproduction of standardized mass culture but also the noneconomic effects of cultural industries and their relations with broader political and social frameworks, including governments.

Popular Culture, High Culture, and the Cultural Industries

What constitutes "popular culture" and how does it relate to "high culture" and "cultural industries"? Literature concerning contemporary culture typically distinguishes between popular and high culture. Popular culture refers to products that are purchased and activities that are practiced by large numbers of "ordinary" people. At the root of the popular is an attraction to a certain practice, event, or phenomena that resonates with people's everyday lives. High culture, on the other hand, is a term that suggests two types of distinctions: in class terms, between the culture of the elite and that of the lower classes; and in aesthetic terms, between serious, "true" art that an artist produces autonomously as a form of self-expression, and commercially produced art designed to appeal to a mass audience (Crothers and Lockhart 2000, 129; Payne 1996, 415).

In Japan, however, as Dolores Martinez explains (1998, 1–18), the distinction between popular culture and high culture is less evident in everyday life. Many practices that were once labeled as elitist have become the domain of a huge middle class. Moreover, arts that originally represented high culture, such as *waka, haiku,* or *ikebana,* are currently practiced or consumed by a large cross-section of society, and in this sense are already popular (Slaymaker 2000, 3; Torrance 2000, 17–43). On the other hand, some arts that initially started as popular, such as *kabuki* theater and woodblock printing, are now considered to be aspects of elite culture that embody traditional values. In other parts of East Asia as well, Western-style distinctions between high and popular culture are less relevant to the ways people view mass-produced cultural commodities, since products and practices from both high and popular origins are being widely disseminated and consumed (Chua 2000, 28–29).

Distinctions between popular culture and high culture are not relevant to this book's investigation, since practices and innovations extracted from both high and traditional sources have become commodified and commercialized, eventually entering the domain of a large group of consumers. Therefore, in this study *popular culture products* and *cultural commodities* refer to cultural products that have been created by industrial means of production and offered for sale through a mass market, particularly products related to leisure activities and consumed by large numbers of people. More specifically, popular culture relates to artifacts, arts, activities, and institutions associated with music, animation, comics, television programs, movies, video games, and fashion (magazines, clothing, accessories). A wider definition might include fields and products such as amusement parks, foods, tableware and other household goods, toys, architecture and design, stationery, and idol culture (Table 1.1).

Cultural industries, sometimes referred to as "creative industries," "copyright industries," "cultural products industries," or "content industries," are industries that provide the organizational framework for turning art and cultural creativity into consumer products. They manage and circulate creativity and generally concern themselves with selling a particular kind of product or service. Cultural industries may be organized as large, medium-sized, or small-scale enterprises. Like all businesses, they have an interest in supporting conditions that will allow themselves to generate profit.[4] In practical terms, cultural industries include organizations, networks, and individuals that directly engage in innovating, producing, manufacturing, or marketing cultural commodities such as music, movies, television programs, animation, video games, and comics (Otmazgin and Ben-Ari 2012, 6–7).

It should be noted that the definition presented here is very different from that of the original term "cultural industries." Originally, the term was used narrowly, in association with critique of mass entertainment by members of the Frankfurt School. Theodor W. Adorno and Max Horkheimer coined the term in the late 1940s and used it to signal their disapproval of the use of media as a means of spreading propaganda, and to emphasize problems generated by the industrialization of culture. According to their view, art loses its traditional value, spirituality, and overall moral high ground when it is repackaged as a mass consumption commodity. Advocates of the Frankfurt School's ideas argued that the commercialization of culture ruins individual artisanship and leads to the fragmentation of society into subgroups based on consumption patterns and lifestyles (see Adorno 1991; Adorno and Horkheimer 1973; for further discussions about this term, see also Gripsrud 1998; Hartley 2005, 10–11).

The term "entertainment industry" is sometimes used to include business activities in the fields of music, movies, broadcasting, toys,

TABLE 1.1 List of Popular Culture Products and Fields

Products and Fields	Methods of Consumption
Music, animation, movies, video games, television programs, radio programs, comic publications, caricatures, magazines, food culture, karaoke, adult movies, fiction, fashion, idol culture, sport, amusement parks, architecture, design, visual and electronic machines (like pachinko).	CDs, VCDs, DVDs, MDs, VHS cassettes, books, magazines, accessories, clothing, posters, pictures, airwaves, Internet, broadband, cellular phones.

games, sports, performing arts, and amusement or theme parks (Payne 1996, 129–132, 175). The idea of an "entertainment industry" comes from economics and refers to businesses whose aim is to profit from leisure activities. It is generally not used in the discussion of noneconomic activities and suggests an exclusive interest in business matters such as management structures and trade practices. On the other hand, when we talk about the music, movie, television, or animation industries as "cultural industries," we imply that we are interested in more than just economic performance, management structures, or mere mechanical reproduction of standardized mass culture products that have been transformed into commodities by the penetration of capital; rather we are more likely to be interested in a critical inquiry into the practices of these industries within a broader political and social framework.

For the purposes of this book, the term "cultural industry" is used to refer to the business of converting artistic creativity into a marketable cultural commodity. Cultural industries extract, produce, and market a wide spectrum of products and activities. In economic terms, their activities lower the cost of commodifying by turning creativity and art into a massive production (Hartley 2005, 8). Nevertheless, analysis of cultural industries should not be limited to conventional economical understandings. Focusing only on economic activities or only on the cultural significance of those activities could lead one to overlook the vast socially and politically relevant effects they engender.

In addition, this book pays careful attention to differences between cultural industries and other industries. As we shall see, the production of popular culture has characteristics that distinguish it from other types of production, and these characteristics have important organizational consequences.

The Distinctiveness of the Cultural Industries

According to Shalini Venturelli (2005, 292–293), Adam Smith was the first scholar to propose a commercial-industrial understanding of culture. In *The Wealth of Nations* (1776), Smith cast manufacturing and producing institutions as the collective basis of social life, thus recognizing modern industrial institutions as a new cultural system. With this understanding, cultural goods can be treated in a similar fashion as any other category of industrially produced products, subject to the same forces of supply, demand, and economies of scale. Venturelli argues that the same economic models can therefore be used to explain contraction or expansion in the production of different types of cultural commodities since they, like other manufactured products, are subject to fluctuations in consumer demand.

I agree with Venturelli's view that the tools used to analyze other manufactured goods and services can provide some intellectual and empirical grounds for examining the production and distribution of commodified culture. But these tools alone are not sufficient for full analysis of cultural industries or their products given the peculiar nature of their work, that is, creating things that have cultural and social value as well as economic value. Therefore, I look closely at the connection between "culture" and "industry" in order to provide analytical grounds for examining the production and marketing of popular culture in East Asia and the organizational transformations they entail.

As I have mentioned, in some respects cultural industries share the same logic as industries that produce more tangible and practical goods, such as automobiles or washing machines. Fundamentally, they all engage in the production of commodities within a capitalist system. Their production is economically motivated, industrially constructed, requires labor, and is related to market demands. They all operate by obtaining necessary technology, resources, and equipment, followed by the manufacturing, marketing, and consumption of final products. Expansion of any industry into foreign markets is usually driven by cross-border market incentives and opportunities.

Despite these similarities, cultural industries tend not to fit neatly into any of the conventional categories used by academics regarding "culture" on the one hand or "industry" on the other. Cultural industries are obviously different from primary industries such as farming or mining, but it is not clear whether they should be categorized with secondary (manufacturing) or tertiary (service) industries. Venturelli (2005, 393–394) directly addresses this challenge: "The economics of ideas and cultural expression cannot be explained by the economics of mining, metals, minerals, agricultural commodities, or the manufacturing of consumer products." Indeed, cultural industries possess quite a few special characteristics that distinguish them from "other" industries. These differences, which I enumerate below, relate to the processes of commodification and production, as well as to the patterns by which those processes are expanded and adapted to new places. Thus, any analysis of cultural industries and their wider politicoeconomic effects should consider the possibility that the distinctive nature of these industries might influence the ways in which they operate.

First, production in the cultural industries is premised upon the cultivation and valorization of creativity much more than in other industries. Most cultural industries are directly dependent on a steady flow of creative juices that must be extracted and "bottled" if the business is to succeed. There is therefore relatively loose control over creative input. Producers and technicians have considerably more autonomy, albeit within the strictures of established formats and genres, than their counterparts in traditional, more rigid factory production line settings that are characterized by rational, systematic, highly organized processes (Negus 1992, 46).

Cultural industries must provide working environments that adequately accommodate creative personnel, whose habits generally differ from those of workers in other industries. People who create culture, such as musicians, animators, scriptwriters, and other artists, often have irregular schedules and cannot be effectively forced to keep "usual" working hours. They may require an individually tailored work environment to stimulate, or at least to avoid stifling, their creativity. In this sense, cultural industries resemble knowledge industries, such as software design. Since cultural industries trade in human innovation, they must construct dynamic and flexible working environments in order to induce their creative talent to do their jobs effectively and stay ahead of the competition. Of course, once the master copy of a final product is complete, be it a CD, a television program, a magazine, or a DVD, the reproduction stage is typically as coldly industrialized as in any other industry (Hesmondhalgh 2002, 55–56).

The second distinctive trait of creative industries is the generally much lower level of equipment investment required to launch a creative business and a much smaller gap between amateurs and professionals in their respective degrees of reliance on production technology. In the automobile and electronic industries, for instance, there is a clear division between professionals and amateurs. In addition to the level of education and/or technological skills, this difference is determined by access to enormously expensive manufacturing equipment and resources. In the cultural industries, however, relatively low-cost modern production equipment offers the possibility that individual creators—who make up the heart of these industries—can reach mass audiences on their own. Relatively affordable digital equipment, including cameras, musical instruments, and video editing equipment, enables the initial transformation of creativity into commodity at relatively little cost. Once that is accomplished, the Internet can facilitate the marketing of packaged cultural content. In Japan, many "indie" musical productions are initiated and commercialized without the use of mainstream distribution centers or studios. New artists can make themselves known by employing nonmainstream channels such as social media or street shows—at least until a contract is offered by a large music company (Ugaya 2005, 208–213). In short, cultural industries present opportunities for the expression of individual creativity to a degree unknown in most other manufacturing industries.

Third, just as there is a relatively small distance between creators and producers in cultural industries, so too there is a relatively small distance between producers and consumers. Of course, in any market system, producers must make products available in response to consumer demands. Like their counterparts in finance, trade, or manufacturing industries, people who work in the cultural industries form new ventures and establish new organizations to meet existing demand and generate profits. On the other hand, they work in an especially dynamic environment where consumers tend to change their minds swiftly and where products tend to have exceptionally short lifespans (consider, for example, the lifespan of a music CD or television drama). Their work is thus affected not only by macroeconomic conditions that cause fluctuations in consumption, but also by sometimes frenetic changes in popular styles and fashions (Otmazgin 2011a, 262–263). Cultural industries need to circumvent the rigidity associated with established organizations in order to shorten the distance between consumer demands and product introduction. Toward this end, cultural industries and their agents must always keep their antennae up to catch new cultural trends and preferences, find creative ways to promote their initiatives, receive feedback from the market, and react swiftly.

This need for speed has important organizational implications. It sometimes requires large companies to reconfigure themselves to act like small companies in terms of addressing market niches and creating close, even intimate relationships with consumers. Multinational companies, for example, need to decentralize their decision-making functions if they want to keep up with the rapid pace at which the popular culture market changes. Companies need to be able to quickly identify unmet needs and business opportunities and act swiftly to put together the resources necessary to address them.

The construction and advancement of new cultural industries are also less hampered by technological constraints as they make use of relatively low-cost replicating equipment. The technology that enables the creation, production, and transfer of many cultural products is available in relatively user-friendly, low-cost formats compared to the equipment and expertise required to mass produce automobiles, semiconductors, or even cans of soup. (The ready availability of reproduction equipment also makes copyright enforcement difficult.) In this way, the development of new cultural industries is made easier through duplicating, mimicking, or acquiring production formats and knowledge that can be used to produce locally drawn cultural content. It is also relatively easy and cheap to forecast initial market demand. The Internet, mobile phones, and pirating operations are powerful media for advancing both the dissemination and consumption of new cultural products.

In other words, there is much easier access to the means of production than in most manufacturing industries. True, producing a television program or a successful music album usually requires considerable resources. Professionals and technicians are needed for filming, recording, editing, and "finishing" the product, and they require expensive equipment. It is still possible, however, to produce an album, television program, or even a full-length movie independently of mainstream industry at a relatively low cost, and to find an audience for it through niche channels, alternative studios, and/or in cyberspace (YouTube, Facebook etc.). In the case of television programs, for example, it is possible to find an interested party to record and distribute an independently produced program through the Internet. This makes it much easier to break into the business of producing or distributing audiovisual cultural products than it would be to start, for example, a new automobile or electronics manufacturing company.

These "special" characteristics of cultural industries—the strong focus on creativity and ease of technological access—may explain the relative ease with which cultural industries in East Asia have been able to learn from and imitate the Japanese model to develop their own cultural industries. While equipment, experience, and knowledge constitute important advantages for more developed cultural industries, it is much easier for competitors in less developed regions to catch up in the cultural industries compared to conventional industries. A newly developing cultural industry still needs to create the conditions needed for producing and managing creativity and to obtain the technologies required for manufacturing products, but the necessary investment is relatively small. In this sense, it is easier for a country to develop its own cultural industry, in terms of constructing a production line and obtaining the necessary resources and technologies, than, for instance, to construct its own successful automobile, electronics, or space travel industry.

Meanwhile, this same "specialness" presents new challenges to policy makers and makes it more difficult for governments to support the development of their own cultural industries and to direct their outcomes. Conventional methods of fostering the development of manufacturing industries, such as investing in research and development or in human resource training or technological and physical infrastructure, do not necessarily work to promote artistic and cultural creativity that thrives on freedom and flexibility. As we shall see in chapter 4, intellectual property protection is also more difficult to enforce given the relative ease of replicating products like CDs or DVDs and delivering cultural content through the Internet.

CHAPTER 2

//////////////////////

Popular Culture and
the East Asian Region

Throughout most of the twentieth century, "East Asia" was a relatively divided region.[1] Apart from the geographical entity, East Asia existed as a construct of the mind and as the object of attempts to force or promote solidarity among Asian people.[2] As a matter of custom, many people tend to draw the boundary of East Asia along the western coasts of Myanmar, Thailand, Malaysia, and Singapore, leaving out the South Asian subcontinent (Purnendra 2000, 208). Geographically speaking, East Asia consists of a land mass that includes Mongolia, the Russian Far East, the Korean Peninsula, China, Japan, Myanmar, Thailand, Laos, Vietnam, and Cambodia, plus various islands and territories south and east of China: Taiwan, Hong Kong, Macau, the Philippines, Brunei, Malaysia, Indonesia, and Singapore.

Given the sheer variety of people, languages, beliefs, and customs, it is obvious that East Asia does not constitute a coherent region. Japan and Laos are two examples of how extremely different two East Asian countries can be: Japan is the world's third largest economy, with a per capita gross domestic product (GDP) of more than US$34,000 (as of 2011), while Laos is one of the world's smallest economies with a per capita GPD of just US$2,800. Japan is a constitutional democracy, while Laos is officially a communist state that has been ruled by a single, nonelected party since 1975. Japanese cities are some of the most densely populated places in the world, while Laos is one of the world's least populated countries. The majority of the people of Laos are Buddhists, while most Japanese regard themselves as nonreligious. The languages of the two countries are also different.

Despite these kinds of differences, the countries of East Asia have grown significantly closer together over the past three decades. A new international movement away from the American- and Soviet Union–dominated politics of the Cold War era, together with continuously evolving political and economic integrating forces, have provided the right incentives for this region's markets to converge and for its governments to band together. Regional cooperative frameworks have been established, with ASEAN (Association of Southeast Asian Nations) and ASEAN Plus Three being the best-known examples. Politicians and academics have predicted the formation of an integrated regional community and have repeatedly debated ambitious ideas for engineering a normative regional order that would validate those predictions (Acharya 2000; Ba 2009). The period following the financial crisis of 1997–1998 brought further acknowledgment of the need to cooperate in order to maintain political and economic stability in the region.

Moreover, globalization and economic development have reinforced East Asian cities' and citizens' connections to global markets, sources of capital and information, and transnational flows of popular culture. Cities such as Shanghai, Hong Kong, Tokyo, Seoul, Singapore, Kuala Lumpur, Jakarta, Taipei, Manila, and Bangkok have become active participants in the global and regional economies, as well as hotbeds of cultural innovation and mingling. A few decades of economic growth also contributed to widespread urbanization and the cultivation of a sizable urban middle class that shares similar leisure-time needs. Curiously, while vast differences remain at the country-to-country level, big cities in East Asia increasingly resemble one another as their residents share similar types of employment, education, lifestyles, and consumption patterns and aspire to the same standard of living. This is most noticeable in mainland China, Indonesia, Malaysia, Thailand, and the Philippines, where growth in major cities has created a new geography that transcends national borders and has widened the culture gap between urban and rural areas. In short, "East Asia" has become more closely integrated in the past half-century than ever before.

In the field of popular culture, East Asia of the past two decades has experienced a flowering rooted in the growth of its economies and booming consumerism, and manifested in massive new cultural innovation, production, dissemination, and consumption. In East Asia, as in other parts of the world, American popular culture continues to loom over the markets, reaching those who are able to pay the price. Local and regional cultural confluences, though, have also developed and intensified, substantially decentralizing the world's cultural structure and refuting the notion that East Asia's cultural scene should slavishly follow that of America. In the process of this development, entrepreneurs, companies, and promoters in East Asia have formed alliances that endorse the emergence of a regional market for culture, connect individuals and communities, and provide cultural content to the imagery of the region.

The recent emergence of "pan-Asian" movies is a good example of ambitious coproductions that affect not only the construction of a regional market for popular culture but also the way people have come to think about "Asia." These movies combine a mixture of motifs and influences extracted from various localities and traditions across Asia. Movies such as *Crouching Tiger, Hidden Dragon*; *Lust; Caution*; and *Hero* were produced and marketed throughout East Asia. Other coproductions not bound to a single market in terms of production and marketing, such as *Jan Dara, 2046, Initial D, The Promise, Perhaps Love,* and *Musa,* involved actors and staff members from South Korea, China, Hong Kong, Japan, and Thailand. Transnational movie production in East Asia began with the making of Japanese propaganda movies in the late nineteenth century and increased during the Pacific War (Kinniya 2009). Large-budget movies with multinational casts, however, are a relatively new phenomenon. These modern multinational movies succeed commercially as movies identified and offered as "Asian" to people both in Asia and in the West.

This chapter defines the boundaries of the East Asian region for the purposes of this book and examines those of the region's sociocultural characteristics that are relevant to our discussion of popular culture. For this discussion, it is more appropriate to define East Asia as a region composed of large cities, especially those that function as economic and / or cultural centers, as opposed to a region composed of entire nations. Thus, the East Asian region that I refer to in this book should be construed as consisting of the wealthier countries of Northeast Asia (Japan, South Korea, and Taiwan), and large swathes of territory inhabited by middle-class people in cities throughout Southeast Asia and mainland China, particularly Hong Kong, Singapore, Shanghai, Bangkok, Kuala Lumpur,

Jakarta, and Manila. I realize that this definition is controversial in that it excludes large groups of people who cannot afford an urban lifestyle.

Nevertheless, for the purpose of our discussion on popular culture, this book conceptualizes a multicentered East Asian region made up of cities and urban areas. It suggests that regionalism may not apply to all parts of a region equally, but rather only to certain population groups. Regionalization may indeed lead to the integration of communities through increasing trade and communication, but that process is likely to be uneven in both its intensity and its geographical scope within a region. In East Asia, it seems that one part of the population—overwhelmingly the urban middle class—has become more "regionalized" than others due to its openness to participation in international economics, culture, and politics. It is therefore more useful to talk about scales of regionalism in various regional formations that cut across political borders, rather than a single, homogeneous political entity made of entire nation-states.

The first part of this chapter reviews theories of regional formation. It briefly addresses some of the major theoretical and analytical foci that touch directly on the nature of region making and defines the terms "regionalism" and "regionalization" as used in this book. The aim here is not to analyze the various factors affecting regional formation or to discuss the historical evolution of the East Asian region in depth. Rather, it is to emphasize that conventional ways of characterizing region-making processes need to be amended in favor of a more dynamic perspective that considers a wider variety of regionally embedded practices, including those in the field of popular culture.

Next, the chapter proposes a new way of looking at the East Asian region that underscores the growing fragmentation between urban and rural areas. It focuses on big cities as cornerstones in regional construction and emphasizes the growing similarities between the various big cities of East Asia and the middle-class populations that inhabit them. Regions, it is proposed, may be bound not only by alliances designed to promote regional economic activity or security, but also through the propagation of common social and cultural practices and behaviors shared by different people in geographically proximate areas.

Third, the chapter examines the specific role that popular culture plays in drawing East Asia's cities and their inhabitants closer together. It analyzes the creation of regional popular culture markets by looking at the process by which confluences of culture have diffused throughout

East Asian markets in the decades surrounding the 1990s and by looking at regionwide collaboration in the making and marketing of movies,
music, and television programs. I argue that popular culture contributes
to the regionalization of East Asia not only at the institutional level, that
is, by connecting companies and other entities involved in the making
and marketing of popular culture commodities, but also at the personal
level, by offering—at least to a large sector of the region's urban population—shared experiences that can lead to the cultivation of common
lifestyles and conceptions.

Regionalization and Regionalism in East Asia

The majority of studies of region making in East Asia have concentrated
on the process of building regional institutions and viewed regionalism as the outcome of trade mechanisms and regime buildup initiated
by national governments (Liu and Régnier 2003; Yoshimatsu 2008, 24).
Others argue that "regional dynamism" and cross-border economic activities, more than formal agreements between governments or a shared historical or cultural "Asian" background, have promoted formation of the
region (for example, Aggarwal 1993; Ball 1993; Buzan 1998; Frankel and
Kahler 1993; Frost 2008; Funabashi 1993; Harvie, Kimura, and Lee 2005;
Lincoln 2004; and Pempel 2005). This sort of economic-led regional dynamism continues despite an obvious lack of strong regional institutionalization in East Asia—especially when compared to that classic exemplifier
used by scholars of region making: the European Union (EU). There is
instead an emphasis on informal, negotiated, and inclusive approaches
toward regional policy (Frankel and Kahler 1993; Katzenstein 2005).

Before proceeding with our investigation of what constitutes the East
Asian region, we first need to define the term "regionalization" as used
in this book and distinguish it from overlapping terms like "integration"
and "regionalism." This is necessary because in recent decades these
terms have become the subject of debate among various branches of the
social sciences, especially since the rise of "the new regionalism" in the
1980s. Like "globalization," "regionalism" fostered an academic growth
industry that drew participation from a number of social science specialties including European Studies, comparative politics, international
economics, international political economics, and international relations (Hettne 2005, 543–546). But these various disciplines have different

interpretations of what actually constitutes a "region." According to Björn Hettne (2005, 544):

> In the field of geography, regions are usually seen as subnational enti-
> ties, either historical provinces (which could have become nation-
> states) or more recently created units. In IR, regions are often treated
> as supranational subsystems of the international system. . . . The mini-
> mum definition of a world region is typically a limited number of
> states linked together by a geographical relationship and a degree of
> mutual interdependence.

In short, these terms have been used extensively and diversely in academia—as well as by politicians and journalists—so we need to define exactly what they mean.

Literature in the field of international relations uses both regionalism and regionalization to describe the process of regional organization or region making in a geopolitical area encompassing more than two states. Regionalism and regionalization are both advanced forms of integration that describe an intensive level of regional connectivity and a high level of institutionalization in three or more geographically proximate states, but the two terms are intrinsically different from each other. Regionalism refers to ideological and rhetorical concepts of regional institutional-ization and regional identity. Regionalism also represents a *deliberate* attempt by states or their agents to create formal mechanisms for deal-ing with common issues in the pursuit of mutual benefits. Holly Wyatt-Walter (1995, 77) defines regionalism as "a conscious policy of states or sub-state regions to coordinate activities and arrangements in the greater region." Regionalism is often used as a response or as a challenge to glo-balization, to indicate a world with a stronger regional focus (Hettne et al. 1999; Mittelman 1996; Oman 1994).

Regionalization, on the other hand, describes an *undirected process* that increases proximity among markets and communities in three or more geographically proximate economies. Under this definition, regionaliza-tion precludes ideological discussions about the formation of regional identity or the evolution of political communities. Regionalization is driven by market forces and actors from the private sector and devel-ops from the bottom up as a result of social processes (Blechinger and Legewie 2000, 299–301; Higgott 1998, 339; Hurrell 1995, 39; see also

Buzan 1998; Gamble and Payne 1996; and Pettman 1999). The differences between regionalism, which is essentially government-driven community building, and regionalization, which is more "spontaneous" (Frost 2008, 14), are clearly summarized by T. J. Pempel (2005, 19):

> Regionalism involves primarily the process of institution creation. It occurs most conspicuously when nation-states come together through top-down activities—deliberate projects involving government-to-government cooperation. New institutions are designed to deal with transnational problems that confront several nations in common. . . . Regionalism thus involves national governments concluding that their interests are sufficiently congruent with one another to subordinate elements of their nominal national autonomy. . . . Regionalism, in short, has at least three key elements: it is top-down; it is biased toward formal (usually governmental) agreements; and it involves semi-permanent structures in which governments or their representatives are the main participants. . . . Regionalization, in contrast, develops from the bottom up through societally-driven processes.

Realist, institutional, and cultural theoreticians have all emphasized different aspects of regional formation. Realists view regionalism as a strategy used by groups of states to increase their economic and political strength. They claim that states interact in an anarchic environment and that much of their behavior is determined by the possibility of conflict. They reason that states tend to group into alliances to defend themselves against common enemies. For institutional theorists, institutionalization and economic activity (whether preceding, following, or concurrent to one another) are the main forces that propel regionalization and regional formation. The EU is held up as an example of an entity that started out working to formulate trade between Western European countries following World War II and evolved into today's EU with its own institutions, currency, and economic and political agendas. Increased interest in the concept of "identity" has also aided the study of regionalism by suggesting that a subjective sense of belonging can be a powerful motive for forming regions and by emphasizing the role of shared cultural and historical narratives in this process. Beginning in the late 1990s, there has been a proliferation of studies in leading IR journals that analyze how norms are shaping the Asia-Pacific region (Jones and Smith 2007, 173). The best-known example in this group is probably Samuel P. Huntington's assertion about the clash of civilizations. He charted a broad and diverse Asian region that encompasses the entire area between Japan and India (while excluding both "Japanese" and "Hindu") and serves as home to "Confucian" civilizations (1993, 25).[3]

The heterogeneity of East Asian ethnic groups, customs, and beliefs, as well as the variety of political systems and levels of economic development found in the region, demands a more specifically applied regional understanding. In today's diverse and dynamic East Asia, it is inconceivable that regional formation might be explained solely on the basis of formal government agreements, institutions, or the search for a common identity, while ignoring the full range of dynamic socioeconomic-centered processes and developments that construct mechanisms for region making, such as those related to consumption, technology, and popular culture. For this reason, as Amitav Acharya (2010, 1001) argues regarding Southeast Asia, a regional perspective should be based on a marriage between disciplinary and area studies approaches.

Constructivist theories, which take note of these various factors, are more useful in understanding the complexity of regional formation in East Asia. They acknowledge a wide range of factors that might affect regional formation and do not base arguments on any single factor at the expense of other important factors. Moreover, constructivist theories employ a specifically applied regional understanding to categorize various factors and processes that are linked to regionalization and regional formation and effectively determine a proper balance between them, separating the important points from the insignificant points. This approach is helpful for navigating the various political, economic, and social-centered processes and developments in East Asia and evaluating their importance to the understanding of regionalization and regional formation. T. J. Pempel's work (2005, 2) exemplifies this integrative approach:

> The focus on East Asia's lack of integration grows largely out of the high level of attention given to the actions of the region's governments and to the cooperative or conflictual interactions of nation states. . . . Yet a strikingly contradictory view of the East Asian region emerges when one looks at linkages beneath the level of state actions. In that picture, despite the overwhelming structural impediments to integration, East Asia has in recent years become considerably more independent,

connected, and cohesive. This increased cohesiveness has been driven by developments, among other things, in trade and investment, cross-border production, banking, technology sharing, popular culture, transportation, communication, and environmental cooperation, as well as in crime, drug, and disease control.

Some scholars and politicians in East Asia have argued for the formation of a region on the basis of "Asian values." The Asian values discourse prompted an ambitious investigation into the imagery of "Asia" as a regional concept. According to Asian values arguments, in spite of the vast cultural and economic differences within the region, an Asian community can be consolidated by extracting common values and norms that emphasize, among other things, the primary importance of the family, communitarianism, thrift, social cohesion, consensus, and the value of education, as well as politically oriented values such as respect for authority, avoiding public conflict, and accepting the primacy of the group (Acharya and Rajah 1999; Kim H. J. 2004). Encouraged by the region's rapid economic development, proponents have leaned on Asian culture, values, or history to describe East Asians as going through a process that shapes them as a collective and attempts to incorporate Asian collective values into a regional policy (Liu 2003, 5–6; Yoshimatsu 2008, 16). In many of these works, the EU is mentioned as an example and a model (e.g., Mahathir and Ishihara 1995; Mahbubani 1995; Ogura 1999).

The search for Asian values, however, has been criticized as no more than an ideological gloss for political authoritarianism in East Asia's pseudo-democracies (Emmerson 2000). Even advocates acknowledge that the rise of a shared Asian consciousness and identity is a new creation and that a multitude of different, coexistent cultural references prevent Asia from being conceptualized as a homogeneous space. In the years following the Asian financial crisis of 1997–1998, the project of constructing a regional identity and an Asian way lost much of its luster. Repeated economic, political, and cultural challenges, as well as East Asia's integration into the wider Asia-Pacific region, brought the project of constructing an Asian identity to an unmistakable halt. Mahathir Mohamad and Lee Kuan Yew are no longer in power, and Malaysia and Singapore, once enthusiastic proponents, have pulled away from endorsing regional unity, engaging instead in discriminatory free trade agreements with individual countries.

Contesting Conventional Understandings of East Asian Regionalization

Arjun Appadurai challenges the theoretical understanding of regional formation, arguing that "the large regions that dominate our current maps for area studies are not permanent geographical facts. . . . Regions are best viewed as initial contexts for themes that generate variable geographies, rather than as fixed geographies marked by pre-given themes" (Appadurai 2000, 7). In this sense, academic interaction is as important as "hav[ing] elaborated interests and capabilities in constructing world pictures whose very interactions affect global processes" (ibid., 13). Here Appadurai conveys the idea of regional formation being a matter of attribute rather than framing. Although Appadurai does not clearly explain how regions should be delineated and defined, his vision is far-reaching in the challenge he presents to the plethora of theoretical literature.

The study of regionalization and regional formation in East Asia requires a methodological and interdisciplinary pluralism that considers a variety of possible regionalizing factors, including new definitions for regions. As contested by Peter J. Katzenstein, "geographic designations are not 'real', 'natural', or 'essential,'" but are "socially constructed and politically contested and thus open to change" (1997, 7). Regions are creations that are initiated and developed by people's consciousness and practices as well as by a variety of actual and potential participants. Regions are not necessarily limited in scope; they are neither defined solely by geography nor predetermined only by intentions or by the formal boundaries of nation-states.

East Asian regionalization has a few conspicuous characteristics. The first is that it is essentially market-driven and involves little formal institutionalization. In many cases the state responds to powerful market forces, and formal agreements follow de facto regionalization already created by nonstate actors. A number of studies have accounted for the dynamism of the economy in East Asia vis-à-vis the stagnation of the region's formal political institutions, suggesting that market-centered processes have been the main propellers of East Asia's regionalization (for example, Frankel and Kahler 1993; Frost 2008; Haggard 1997; Hatch and Yamamura 1996; Katzenstein and Shiraishi 1997; Pempel 2005; Petri 1993).

Take intraregional trade for example. Intra–East Asian trade has increased from 11.3 percent of total world trade in 1975 to 19 percent in

1985, to 25.6 percent in 1995, and to 25.7 percent in 2001. Intraregional foreign direct investment (FDI) in East Asia (as a part of global FDI) has also increased, from 4 percent in 1980 to 8 percent in 1994 (Chirathivat 2003, 2–3; Urata 2003, 7–13). A comprehensive study by the World Bank found that since the mid-1980s, East Asian intratrade has been growing more rapidly than intratrade in North America or the EU, and at a rate roughly double that of overall world trade. According to this study, trade relations between most East Asian countries have been growing sharply in terms of both intensity of trade and importance to the global economy (Ng and Yeats 2003).

Another study, conducted by the Asian Development Bank (2008, 42–64), found that intraregional trade and FDI have grown since the Asian financial crisis of 1997–1998 as a result of the East Asian region's exceptional economic growth, its network-based production systems, and investment and labor flows associated with these systems. Industrial relations in East Asia have also become closer. The ratio of parts and components trade (PCT) to overall manufacturing trade increased from 24.3 percent in 1996 to 29.4 percent in 2006. PCT is especially significant in ASEAN, where it rose from 35 percent in 1996 to 43 percent in 2006, and nearly doubled in the People's Republic of China (PRC), from 12.5 percent to 24 percent over the same period.[4]

At the same time, however, the level of institutionalism in East Asia remains low, especially in comparison to the EU, which is by far the most institutionalized of all regions today (Johnston 2003, 108–109; Munakata 2006, 3–4). For this reason, the comparison to the EU in studies of regionalism has been criticized as a Eurocentric view counterproductive to the development of new conceptual frameworks for explaining region making. As Breslin and Higgot (2002, 11) remark, "The EU, as an exercise in regional integration, is one of the major obstacles to the development of analytical and theoretical comparative studies of regional integration." Even though regional institutions such as ASEAN and the Asian Development Bank have been formed and the level of intraregional cooperation has increased, regionalization in East Asia operates predominantly through informal market institutions and is largely uninterested in political solutions at the regional level (Katzenstein 2005, 136–148).

The formation of ASEAN is perhaps the best example of the rigidity of state-led region making in East Asia. ASEAN began more than forty-five years ago, when five countries—Indonesia, Malaysia, the Philippines, Singapore, and Thailand—signed the ASEAN Declaration on August 8, 1967. It took another thirty years for ASEAN to encompass all the countries of Southeast Asia, admitting Brunei in 1984, Vietnam in 1995, Laos and Myanmar in 1997, and Cambodia in 1999. ASEAN has worked to peacefully resolve disputes between its member countries and currently places great importance on encouraging Southeast Asian states to think more regionally. But ASEAN has been largely unsuccessful as an economic institution because its members have been unwilling to put their national interests aside for the sake of wider regional interests. ASEAN impotence was exposed during the 1997–1998 financial meltdown, when its leaders engaged in unseemly mutual recriminations rather than banding together (Jones and Smith 2007, 168–175). In the beginning of the twenty-first century, ASEAN was still, in the words of Shaun Narine, "a loosely structured organization, representing Southeast Asia in international forums on uncontentious issues on which its members have reached consensus" (Narine 2002, 193; see also Vatikiotis 1999, 79–81).

Cities' Role in the Making of a Region

Aside from being essentially market-driven and involving a low level of institutionalization, regional construction in East Asia is intrinsically different from that in Western Europe in another important way: in Asia, regionalization is centered on translocal relations between cities and middle-class consumers rather than between entire nation-states. The East Asian region defined in this study is thus more an array of urban centers and marketplaces bound by economic, social, and cultural forces rather than a strictly geographically defined area marked by national boundaries or constructed by state-to-state agreements. Therefore, in our analysis of popular culture it is more appropriate to discuss the interactions and participation of cities, individuals, communities, and subcommunities in a formal as well as an informal manner rather than to address a region that is construed solely as a collection of nation-states.

More to the point, the focus on cities bears a few important implications for exploring new modes of regionalization and region making that goes beyond the conventional definitions favored by current IR theorists and beyond the typical reliance on "national" versus "global" as the only frameworks for analysis. First, the concentration of economic and cultural power in cities has an impact on how the region is being built. Because cities have a high concentration of influences from inflows of culture, trade, tourism, and migration, they serve as dynamic centers of creativity and as spaces for social and cultural interaction. It is in cities that cultural and social transformations are most prolific, and consequently cities are where construction of intraregional and extraregional consciousness culminates. The branding of cities as an alternative reference to the nation-state therefore introduces a new concept of "community" as not only a group of people living under the banner of a nation-state but also communities of urban residents living in different cities in different countries bound by certain behaviors and practices.

China's coastal cities (Shanghai, Guangzhou, Qingdao, Tianjin, Fuzhou, etc.) are a good example. They are active participants in the regional and global economy, but at the same time they demonstrate their growing difference and disconnection from the rest of mainland China. The urban population earns much more than Chinese in rural areas, and they spend more on fashion and popular culture. The shopping centers, entertainment districts, and office blocks of each city closely resemble those of the other big cities in the region.[5] Thailand is another good example. Over the last two decades Bangkok has became as cosmopolitan as other East Asian metropolises such as Kuala Lumpur, Jakarta, or Seoul, while the rest of Thailand, especially the northeast, remains comparatively poor and parochial.

I do not suggest that the division between cities and rural areas is unbridgeable. For one thing, there is constant circulation of people in and out of cities, including migrants, tourists, and students, who help keep the rural population informed about the latest news and trends. There is also a steady flow of people who enter cities and do not leave, which is why the cities keep growing. Moreover, new and old means of communication and information technology, ranging from radio and television broadcasting to the most recent cellular and Internet technologies, help to bridge some of the gaps between physical locations by digitalizing and deterritorizing significant portions of the world economy (Castells 2000b; Hjorth 2009; Mosco 1999, 105). However, the East Asian region is not "flat" in the sense that participation in the wider regional order is much more active in cities and by people who live in cities than it is among people living in rural areas.

Put differently, the increasing importance of big cities has created new hierarchies that cut across the old divide of developed/developing economies and distinguish the economic and cultural magnitudes of cities from those of the rest of the country. Of course, big cities, especially those connected to marine trade, have been the focal points of cultural exchange since ancient times, in East Asia as elsewhere (see Frost 2008, 41–46; Hamashita 2008, 87–90; Haneda 2009). Today, however, cities are connected to other cities to an extent and at a speed unprecedented in history. The result is a special sense of connectedness, along with a growing resemblance between metropolises that parallels the widening gap between the importance of cities and that of rural areas.

The fact that cities play such an important role in East Asian region making suggests that region making in general is not simply a matter of institutionalization but also of practice. Rather than viewing regionalization as simply the deterritorization and disentanglement of national boundaries by economic, technological, and political forces, we can also see it as something that happens through the cumulative practices of groups of people who, over a period of time, are geared toward some common purpose (Borrie 2005, 15). Consequently, as Alder and Greve argue (2009, 59), the boundaries of regions are determined by the practices that constitute them, a pattern of relations indicative of what Emilian Kavalski (2009, 10) calls "community of practice."

The Role of the Middle Class

The emergence of East Asia's urban middle class has also played a central role in the making of the region. Although the urban middle class does not constitute the majority of people living in East Asia (especially in Southeast Asia and mainland China), they serve as a model for others to follow. The demand they generate for art, food, fashion, entertainment, and the like, and their support for the industries that cater to these demands, fuel the circulation of popular culture and lead to the propagation of common practices and behaviors across cities.

In all major cities in East Asia, the rapid urbanization and consumerism of the past few decades has created busy urban sprawl. The rise of the middle class in these cities, together with increasing flows of goods and cultural streams, has encouraged the construction of bustling shopping malls, department stores, leisure facilities, and cafes, many with a strong cosmopolitan flavor. The emergence of this middle class was nurtured by approximately ten consecutive years of double-digit annual economic growth from the late 1980s and by rising demand for new skills and expertise in fast-changing market-driven economies. Observing this process, Shiraishi Takashi (2006) argues that this East Asian middle class is the product of regional economic development that has taken place under a de facto American empire, over the course of half a century, in successive waves—first in Japan, then in South Korea, Taiwan, Hong Kong, and Singapore, later in Thailand, Malaysia, Indonesia, and the Philippines, and now in China. Similarities in employment, education, consumption, and everyday culture have contributed to what he calls "middle class consciousness," composed of experiences, symbols, and perceptions drawn from life in the city. This urban experience articulates certain aspects of identity and cultivates communalities of conceptions and behaviors, consequently laying new ground for regional integration.

The overwhelming majority of East Asia's middle classes live in cities. Cities offer greater potential for generating employment, greater access to education, health services, and entertainment, and more comfortable, modern living conditions for those who can afford to take advantage of them. The fact that the average income of residents in the Bangkok metropolitan area is four to six times higher than that of the half of the Thai population that lives in the provinces, mainly as peasants and farmers, is illuminating. Even in South Korea in 1997, urban households spent six times as much money on leisure pursuits as did farming households, while in Malaysia the rapid economic growth of the last three decades stimulated the rise of an urban middle class to the point that 64 percent of the country's population had been urbanized by 2004 (Kim 2000; Jamalunlaili 2004; Chan 2000). Other studies confirm that the income and expenditures of people living in cities in Southeast Asia are higher on average than of those living in rural areas (Hattori, Funatsu, and Torii 2002; Shiraishi and Pasuk 2008). These residents are generally educated families whose main providers are technicians, clerks, mid-level or executive-level managers, engineers, accountants, etc.

Consumerism in East Asia's Big Cities

Consumerism is such an important feature of the urban middle class that it is sometimes identified as a "new consuming class" (King 2008).[6] Today's metropolises are marked by conspicuous leisure consumption and the pursuit of pleasure; there is a strong tendency among young, highly educated members of the middle class to actively seek a lavish lifestyle. Although East Asia's urban middle classes inhabit different locations and income differences do exist, a comparable level of consumption is available to most, if not all. They earn enough to buy not only essential food, shelter, and clothing, but also to pay for "luxury" objects and leisure activities, including shopping for pleasure, gourmet foods and dining out, entertainment, and travel (Chua 2000; Torii 2006, 293). Any observer of consumerism in the shopping areas of an East Asian city, be it Hong Kong's Tsim Sha Tsui, Singapore's Orchard Road, Bangkok's Pathumwan area, or Taipei's Ximendong district, can easily testify to the vigorous pace of shopping on the part of both locals and visitors.

This heated consumption advances integration in the East Asian region in two ways. First, it creates a new economy based on products shared by Asians with a high standard of living. Consumerism is integral to the way of life of this middle class, overwhelmingly urban cross-section of the population; it creates a bond between them and others who share the same type of urban lifestyle, while differentiating them from poorer sectors of the population who cannot afford these products. Among this elite segment of the population, consumerism has become an important factor in formulating value—not only in the economic sense but also in the social and cultural sense. Through consumerism, people acquire new perspectives and behaviors that express and articulate a part of their identity.

Second, consumerism influences the kinds of lifestyles that authorities view as appropriate for their citizens. Historically speaking, East Asian governments have not always taken a positive view of consumerism. During periods of high economic growth, governments in the region tended to encourage high levels of saving in order to accumulate capital and reduce dependency on international borrowing (Garon 2006). Consumerism was seen as wasteful and harmful to economic development. Except in Japan, Hong Kong, and perhaps Taiwan, indulging in consumerist culture has generally been regarded as an excessively materialistic pursuit associated with Western values and ideals that are frowned upon in Asia. The official discourse of Southeast Asian countries, especially Singapore, Malaysia, and Indonesia, has long criticized Western values and practices and condemned consumerism as being politically risky and socially destructive (Chua 2000, 9–13). Today, however, most East Asian governments encourage consumption, which is now seen in a positive light because it keeps factories working and keeps the economy moving. As the retail sector has come to constitute a significant part of domestic economies in the region—especially in its more developed economies—the desire to prop it up has led governments in the region to encourage those who have steady employment to spend their money rather than save. No doubt the most extreme example is Singapore, where consumerism has come to be seen as a patriotic duty. As Prime Minister Goh Chok Tong said in his 1996 National Day Rally speech—"Life for Singaporeans is not complete without shopping!" (quoted in Chua 2003, 6–17).

The Cultural World of Cities

In addition to being centers of consumption, East Asia's big cities (Bangkok, Hong Kong, Seoul, Shanghai, Singapore, Taipei, Tokyo, etc.) are also centers of cultural innovation and blending. The constant flow of people into cities feeds urban cultural creativity and localized production and provides a nexus for multiculturalism. Cities thus serve as matrices for the formation of new transnational identities with references outside the nation-state, and they are instilled with what Saskia Sassen calls "a multiplicity of cultures and identities" (2000, 142). People who live in big cities are exposed to the most diverse and intense flows of cultural commodities and images, as well as the perceptions, behaviors, and lifestyles with which they dovetail. In short, we are witnessing the regionalization of taste in East Asia's big cities.

Because they live surrounded by cultural innovation and blending, urban residents are constantly provided with contexts in which they may imagine new spaces. Given that many people in East Asia spend hours every day in front of their television screens, go out to movies, listen to music, and generally spend time and energy on cultural consumption, it seems reasonable to assume that these practices impact their lives and the way they view and conceptualize external influences and places. At the very least, these activities must introduce new ideas and images coming from other places. Urban conditions and practices produce symbolic goods that change people's lives, creating what Pierre Bourdieu calls new "habitués" that have the potential to cultivate an atmosphere of affinity among individuals and arouse feelings of belonging to the same cultural space.

East Asia's Popular Culture Confluences and Alliances

In the past two decades, East Asia has been saturated with a variety of popular culture products and images, especially in the form of movies, music albums, animation series, comic publications, television programs, video games, and fashion magazines. This trend has gradually intensified amid waves of economic and consumerist growth in the region. Cultural products have been reaching consumers across national and linguistic boundaries and substantially decentralizing the region's popular cultural structure. In the process, entrepreneurs, companies, and promoters have collaborated to form alliances that endorse the emergence of a regional market for popular culture (Berry, Liscutin, and Mackintosh 2009; Chua 2004).

Before looking more deeply at the dramatic changes in East Asia's popular culture market in recent decades and how popular culture has contributed to regionalization, it is important to note that East Asia's popular culture markets have emerged against the backdrop of a remarkable half-century of economic growth and booming consumerism. More specifically, the construction of regionwide popular culture markets is related to four economic and social developments that have stimulated the transfer and consumption of cultural commodities and encouraged the region's cultural industries to cooperate on commodifying culture and delivering it to consumers.

First, in the past two decades, most of the economies in East Asia have developed to a certain degree (to varying degrees, of course) as active participants in both the East Asian regional economy and the global economy. This is expressed in terms of GDP growth, inflow of investment, and trade links with other countries (Lincoln 2004, 25–113; Ng and Yeats 2003). According to a study by the Asian Development Bank (2008, 27–28), in the four decades from 1956 to 1996, living standards in sixteen Asian economies grew at an unprecedented average of 5 percent, while the world as a whole grew at an average of only 1.9 percent.[7] North Korea and Myanmar obviously did not fit this pattern, as their leaderships placed priority on avoiding regime collapse rather than on becoming active participants in the regional economy of East Asia.

Second, flourishing consumer cultures have evolved in the economies of Japan, Hong Kong, Singapore, Taiwan, South Korea, Malaysia, Thailand, the Philippines, China, and Indonesia, where there is a large pool of middle-class consumers with considerable disposable income and a strong desire to consume (Shiraishi 2006). As discussed earlier, economic growth in the region over the past twenty years has spawned an affluent urban middle class in each of these countries. In many East Asian urban communities, people no longer have to work all day long or expend the bulk of their income to acquire life's basic necessities. Rather, increased purchasing power has allowed them to enjoy a more varied diet and indulge in leisure-time pursuits. This middle class has acquired a taste for luxury goods, including imported cultural goods (Chua 2000; Hattori, Funatsu, and Torii 2002).

The third development that has stimulated the cultural commodities business and encouraged regional cooperation in delivering commodified culture is that there has been sufficient dissemination of technological means of reproducing, accessing, and consuming cultural content in East Asia over the past three decades. This includes access to satellite TV and inexpensive devices such as music and DVD players. By the end of the 1990s, 86 percent of all households in Hong Kong and Singapore owned VCRs; 80 percent in South Korea; 76 percent in urban Vietnam; 61 percent in Guangzhou; 58.7 percent in Malaysia; and 57.1 percent in Taiwan. Today, every household in Hong Kong and Guangzhou has a color television, as do 95 percent of households in China's large urban centers, 99.5 percent in Taiwan, and 96.5 percent in South Korea. In Vietnam, 93 percent of urban dwellers own a black-and-white television set (*Adweek Asia*, December 4, 1998, March 16, 1999).

Before Internet access became widespread in Asia, dissemination of cheap reproduction and consumption devices was especially effective in stimulating regional circulation of pirated popular culture commodities, mainly in the form of CDs, VCDs, and DVDs. Piracy—both physical and online—has played an important role in fueling regional circulation of popular culture in East Asia. This was especially true during the Asian popular culture market's formative years in the 1990s, which I will discuss in more detail later in this chapter. Although illegal, pirate operations have been effective in distributing fake cultural commodities across nation-state boundaries, and they often succeed in introducing consumers to popular culture products that their governments try to censor. The flexibility of networks supplying illegally reproduced products, and imported popular culture's attractiveness in the eyes of consumers, have made it almost impossible for such government restrictions to succeed.

The result has been heavy, unsupervised traffic of popular culture commodities and content across markets.

Fourth, there has been a gradual relaxation of political control over the flow and consumption of popular culture. East Asia has a history of restricting importation of popular culture. American and Japanese cultural products, in particular, were banned at times due to concerns that their influence could harm local traditions and values (Chua 2000). Most governments in East Asia, however, have eased most of their restrictions on the importation of culture after realizing that their attempts to direct the flow of culture were futile. In the twenty-first century, only North Korea continues to officially restrict citizens' access to cultural products, although in recent years a small black market for smuggled cultural products has sprung up even there.[8]

Confluences of Popular Culture in East Asia

The four developments outlined above have encouraged transnational dissemination and reproduction of American, Chinese, Japanese, and Korean popular culture products. One can find the same selection of imported popular culture products in virtually every big city in East Asia, where they are regularly disseminated, indigenized, hybridized, and consumed. At the same time, there is an unmistakable imbalance in the regional production and distribution of popular culture. The vast majority of popular culture commodities originate in a small group of wealthy economies in Northeast Asia (Japan, South Korea, Taiwan, and Hong Kong), while the poorest economies with less developed cultural industries rarely export their popular culture on a massive scale. Cultural production and dissemination remains asymmetric in spite of progress achieved by cultural industries in less wealthy parts of East Asia, such as Thailand and Indonesia, and in spite of the relative ease with which cultural content can be transferred by using accessible devices and communication technologies such as satellite TV or the Internet.

In East Asia, as in other parts of the world, American popular culture continues to loom over the markets. American products are marketed successfully wherever local incomes have risen to the point that people can afford them. Although Asians across the region continue to prefer musical artists who sing in their local language, American music accounts for between a fifth and a third of domestic sales in Japan, Hong Kong, Taiwan, Singapore, South Korea, and Thailand. In most of East

Asia, movies from Hollywood remain more popular than those from any other source. In Hong Kong, imported movies account for approximately 60 percent of the market, and 80 percent of the imports are American. The Chinese government allows a quota of twenty foreign movies to enter the country each year, and American movies regularly occupy the top slots in the box office. In Singapore, Taiwan, South Korea, and Thailand, American movies account for between a third and a half of the movie market. American television dramas, such as *ER, Friends, Sex and the City,* and *Desperate Housewives* are broadcast by local television stations throughout the region.[9]

Despite America's global dominance, regional popular culture confluences have developed and intensified, substantially decentralizing the world's cultural structure and refuting the notion that East Asia's popular culture scene must necessarily imitate that of America. In the past two decades, Beijing and Shanghai have emerged as China's incubator sites for cultural production, especially of animation, digital television, and video games, in spite of sporadic interference from the state censor (Keane 2006, 850). Chinese pop music, in both Mandarin and Cantonese, is increasingly popular among young Chinese audiences throughout East Asia. Taiwan recently replaced Hong Kong as the regional hub of Mandarin-language pop music and is the source of approximately 80 percent of sales of Mandarin music worldwide. Musical artists from Taiwan, Hong Kong, and Singapore promote their music intensively in Asian markets and have become especially popular in cities with predominantly Chinese populations. For example, Taiwanese popular singer Chang Huei Mei (popularly known as "Ah Mei") is supported by fans throughout East Asia although the Chinese government banned her music and image. Jay Chow, another Taiwanese-born singer-songwriter, has successfully marketed himself as a pan-Chinese artist and is now the most popular singer in China in terms of album and concert sales (Fung 2005). Kelly Chen, a Hong Kong–based singer and actress, is another superstar who is well known to every Chinese pop music or Chinese drama fan in Taipei, Shanghai, and Bangkok. The culture and entertainment sections of local newspapers in Taiwan, Hong Kong, Singapore, and Shanghai always feature Chinese musicians from across Asia, providing daily reports about their music and lives. Some of these artists are no longer considered to be only Taiwanese, Hong Konger, or Singaporean, but rise to the status of Asian-Chinese idols who contribute to the creation of pan-Asian Chinese pop culture.

Hong Kong is another central player in the making of Chinese popular culture. In the 1990s, Hong Kong–made TV programs, featuring kung fu epics, musicals, and feature films, tended to attract ethnic Chinese viewers across Southeast Asia. Dubbed versions also performed well among Malay, Thai, Cambodian, Vietnamese, Korean, and Japanese audiences—in addition to Taiwanese and mainlanders (Curtin 2007, 112). Hong Kong is estimated to have the third largest movie industry in the world, after America and India. In 2003, seventy-nine Hong Kong movies were released with an aggregate box office net of US$419 million and export value worth US$1,050 million in the form of videotapes, laser discs, and other compact discs (Film Service Office Hong Kong 2004). Hong Kong movies have strong international appeal, especially action comedies and other films that feature martial arts. Actors such as Jackie Chan, Chow Yun-fat, Jet Li, Michelle Yeoh, and Leslie Cheung have become international stars whose movies are widely available across East Asia, in theaters as well as on VCD and DVD, in media shops, and more recently online. Some of these actors have also starred in Hollywood movies.

Since the turn of the century, the Hong Kong movie industry has specifically targeted the emerging mainland China market. In June 2003, with the support of the Hong Kong government, the Mainland and Hong Kong Closer Economic Partnership Arrangement (CEPA) was signed to allow Hong Kong producers to export Chinese-language films to China without being subject to import quotas. Since January 2005, these movies have been completely exempt from import tariffs (Film Industry of Hong Kong 2006).

During the past three decades, Japanese music, television programs, animation, and comics have carved out a key position in East Asian markets and introduced young East Asians to a variety of new consumption opportunities and lifestyles. Many Japanese musical artists are widely known throughout East Asia. By 2005, young singer-songwriter Utada Hikaru sold more than one million copies of her three albums in Thailand alone.[10] Other prominent singers, such as Chage and Aska, Sakai Noriko, Chiba Mika, Matsuda Seiko, Nakamori Akina, Namie Amuro, and Hamasaki Ayumi, have reached superstar and cultural idol status, at times extending their influence on young East Asians from music to fashion by becoming fashion models.

Japanese television dramas and variety programs have also achieved lasting popularity and have become an integral part of East

Asia's television scene. Japanese television dramas such as *Tokyo Love Story, Long Vacation,* and *Yamato Nadeshiko;* Japanese variety programs and cooking shows such as *Iron Chef;* and especially Japanese animation such as *Doraemon, Tiger Mask,* and *Detective Conan* have been continuously broadcast on public television and cable channels in Hong Kong, Singapore, Thailand, Malaysia, and Indonesia, and more recently in Taiwan and South Korea.

Korean popular culture is also making its mark on East Asia's cultural scene, leading observers and fans to refer to its rapid spread as "the Korean Wave."[11] In less than a decade, South Korean television dramas, movies, music, and fashion have gained immense popularity throughout East Asia, offering a variety of new images and consumption opportunities. South Korean idols have become phenomenally popular throughout the region, thanks to a marketing strategy that mixes television exposure, commercials, and music (Chua and Iwabuchi 2008). Won Bin and Song Seung-hun, for example, became widely known to young East Asians by acting in the hit television drama *Autumn Fairy Tale* (2000). Other South Korean idols who gained fame in the same way include Jang Dong-gun (*Friend*), Cha Tae-hyun (*My Sassy Girl*), Lee Jung-jae (*Il Mare*), Kyon Sang-woo (*My Tutor Friend*), and Bae Yong Jun (*Winter Sonata*).

The recent regard for South Korean popular culture has had a strong economic impact in addition to kindling an interest in Korean culture among many East Asians. Korean television broadcast exports jumped from US$8,318,000 in 1997 to US$18,920,000 in 2001, and to US$71,461,000 in 2004. The trend has also boosted tourism to the country (Shin 2008, 21–27). In 2004, for example, Korean Airlines reported a major increase in passengers headed for the ski resort where the popular television drama *Winter Sonata* was filmed, generating US$950 million in revenues.[12]

India's Bollywood is another industry that successfully exports its movies to East Asia, especially to rural areas.[13] Bollywood produces more than eight hundred new movies every year—more than double the number of feature movies produced in the United States! Bollywood exports films, music, and fashions, especially to Central and South Asian consumers in Pakistan, Bangladesh, Sri Lanka, and Nepal. Theaters featuring Bollywood movies have come to serve as community foci for South Asians, as well as a way for them to stay in touch with their culture. The diffusion of Indian popular culture in East Asia is also based on reproduction and distribution of pirated CDs, VCDs, and DVDs containing

Indian movies and music (Bose 2006; Mehta 2005). In Southeast Asia, Bollywood's influence is most prevalent in rural areas, but it is also growing popular among urban members of the Indian diaspora. Bollywood movies and music are standard fare offered at retail outlets in places such as Singapore, Malaysia, and rural Indonesia.

The fact that the majority of popular culture products come from the richest economies of Northeast Asia (Japan, South Korea, Hong Kong, Taiwan) does not mean that the intraregional flow of popular culture is one way. In recent years, a few productions originating in Southeast Asia became popular throughout the region, diversifying and redirecting the regional circulation of popular culture. A good example is the Mandarin-language drama serial *The Little Nyonya* (November 2008–January 2009), which was made in Singapore and bought and screened in Malaysia, Thailand, Vietnam, Hong Kong, and Shanghai. Another example is the penetration of Filipino popular culture into non-Filipino cities and other parts of the region, especially in places with high concentrations of Filipino workers (Hong Kong, Singapore, Taiwan, etc.). Filipino movies have been heavily exported over the past two decades, especially to East Asia (Tolentino 2013). Examples of more complicated movements of popular culture include Malaysian-born actors (such as actress Michelle Yeoh), directors (such as Tsai Mingliang) and musicians (such as singer Aniu) who shot to stardom in Taiwan or Hong Kong before they gained recognition at home.

As a result, today's urban East Asian consumer may have popular culture preferences deriving from multiple national sources. Millions of youths in places such as Hong Kong, Seoul, Shanghai, and Jakarta covet the same hot fashions from Tokyo, listen to the same genre of American pop music, watch Chinese dramas on television or DVDs, read Japanese comic books, and go with friends to watch the latest Korean movie. Heavy traffic in popular culture throughout East Asia has been insinuated into the pan-Asian urban cultural context and into the daily life of East Asian people.

Regional Media Alliances

Concurrent with the heavy circulation of popular culture products, regional collaborations among media companies and promoters have created alliances that have had a significant impact on the East Asian popular culture market. These collaborations are generally motivated by entrepreneurs in search of new business expansion opportunities and encouraged by the expansion of East Asia's cultural market in the decades surrounding the 1990s. From an organizational point of view, such collaboration interlocks companies, networks, and producers engaged in various stages of popular culture production and commercialization. These partnerships consequently endorse expansion of East Asia's culture markets, and they expand and strengthen regional cooperative links as they commercialize popular culture.

By creating shared products, images, and genres labeled "Asian," these alliances demonstrate that the East Asian region is a major source of creative production in its own right, in addition to its great potential as a destination for the consumption of popular culture commodities (Otmazgin 2011a). Since the cultural commodities and genres produced by these alliances are deliberately depicted and commercialized as Asian, they also provide a context for people to develop new images of Asia.

The coproduction of so-called pan-Asian movies is perhaps the best example of these collaborations. These large-budget, multinational movie productions dovetail a mixture of Asian and Western motifs or incorporate narratives that appeal to both East Asian and global audiences. This kind of coproduction also makes good economic sense. Low production costs in "cheap" places such as China, Thailand, or Malaysia provide ample incentive to relocate production. The existence of potential consumers in both the regional and global markets encourages marketing strategies that target the widest range of audiences in East Asia and beyond.

The best-known examples of pan-Asian movies employed multinational staff members and actors from South Korea, China, Hong Kong, Japan, and Thailand. Examples are *Crouching Tiger, Hidden Dragon; Hero; Jan Dara; 2046; Initial D;* and *Musa.* Other notable examples include Zhang Yimou's *House of Flying Daggers* (2004), He Ping's *Warriors of Heaven and Earth* (2003), Tsui Hark's *Seven Swords* (2005), Jackie Chan's *The Myth* (2005), Chen Kaige's *The Promise* (2005), Jacob Cheung's *Battle of Wits* (2006), Lin Yu-Hsien's *Exit No. 6* (2006), Jin-ho Hur's *A Good Rain Knows* (2009), and Chao-Bin Su's *Reign of Assassins* (2010) (Jin and Lee 2007, 41; Shim 2013, 60-65). Hong Kong has been a key player in this trend. According to Hau and Shiraishi (2013), between a third and a half of the movies produced in Hong Kong in the years 2004 and 2006 were cofinanced by companies from other Asian countries. Since the 1990s, actors from Taiwan, mainland China, and more recently Japan have been employed in Hong Kong movies. More non–Hong Kong directors have also become involved in recent years, especially since 2004.

More East Asian collaborations are taking place in the field of music as well, leading to the creation of new musical genres and pointing to the rise of an East Asian popular culture. More than broadcasting media, music producers in East Asia primarily tend to aim for regional rather than global acceptance. An important player is Channel V, an Asian version of MTV that enjoys phenomenal popularity across East Asia. The channel continuously introduces local and international pop and rock music to its broad-based cable television audience. Channel V's music programs often offer a category of music it calls "Asian music," which includes the pop music of a variety of East Asian music artists and bands.

Music collaborations also take the form of Asian-labeled albums known as "constellation albums." In 2005, for example, JVC Hong Kong produced its own music compilation featuring songs from some of the company's most famous artists. The Hong Kong subsidiary of major Japanese record label Avex Trax went a step further in 2004 with the launch of *The Best of J Pop,* a music CD bundled with a bonus VCD that was so popular it stayed in the top ten on UK-based music retailer HMV's foreign music chart for approximately three months. The album was not sold in Japan, but instead focused on the non-Japanese Asian market from its inception and was marketed as Asian rather than Japanese music. Following its success in Hong Kong, the album was further marketed in Malaysia, Thailand, Singapore, and Taiwan through Avex Trax/ HMV subsidiaries in those locations.[14]

In 2004, Sony Music Entertainment produced a two-volume pop music collection featuring Japanese, Hong Kong, Taiwanese, and South Korean artists. The album's success led to the production of new volumes in 2005, including Thai music. In an interview in 2005, a senior Sony official in charge of strategic thinking in Asia told me that the company wanted to create a pan-Asian musical genre targeted at audiences from various nations and language groups across Asia, and the official expressed confidence that in the long term this market would grow. To support this effort, the company encourages its regional offices to produce constellation albums that emphasize transnational collaboration between musicians. In a separate interview, Sony's legendary producer Tanaka Akira surmised that one of the best places for collaborative music productions is the Asian market, especially in areas inhabited by Chinese and Malay speakers. He also saw potential for other creative collaborations, such as a joint effort of musical artists from Okinawa (Japan) and Indonesia, to be marketed in both countries.[15]

Not many transnational alliances have materialized in the field of television, as high production costs impeded most such attempts before they could get off the ground. Unlike in other parts of the world, coproduction of television programs is a relatively new phenomenon in East Asia, despite a handful of examples of coproduced television programs in the 1980s and early 1990s, consisting mainly of documentaries produced by Japanese and Korean partners. Nevertheless, some major TV companies have more recently tried their luck in spite of significant financial risk. The importance of these collaborations lies mainly in their entrepreneurial exploration of the potential for joint cultural productions in general and in their forging a vision for cultural industries to look beyond their immediate domestic market. According to Jin and Lee's study (2007, 33), the companies most active in transnational coproductions at the turn of the twenty-first century included TBS and Fuji TV (Japan), SBS, KBS, and MBC (Korea), MBC and CCTV (China), and Jet Tone Films (Hong Kong). Many television companies in East Asia, however, remain wary of getting involved in expensive transnational television program production. They prefer to purchase and localize imported television content or serve as subcontractors for foreign productions.[16]

Japanese and South Korean television companies have collaborated on a few projects since the late 1990s. The fact that Japanese and Korean broadcasters can work together at all in spite of considerable financial risk and political and historical differences is an important indication of the potential for cultural collaborations. Examples of successful television dramas coproduced by Japanese and Korean companies include *Friends* (2002), *Sonagi, an Afternoon Showers* [sic] (2002), and *Star's Echo* (2004). All three depicted stories of young love that transcended national boundaries, cultural differences, and various difficulties. And in all three, Japanese heroines and Korean heroes succeeded in both romance and work.

In recent years, Star TV has become Asia's biggest transnational television broadcasting venture. The India-based broadcaster owns a wide variety of entertainment, news, and sports channels that give it access to a potential pool of consumers in three hundred million homes from China to India. The company favors localizing existing content and broadcasting it in Asian languages, especially in Mandarin (Sinclair, Jacka, and Cunningham 1997). For example, Star TV broadcasts Mandarin-language dramas, news, and talk shows in Taiwan and mainland China, and a variety of other TV programs for audiences in Thailand, the Philippines, and South Korea. It also syndicates several popular shows from the United States and United Kingdom (such as *Desperate Housewives, Boston Legal, The Simpsons,* and *Heroes*) to appeal to English speakers in South and East Asia.

The Impact of Piracy

Piracy in East Asia plays a conspicuous role in promoting regional confluences of popular culture by facilitating and accelerating the diffusion of popular culture products and images despite restrictive conditions. Piracy, or illegal reproduction of copyrighted material, both physical and online, has been highly instrumental in getting banned material past government censors and into the hands of consumers who would not otherwise have had access to it. Since the 1990s, piracy in East Asia has been helped by lax state enforcement of intellectual property laws and driven by strong demand for illegal cultural products (Pang 2006).

During the formative years of the Asian popular culture market in the 1990s, East Asia, excluding Japan, was the scene of the world's biggest music piracy markets, including brisk markets for pirated music in China (then the world's biggest market for pirated goods), Taiwan, Indonesia, Malaysia and Thailand.[17] According to the International Federation of Phonogram and Videogram Producers (IFPI), in 2000, illicitly copied music accounted for at least 90 percent of the entire domestic music market in China, 85 percent in Indonesia, at least 50 percent in Taiwan, Malaysia, Thailand, and the Philippines, and at least 30 percent in Hong Kong, Singapore, and South Korea. East Asia's lucrative piracy markets are based on low manufacturing costs and adroit transfer of products to a large pool of potential customers. Products such as comic books, music, and visual images (TV programs, animation, video games) can be reproduced and disseminated using relatively simple technology, certainly simpler than with products such as automobiles or electronic devices. A recorder is all that is needed to burn pirated CDs, VCDs, and DVDs and to illegally record and distribute television programs.

In recent years, popular culture has also become available online, often illegally, as the Internet has emerged as a powerful medium for delivering and consuming cultural content. According to a study commissioned by MTV Networks Asia, mobile phones are commonly used by young Asians for downloading digital content, with the most popular types being songs and ring tones.[18] According to another survey commissioned by MTV Networks Asia, at least 55 percent of youngsters interviewed, especially in China, the Philippines, and Thailand, admitted they have downloaded music without paying (The Asia Pacific Music Forum 2008).

While physical piracy was the main form of dissemination of popular culture in Asia in the 1990s, in recent years online piracy has become more prevalent. According to the IFPI, for every music track bought online, twenty are downloaded illegally and many music albums appear online even before their formal release in shops or on the radio.[19] Online piracy is more difficult to trace, since locating servers that allow illegal downloading, especially when they are located in other countries, is much more complicated than locating equipment that produces disks or tapes. Operators of both physical and online pirating businesses have continued delivering popular culture across national boundaries since the early 1990s, for the most part undisturbed by law enforcement agencies.

East Asian governments have sometimes restricted the importation of certain cultural products on the grounds that their content was morally or politically harmful. In the Philippines for example, imported comics and TV animation were often banned because of their violent content or because they threatened to overshadow productions supported by the Marcos regime. In Malaysia, the Ministry of Interior must examine imported comic books to see if they pose any educational or political risk before approving their distribution. Since 2002, the Ministry of Culture in Thailand has been engaged in a vigorous campaign to restrict violent or vulgar pornographic cultural products.

Censorship in East Asia was sometimes aimed at preventing "cultural imperialism" as a late reaction to colonization. This was the case with the ban on importation of Japanese culture to Taiwan and South Korea for decades following World War II. Taiwan banned the importation of Japanese music, movies, and television programs after Japan officially re-established diplomatic relations with the People's Republic of China in 1972, but it gradually began to allow Japanese culture in after 1993. Since 1998, the South Korean government has also been easing its ban on the importation of Japanese culture, although a few restrictions remain on the broadcasting of television programs and movies from Japan.

Meanwhile, government censorship and restrictions aimed at preventing the infringements of copyright on popular culture products have never been effective. Consumers' attraction to popular imported products, the ability of underground networks to supply them, and hugely popular markets selling pirated goods have made it difficult to enforce government restrictions. As any visitor to a major East Asian metropolis in the 1990s would have noticed, an abundance of pirated versions of prohibited products were available from street vendors and in shops. In spite of censorship of adult movies, pirated versions were openly mass-marketed in places such as Hong Kong's Ho King and Sino Center and Bangkok's Pantip and night market. Even in Singapore, where media piracy is relatively low and copyright enforcement is strict, pirated products do exist, both locally and in nearby Malaysia.

Taiwanese and South Korean restrictions on Japanese popular culture were not effective either. In Taiwan, Japanese songs and video programs were widely heard and rented in most music and video rental stores, and Japanese fashion magazines (or translated Chinese editions) were readily available, even from street vendors, despite the official restrictions (based on testimonies in Ching 1996, 189; and Iwabuchi 2002, 138–139). Throughout the 1990s, Japanese music constituted approximately 30 percent of products on the South Korean illegal music market (METI 2002). Pirated music was estimated to occupy more than 30 percent of the country's overall music market, with illegal versions of Japanese music alone reaching as much as 10 percent of South Korea's entire music market, both legal and illegal. In addition, karaoke bars and the Internet made Japanese music and television dramas even more abundantly available in South Korea as they easily bypassed the government's restrictions on offering Japanese culture to consumers (Ōtake and Hosokawa 1998, 186–187; Pack 2004).

One important effect of piracy in East Asia has been that it forced governments and organizations in the region to cooperate. Governments in East Asia have been continually warned of the damages piracy inflicts on their countries' economies and of the need to improve enforcement of copyright laws. The Japanese government, for example, began emphasizing the importance of enforcing intellectual property rights; it raised the issue in FTA talks with Singapore and Thailand and repeatedly alerted its neighbors about infringement of Japanese copyrights in Asia (JETRO 2002). Multinational and regional music and television companies have also been helping to fight piracy of their products. They have established local and regional federations to promote awareness and enforcement of antipiracy laws and have ardently lobbied governments to get them to articulate copyright protection measures.[20]

Conclusion

This chapter proposes an alternative way of looking at the East Asia region, highlighting its sociogeographical densities and the dynamics of popular cultural flows within its register. I started by showing that the regionalization process in East Asia is driven by market forces, rather than by the political will of governments, and that the East Asian region can also be construed as an area defined by cross-border relations between cities and their residents, rather than an area consisting only of entire nation-states. I emphasized the importance of cities in our understanding of the newly created hierarchies of East Asia and described the widening gap between residents of big cities and residents of nonurban areas, especially in Southeast Asia and mainland China. I then described a process of region making initiated by ongoing reciprocity between the economies and popular cultures surrounding East Asia's largest cities. I showed that a dynamic East Asian popular cultural market has been in the making for the past two decades, bolstered by a rapid flow of cultural commodities and by cooperation in visual and sound productions, as well as by piracy.

The regionalization process in East Asia has a few conspicuous features. First, compared to regionalization in Western Europe, the process in East Asia is engendered less by institutional arrangements revolving around the search for a common future. Rather, at the heart of the East Asian process lie market forces that promote the construction of new economic and cultural linkages. Second, regionalization in East Asia is essentially taking place in cities and consists largely of transnational relations between cities and their middle-class consumers, rather than encompassing entire nation-states. While national boundaries are being blurred in both Western Europe and East Asia, the regionalization taking place in East Asia is fragmented in the sense that a certain segment of the population (overwhelmingly the urban middle class) is more "regionalized" than those who live in rural areas. In this sense, the increasing connectedness between cities and people in East Asia is not evenly spread, but is instead a socially selective process that is not necessarily relevant to the entire population of a given country, but only to parts of it.

How does popular culture contribute to our discussion of regionalization in East Asia? As we have seen, a transnational flow of popular culture has been reaching urban consumers, and companies, networks, and individuals have been collaborating on a regionwide basis. This transplanted popular culture finds the richest soil in the hearts and minds of the younger generation of Asia's developing countries—a generation that is generally better educated than the previous one and will someday lead the nations of Asia. As successive generations of consumers mature, popular culture spreads its roots throughout society, young and old. This cultural diffusion can lead people to feel that they are a part of a single region defined by the proliferation of a common popular culture.

Popular culture is a powerful engine that helps make East Asia into a region. Regional circulation of commodified culture encourages the creation of shared popular culture markets. These establish East Asians, especially city dwellers, in a new cultural realm constructed by common popular culture products and images, and thus enable the dissemination of communalities of conceptions and ideas. The dissemination and consumption of popular culture constructs new frameworks for delivering images, ideas, and emotions, which can stimulate feelings of belonging to the same cultural space and convince people in places such as Hong Kong, Japan, Bangkok, and Jakarta that they live in a unified cultural domain.

There is little doubt that when people grow up consuming the same popular culture, it engenders a special bond or a special sense of kinship between them. Given the large number of people in East Asia who spend many hours every day in front of a television, go to movies, listen to music, and generally invest in cultural consumption, it seems reasonable to expect that these practices will have an impact on their lives and perceptions, introduce new images and options, and create new social and symbolic references. We can well imagine popular culture, along with the practices and discourses it gives rise to, creating a sense of "we-ness," to borrow a term from international relations scholar Andrew Hurrell (1995, 65).

The chapters that follow will focus on the operations of Japanese cultural industries in East Asia in the decades surrounding the 1990s and their implications for the regionalization process. The investigation starts in Japan by examining the process of cultural commodification, the capacity of the domestic market to produce and export culture, and the Japanese government's responses to these processes. Subsequent chapters analyze these activities and the impact of Japanese cultural industries on the East Asian region.

CHAPTER 3

//////////////

Japan's Popular Culture Powerhouse

It is no exaggeration to say that the world's interest in and admiration for Japanese popular culture has grown dramatically in the past two decades. The reach of Japan's popular culture extends far beyond the island nation's borders; keen interest in Japanese popular culture commodities, especially anime, manga, and video games, is evident not just in neighboring countries, but also in Europe, North America, the Middle East, and Africa. A large increase in the number of students learning Japanese is an indication of the world's fascination with Japanese popular culture. According to the Japan Foundation (2011), Japanese language studies have never been so popular, mainly due to the consumption of manga and anime by young audiences abroad. The number of people studying the Japanese language outside of Japan has increased from 130,000 in 1979 to more than three and a half million in 2009. Any lecturer in Japanese studies can testify that these days it is no longer Japanese corporate culture, managerial techniques, or economic success that draws most students to study the language so much as Japanese contemporary culture and lifestyle.

In addition to its allure from an artistic standpoint, Japan's popular culture is also a big export industry. According to Sugiura Tsutomu's calculations (2008, 141), the export sales of popular culture merchandise together with royalties, service fees, and other income from products such as recorded sounds and images (music, anime, movies, video games), books, magazines, paintings, art, and handicrafts more than tripled from ¥837 billion (US$8.37 billion) in 1996 to nearly ¥2,539 billion (US$25.4 billion) in 2006. This growth rate is impressive given that during the same period Japan's total exports (cultural and noncultural related items) grew by only 68 percent, from ¥44.7 trillion (US$447 billion) in 1996, to ¥75.2 trillion (US$752 billion) in 2006.

Take animation (anime),[1] for example. According to the Japanese Ministry of Economy, Trade and Industry (METI)[2] (METI 2003, 8–9), approximately 65 percent of the world's production of animated cartoon series takes place in Japan, where estimated annual sales of licensed goods amount to US$17 billion. According to the Japan External Trade Organization (JETRO), anime sales in the United States alone generated US$2.929 billion in 2007 (JETRO 2009). Japan is also a world leader in comic publications (manga).[3] Sales in the United States are estimated to have increased from US$50–60 million in 2002 to US$90–110 million in 2003.[4] Manga is also extremely popular in East Asia, where it is consumed in large quantities (both in Japanese and in local languages) and serves as a model for local comic industries (Hu 2010, 141–150). In South Korea for example, it is estimated that nearly 80 percent of the comic books sold in the market are translated from Japanese (Yamanaka 2010, 50). The video games industry is similarly dominated by Japan. Three Japanese companies, Sony, Nintendo, and Sega, lead the world video games market despite competition from Microsoft's Xbox. In 2006, international video game sales rose 20 percent from a year earlier to US$32 billion, of which US$22 billion were North American sales (Digital Content Association of Japan 2009, 176–178).

Japan's extensive popular culture exports and worldwide imitation of Japanese popular culture commodities and genres are the results of Japan's cultural industries' many years of experience commodifying and commercializing culture in their home market. The Japanese market provides ample industrial and social infrastructure for supporting cultural industries and serves as an excellent testing ground for their products. The skills and abilities cultivated by producing high-quality popular culture products in their domestic market became an advantage that later paved the way for entry into foreign markets. After all, a new genre of goods cannot immediately become export-led, but needs to go through a maturing process that nurtures its competitiveness.

This chapter examines processes of popular culture commodification in Japan and analyzes the capacity of the domestic market to manufacture and export anime, movies, video games, television programs, music, and manga. The central argument presented here is that the structure and size of the Japanese market and the experience Japanese cultural industries gained in the domestic marketplace has helped build their competitiveness and has stimulated their expansion to overseas markets since the 1980s.

The chapter is divided into four parts. The first part examines the structure of Japan's cultural industries and analyzes the process of cultural commodification based on examples from music, television, and manga. The analysis provides a broad picture of Japan's popular culture industries and the main features of popular culture production. The second and third parts provide an overview of the enormous capacity of Japan's cultural industries, for production and consumption in part two, and for export in part three. This overview is important in the context of this book because it underscores the industrial foundations of Japan's cultural industries and their ability to manufacture commodified culture and market it on a massive scale. The last part looks at the Japanese government's involvement in the production and export of popular culture and its initiatives to support the sector. It emphasizes the point that success of the private sector in the 1990s convinced the government that cultural industries can facilitate industrial progress, improve the economy, and help the nation attain "soft power"[5] by boosting its image abroad.

Image Factories: Japan's Popular Culture Production Mechanisms

The commodification and marketing of culture is not, of course, unique to Japan. Many countries have commodified and industrialized culture to some degree, whether for purposes of entertainment or propaganda (Mulcahy 2006). Japan, though, is an extreme case in which a wide variety of forms of entertainment are highly commercialized. According to Donald Richie (2003, 10–31), one of the most prolific writers on Japanese society and culture, Japan is an "image factory," with an unusual capacity for inventing and commercializing cultural innovations and fashion trends, both native and imported. Richie says Japan is unlike other countries in the degree to which these processes are exaggerated and highly visible.

Indeed, the Japanese industries have their own sophisticated and highly efficient way of translating artistic innovations into accessible consumer products and marketing them to specific audiences. Essentially, this way is an industry-driven process that entails extracting and indigenizing creativity, images, fashion trends, material pleasures, and fads, and then producing, standardizing, and marketing a related line of products. Although imaginative innovations are at the heart of these creations, they are commercially worthless unless they are packaged in a way that marries cultural ideas and sensibilities with economic logic.

Japan's cultural industries have evolved into organizations that are highly effective at producing and commercializing popular culture. At first, many of Japan's cultural industries, such as anime, video games, pop music, and television programs, were based on Western technologies and influences that entered the country after World War II. Most Japanese popular culture products found in the market today still combine the strengths of both imported technologies and local culture (Low 2009; Mōri 2009; Nakamura 2004; Pope 2012). Eventually, however, Japan's cultural industries began to seek new creative fodder that would allow them to satisfy domestic demand. In the process, they stopped merely imitating Western popular culture and became world-class innovators of popular culture in their own right, with anime, manga, and video games being the best-known examples.

Although there are a few mammoth enterprises, the overall structure of Japan's cultural industries is not oligopolistic. The process of innovation, development, and commodification is shared by a number of competitive players and includes thousands of small companies and venture start-ups that are vital to the process of popular culture production. There are five key TV stations, approximately forty record companies (of which the eight largest account for the majority of sales),[6] about ten major publishers, and three main movie companies. The animation industry, however, comprises approximately 650 production and postproduction companies that employ about 5,000 animators. The comic industry employs about 4,000 cartoonists and 28,000 assistants, while the video game industry is made up of 146 mainly small companies that together employ a creative population of some 18,500. There are no fewer than 127 terrestrial TV stations plus 547 cable TV companies, almost all involved in television production to one degree or another. As of 2004, there were 73 music production companies, 85 major recording studios, and approximately 2,400 other registered companies engaged in various stages of commodifying and commercializing music—in addition to thousands of so-called "indie" (independent) companies involved in alternative, small-scale productions of music and visual images (JETRO 2004a; JETRO 2006; Dentsū Communication Institute 2005, 68–69; Nakamura 2003). A substantial number of the people who contribute to popular culture production are not directly beholden to the biggest enterprises.

As the nucleus of Japan's cultural industries, Tokyo is where many of the products are initially conceived, produced, and marketed. Tokyo's "pop culture triangle" includes the Akihabara, Shibuya, and Harajuku districts, where artists and agents interact and explore new production possibilities. Shibuya, Shimokitazawa, and Kichijoji are the most prolific locales for the making of contemporary Japanese pop music. Approximately 80 percent of Japan's animation companies operate inside the city of Tokyo, together with all the major newspapers and publishers (Association of Japanese Animations 2005). The core divisions of the five key Japanese TV stations, namely Asahi TV, NHK, Fuji TV, TBS, and NTV are also located in Tokyo (Capel 2004; Ugaya 2005, 152–154).

Osaka is another important cultural hub. Many of Japan's biggest *talento* (media personalities) were nurtured by Osaka-based production companies and talent agencies. The most famous of these is Yoshimoto Kogyo, a talent agency with more than two hundred salaried employees that has dominated comedy entertainment in Japan for decades. The company constantly seeks new faces and raw material. Yoshimoto Kogyo's schools in Osaka and Tokyo train thousands of aspiring celebrities every year (Stocker 2001, 251–257). Although performers and creative personnel come from every part of Japan, their creative work is concentrated in Tokyo and Osaka.

Several characteristics of Japanese-style popular culture production help make it a highly effective means of commodifying and commercializing popular culture. The most prominent characteristic is that a good deal of creativity in popular culture is facilitated by close reciprocity between the industry and its audience. The creative stage is often occupied by an individual performer, but the development of creativity into commercial products and its translation into commodities is undertaken by an agent or mediator assigned by the established industry. The partnership between artist and industry constitutes an effective mechanism for commodifying and commercializing diverse forms of art and culture. These relationships are very active, but they are not sequential as with manufacturing noncultural commodities at a factory. Rather they are characterized by continuous engagement between audiences/

consumers on the one hand and agents of established industry on the other. For the cultural industries, these relations are vital to the thrust of their work, that is, establishing a framework for utilizing and valorizing individual creativity and turning it into a commercialized set of products that contribute to corporate success. For the audience, the relationship with the industry presents an opportunity to take part in the creative process and have a say in the final design of the products. For successful amateurs, these relationships provide a chance to exhibit their talents and hopefully to be recruited by the established industry.

Japan's cultural industries have succeeded in fostering a close proximity between professionals and amateurs. Rather than squelching individual creativity and private initiatives, the cultural industries have supported, recruited, and co-opted them to their own advantage. Japanese popular culture production takes place through a bottom-up process that is not only tolerated but embraced by the established industry. Because private and individual initiatives are seen as opportunities rather than as threats, there is room for close reciprocity between creators, culture production companies, and consumers. The bottom line is that creative work is often carried out by individuals who are not a part of the established industry, such as fans, amateurs, temporary workers, and students. Their work is sponsored, guided, and packaged by industry representatives, often for very little compensation.

This style of cultural production is different from the Hollywood model of popular culture production, which is carried out by teams of professional creators, including experienced creative personnel and managers, technical experts, and producers, sometimes assisted by large-scale subcontracting (Aksoy and Robins 1992). The Hollywood model has changed over the years, gradually loosening the tight control the industry used to exert over the production of popular culture before the 1970s. Although Hollywood productions are now carried out by multiple professionals led by project teams (Ryan 1992, 124–134; Storper 1994, 200–216), they are still considerably more centralized than their Japanese counterparts.

Japanese productions are carried out through a much more complex process that involves participation from a large number of closely cooperating innovators and service providers, both professional and amateur. Venture companies are a good example of popular culture producers working in an interactive environment marked by close proximity between professionals and amateurs. An essential player in Japan's cultural industries, venture companies facilitate cultural industries' interactions with semiprofessionals and amateurs and establish the framework necessary for producing a specific project for a larger enterprise they represent. Venture companies are typically made up of a producer or producers who create a specific venture by recruiting creators, obtaining sponsors, and developing distribution contacts. Producers from larger companies provide most of the operating capital and take on the financial risk of manufacturing and marketing the venture's product (Nakamura 2003). Companies that specialize in investing in culture-related ventures sometimes provide additional funds.[7]

Studies of popular televised music shows in Japan exemplify the type of interaction described above, between established culture industries and amateur participants. These music programs are reality shows that include competitive music performances by amateur singers. The audience judges the performances and ultimately selects one performer as the winner, which gives the audience the satisfaction of active participation in the show. Shows like these were extremely popular in the 1970s and 1980s, when they achieved audience ratings of more than 40 percent (compared to 20.9 percent for the highest audience rating for the top 1998 show). The best-known example of this genre is *Sutā Tanjō* (A Star Is Born), a popular star-search program developed in Japan in the 1970s (Iwabuchi 2002). The program was produced by NTV—one of Japan's biggest television stations—in close collaboration with recording companies and talent agencies.

Throughout production of the program, there was also close cooperation between the industry (television station, recording companies, talent agencies) and the audience (studio audience and amateur singers). The program auditioned amateur singers by holding singing competitions that were broadcast live from public halls. Adolescent winners of the singing competitions, having been selected by executives of top record companies and management agencies in attendance at the competitions, were then made into professional music artists and star-idols. Superstars who got their start on the show included Yamaguchi Momoe, Mori Masako, Sakurada Junko, Iwasaki Hiromi, Nakamori Akina, Koizumi Kyoko, and Pink Lady. In the 1980s, other successful music programs included *The Best Ten* (TBS, 1978–1989), *Top Ten* (NTV), *Music Station* (Asahi), *Heisei Meibutsu Ikasu Bando Tengoku* [Paradise for Cool Bands] (TBS, 1989–1991), and *Yuyake Nyan Nyan* (Fuji TV, 1968–1988).

These amateur music television shows are part of a broad trend in entertainment based on joyful interaction between producers and consumers, who both contribute to the final product. In order to achieve optimal exposure for these relatively inexpensive and versatile productions, amateur music shows are highly structured in terms of performer roles and show themes. They have evolved into a new genre of television programming that combines music, comedy, and dance performances with active audience participation. As a result, music has become more dependent on television exposure, and new trends in multifaceted televised music production have emerged (Stevens and Hosokawa 2001, 227–230).

Meanwhile, these shows have also modified the structure of music production by eliminating some of the boundaries between the creative work of professionals and that of amateurs and consumers. Up to the 1970s, there were clear divisions of labor in the Japanese music industry between lyricists, composers, and arrangers, all of whom had exclusive contracts with record companies. Indie music artists, especially those representing rock music, were excluded from mainstream production channels. Amateur programs on television, however, have given these bands a stage on which to debut and become popular, bypassing the established industry and facilitating a shift in the position of music artists vis-à-vis the industry. Noteworthy Japanese bands that benefited from this process and went on to become popular nationwide include *Speed, Max, Glay*, and *Penicillin*. By giving the audience the power to choose winners, these productions broadened the industry's search for talent and created new production opportunities.

The manga business provides another example of how corporate production efforts can coincide with fans' consumption practices. Amateur manga artists and fans of their self-published works, called *dōjinshi*, have become an integral part of the manga industry. *Dōjinshi* producers and consumers joined forces with creative editors and retailers to create Japan's manga business empire. *Dōjinshi* started to appear in Japan in the mid-1970s, when manga fans and amateur manga artists gathered to trade and share the latter's work. Today these groups are well organized, to the point that *dōjinshi* events draw tens of thousands of amateur artists selling their homemade comic books and animation. Special manga markets held in Tokyo each August and December draw a half-million visitors. *Dōjinshi* borrow liberally from existing works. Many times, the characters are indistinguishable from the originals on which they are based, although the stories usually include much more parody, sexual escapades, and violent scenes.

Japanese copyright protections are just as restrictive as American copyright protections, but there is an unspoken understanding between the established manga industry and the *dōjinshi* publishers that allows fans and amateur creators to issue small-scale editions of manga that parody characters and story lines already in the market without being sued for copyright violation. In fact, these operations can reach quite a large scale. For example, at the Super Comic City events in Tokyo and Osaka, hundreds of thousands of books are sold every year in cash transactions totaling millions of U.S. dollars. Despite the growth in scale, the established industry continues to tolerate these activities in the belief that they serve to maintain fresh interest in buying mainstream manga and cultivate a pool of talented manga artists—some of whom will later be recruited by the established industry (Norris 2009; Pink 2007).

This special relationship between amateurs, fans, and the major manga producers allows big companies to tap into the creative process of gifted amateurs, gauge and develop new products, and recruit new talent—all without heavy investment in commissioning polls, conducting surveys among focus groups, or other forms of formal market research. Scouts from big and small manga producers frequent the major *dōjinshi* conventions to seek new talent, and they sometimes contact the artists they find there with job offers. Among the famous professional manga artists who got their start in the *dōjinshi* arena are Takahashi Rumiko, Fujishima Kōsuke, CLAMP, and Akamatsu Ken (Kinsella 2000, 134; Shimoku 2008, 120–129). Takeda Keiji, one of the organizers of Japan's largest *dōjinshi* gathering, explains:

> *Dōjinshi* create a market base, and that market base is naturally drawn to the original work. . . . *Dōjinshi* conventions are also where we're finding the next generation of authors. Publishers understand the value of not destroying this arrangement . . . and *dōjinshi* creators honor their part of this silent pact. They tacitly agree not to go too far—to produce work only in limited editions and to avoid selling so many copies that they risk eating into the market for original works. (quoted in Pink 2007)

Marketplace interaction between professionals, amateurs, and audience constructs a reciprocal system that enables a rational-industrial continuation of individual creativity. This system constantly draws new recruits from the audience to become active participants in the commodification of culture. At the same time, it nurtures cooperation between professionals and audiences in the development of new products. In this way, anyone with a creative idea, a digital camera, and a computer has a chance to become part of the industry that produces commodified cultural products. Audiences are thus constantly drawn into involvement in popular culture production, making consumption an integral part of a cycle of production, rather than merely a final destination.

The Role of *"Freeters"* and *"Otaku"* in the Production Cycle

Another important feature in Japan's popular culture production system is the younger generation, especially *"freeters"* and *"otaku."* The term *"freeter"* (a blend of "free" or "freelance" and *"arbeiter,"* the German word for "laborer") emerged in Japan in the late 1980s in reference to people who work as freelancers or in a series of nonpermanent, perhaps part-time jobs. *Otaku,* another Japanese slang term coined in the 1980s, refers to people (almost always socially inept young men) with an obsessive interest, generally in video games, anime, or manga. These groups have played an important role in developing the country's cultural industries, not only by constituting a community of ardent consumers that spend much of their disposable income on popular culture, but also by acting as a seismograph for the wider market. Consumption-driven generations born after the mid-1960s grew up during a long period of consistent economic growth during the post–World War II period, amid rising demand from a large, domestic, consumer-oriented middle class (sometimes referred to as the "mass middle class"). Between 1950 and 1980, Japan's GNP grew at an average yearly rate of 7.4 percent. By 1980, Japan's industrial production and manufacturing technology had overtaken that of most Western industrialized nations, and Japan had become the world's second biggest economy, following the United States (Jones 1997, 62–68). The economic growth Japan experienced after the mid-1950s nurtured a sizeable middle class with abundant disposable income and leisure demands, and nonessential consumption gradually became an integral part of everyday life, especially for young people (Shiraishi 2005, 40).

At present, most young Japanese who live with their parents no longer spend the bulk of their income on basic food, shelter, and clothing, but devote much of it to the acquisition of consumer goods, such as communication and other electronic devices, popular culture products, and fashion. A survey conducted by *Nikkei Shinbun*, Japan's leading daily economic newspaper, estimated that in 2003, teenagers in Japan spent more than 75 percent of their disposable income on cultural consumption in the form of video games (both hardware and software), anime, music, books, and movies, while people in their twenties spent approximately 40 percent, and people in their thirties and forties less than 30 percent.[8]

Japanese who grew up amid the wealth of postwar Japan, especially *freeters* and *otaku*, have been infused with huge amounts of creative energy without the sense of obligation that their parents had to save and sacrifice for the nation's postwar reconstruction (Kelts 2007, 180). *Freeters* are given credit for much of the exuberant cultural innovation that took place in Japan during the so-called "lost decade" that began at the end of the 1980s. Their decision to opt out of Japan's mainstream "salary-man" employment system provided them with time to engage in artistic and cultural creativity. In 2002, their numbers were estimated to be more than two million, or about 3 percent of the nation's workforce (JETRO 2004b).

Otaku, considered the most passionate of popular culture fans, are no less important to Japan's popular culture production system than *freeters*. The term *otaku* has experienced a transformation of meaning in the past three decades, from initially referring to youngsters obsessed with anime to describing groups of consumerist-oriented fans of a variety of popular culture products and trends. Initially, *otaku* was a pejorative term that was synonymous with social misfit, nerd, or maniac. Over time, however, it has become more accepted and could be used in a more or less positive sense (Azuma 2009, 3–18). Today, this term is generally applied to youngsters driven by a strong interest in contemporary culture and lifestyles, or to those who choose to facilitate social connections through specific, nonmainstream cultural practices such as cosplay. *Otaku* are also heavy users of information technology.

For our purposes, I would like to focus on the role of *otaku* in popular culture production. First, as conspicuously heavy consumers of cultural products, *otaku* constitute a large market for popular culture products. A report by Nomura Sōgō Kenkyūsho (Nomura Research Institute) has estimated that there are approximately 1.31 million Japanese *otaku* who obsessively consume manga, anime, accessories (such as posters and pictures), fashion, and various game and visual software as well as hardware parts worth ¥2,720 billion. This figure does not include consumption by "ordinary people" whom the research does not define as *otaku*. As seen in Table 3.1, *otaku* have considerable consuming power although they make up just over 1 percent of the Japanese population.

Aside from representing a sizable portion of the consumer market, *otaku* also serve an important function as a "safety net" when new products are launched. *Otaku* are likely to be first in line to purchase new products prior to commercial marketing in the wider market. The success of a new product, especially products as short-lived as popular culture, depends heavily on the immediate reaction of consumers. A positive reaction (for example, reports of long lines of people waiting to buy the newest video game console) can stimulate further demand in the wider market. The *otaku* market's role in the launch of a new popular culture product is illustrated in Table 3.2. When a new product is launched, it is only after it has won the *otaku*'s approval that the product is introduced to a wider group of consumers. In the third stage, a successful product becomes a commercial goldmine not only in itself, but also in the form of a host of spin-off products. A successful caricature, for example, can amplify the development and sales of other inspired products, such as video games and animated television series. After a certain period, the products experience a natural decline in popularity and are replaced by new ones (Nomura Sōgō Kenkyūsho 2005a, 2005b).

TABLE 3.1 The *Otaku* Market in 12 Major Fields

Field	Number of *Otaku*	Monetary Value
Comics	350,000	¥83 billion
Animation	110,000	¥20 billion
Idol culture	280,000	¥61 billion
Games	160,000	¥21 billion
PC assembly	190,000	¥36 billion
Audio-visual equipment	60,000	¥12 billion
Mobile IT equipment	70,000	¥ 8 billion
Autos	140,000	¥54 billion
Travel	250,000	¥81 billion
Fashion	40,000	¥13 billion
Cameras	50,000	¥18 billion
Railways	20,000	¥4 billion
Total	1.72 million	¥411 billion

SOURCE: Nomura Sōgō Kenkyūsho 2005b, 52.

TABLE 3.2 The Diffusion of New Products into the Market

1. The *Otaku* Stage	2. Popularization 1	3. Popularization 2	4. Declining Stage
Initial consumption and assessment of new products entering the market	Consumption by a wider circle of consumers	Mass consumption, product diversification, and marketing of related products and accessories	Gradual reduction in consumption and appearance of new products

SOURCE: Nomura Sogo Kenkyusho 2005b, 47.

Moreover, because they are preoccupied with contemporary culture, *otaku* possess abundant knowledge of the latest cultural trends and innovations and serve to filter or herald the diffusion of new popular culture products and trends to the market. In fact, *otaku* are the biggest experts in the field, often more knowledgeable than the producing companies themselves. Figure 3.1 illustrates the relationship between the established industry (often a venture company), *otaku*, and the wider domestic market. In Stage A, the company / venture is in constant communication with the *otaku* market while launching new products to the wider market (Stage B1). The *otaku* market is important in gauging and negotiating new tastes, and the production establishment pays careful attention to the assessments of *otaku*, in both production and launch stages. In some cases, products circulate directly from the *otaku* market into the domestic market and proliferate into the domain of a wider group of consumers (Stage B2).

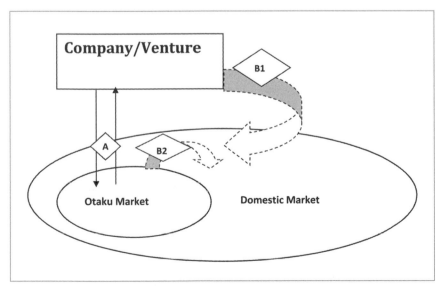

FIGURE 3.1 The Role of *Otaku* in Fostering the Diffusion of New Products into the Market.

The relationship between established industry and *otaku* provides the best examples of active audience participation in popular culture production in Japan and the close proximity between professionals and amateurs. The established industry has wisely used the huge amount of creative energy available in the market for its own purposes, rather than making unilateral decisions about what sort of popular culture consumers want. Although the established industry provides the managerial, financial, and technical resources needed for popular culture production, the industry stays attuned to market needs and takes its cues from an audience that takes an active part in both creative and marketing stages.

Japan's Popular Culture Markets

The scale of Japan's cultural industries is impressive, whether viewed from the production or the consumption side. Despite its decline in some other areas, Japan remains the world's second biggest market for popular culture, after the United States. In 2002, Japan's production of content, including products such as motion pictures, video games, music, books, magazines, and Internet software, represented approximately 10 percent of the world market, compared to America's 41 percent, China's 1.6 percent, and South Korea's 1.2 percent. In 2003, the value of Japanese content production rose 2.3 percent from the previous year to ¥12.7 trillion. By 2007, Japan's share of the world's production of content had increased to 15 percent, compared to America's 51 percent, China's 6 percent, and South Korea's 3 percent. Content industries, however, account for only about 2 percent of Japan's overall GDP, compared to 5 percent in America and the worldwide average of 3 percent, suggesting that Japan's content industries have further room to grow (Digital Content Association of Japan 2005; 2009).

Japan is also number two in the world, following America, in the size of its music market. In 2002, Japan accounted for approximately 18 percent of worldwide music CD sales and 83 percent of sales in Asia.[9] In 2003, sales of recorded music in Japan were estimated at ¥574 billion (Recording Industry Association of Japan 2004). If we include other methods of musical consumption, such as concerts, karaoke, and music downloaded via mobile phones or the Internet, overall revenues from music dramatically increase to ¥1,588.5 billion in 2003 (Figure 3.3). The

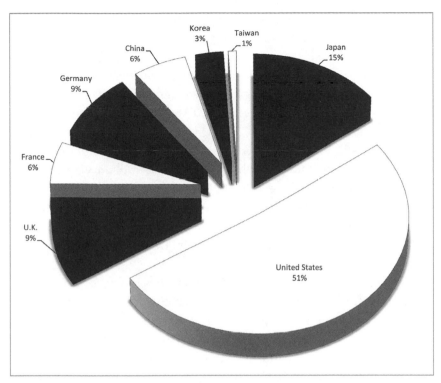

FIGURE 3.2 World Content Market in 2007. (Source: Digital Content Association of Japan 2009)

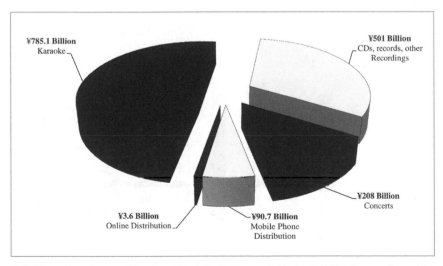

FIGURE 3.3 Distribution of Japanese Music in the Domestic Market in 2003. (Source: Onouchi 2005)

majority of consumers (54–66 percent in 1998–2004) were under the age of twenty-nine (JETRO 2004a).

Japan is the world's third biggest market for movies. In the 1980s and 1990s, it was one of the most prolific movie-producing nations, ahead of Hong Kong and South Korea, although lagging behind India and the United States. In the ten years from 1989 to 1998, Japan produced 255 movies, compared to India's 787, the USA's 591, Hong Kong's 169, and South Korea's 73. From 2001 to 2003, annual revenues from movies were approximately ¥200 billion, with more than 160 million viewers visiting movie theaters every year. In 2004, box office revenues hit a record high, amounting to ¥210.9 billion from more than 170 million moviegoers. In 2009, the figures were similar, with ¥206 billion in revenues and approximately the same number of viewers (Motion Picture Producers Association of Japan 2010).

Japan's video game industry is larger than its movie industry. Japan was not the first to come up with video games—they developed in tandem with computers, primarily in the United States. Japanese video game developers entered the field in the early 1970s with the development of arcade games and the creation of successful games and characters such as Pac-Man (Namco) and Donkey Kong (Nintendo). In 1983–1984, the U.S. console market experienced a devastating crash, generally attributed to a flooding of the market with poor software. Western developers,

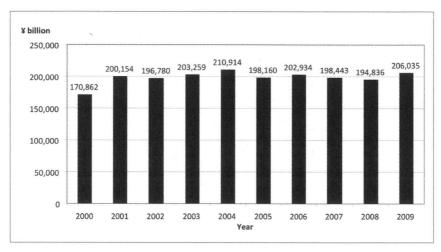

FIGURE 3.4 Box Office Revenues in Japan 2000–2009. (Source: Motion Picture Producers Association of Japan 2010)

heavily impacted by the crash, largely turned their backs on consoles and instead focused on the PC market. The Japanese, however, continued to develop video games for arcades and consoles and dominated the market through the 1980s and 1990s. In 1989, Nintendo, a Kyoto-based company, released the first handheld game to gain mass popularity, the Gameboy. Nintendo has remained the dominant force in the handheld market to this day. In 1995, Sony entered the video game console market with PlayStation, quickly rising to become dominant in market share with that console and its successor, the PlayStation 2. In the start of the twenty-first century, Microsoft entered the console arena while Sega exited it.[10]

At present, two companies—Sony and Nintendo—maintain dominant positions in game hardware sales. In 2004, combined sales of video game hardware and software in Japan amounted to ¥427.95 billion (Figure 3.5). In the same year, Sony's PlayStation 2 and Nintendo's Game Cube accounted for 97.8 percent of sales of nonportable game machines in Japan, leaving Microsoft's Xbox with only a 2.2 percent share (Hamamura 2005). The Japanese market accounted for approximately 16.8 percent of the world's video game machines sales, compared to North America's 46.3 percent, Europe's 28.3 percent, and Asia's 8.6 percent. Moreover, 53.6 percent of Japanese game software was consumed locally, compared to 32.5 percent in North America, 8.6 percent in Europe, and 5.3 percent in Asia (CESA 2004, 68–72). According to a recent survey, Sony's PlayStation and Nintendo's Game Cube accounted for more than 97 percent of video game consoles sold in Japan in 2007, while Microsoft's Xbox claimed only 2.3 percent.

Proliferation of manga in Japan is also enormous. Manga is one of Japan's most widespread forms of popular culture. Manga as a medium existed in Japan as early as the 1920s, but after World War II it emerged as an edgy Japanese art form. In the 1960s, it underwent an immense expansion and gradually transformed into a mainstream industry.[11] Unlike comic books in the United States and Europe, which are almost entirely targeted at children, manga in Japan are widely read in Japan by adults and children alike.

Today, manga has diversified into various genres appealing to different social and age groups and has insinuated itself into Japan's daily life. It addresses a wide range of subjects, including "serious" issues such as history, politics, and technology, as well as "fun" subjects such as fashion, cooking, and humor. The late manga artist Tezuka Osamu (1928–1989),

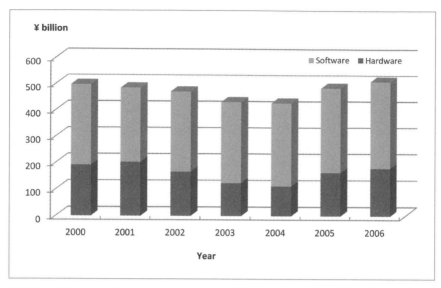

FIGURE 3.5 The Size of the Japanese Video Game Market. (Source: Hamamura 2005)

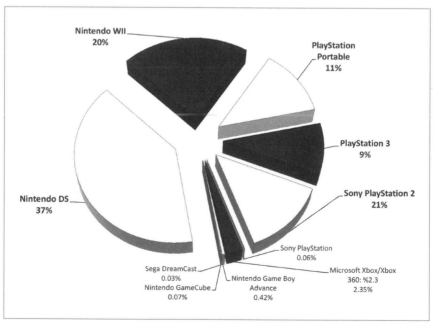

FIGURE 3.6 Video Game Consoles Sold in Japan in 2007. (Source: Dentsū Communication Institute 2009, 103–105)

a major contributor to the rise of Japan's manga industry, churned out sophisticated, artistically appealing pictures coupled with interesting stories. A medical doctor by training, he created no fewer than seven hundred manga series, including *Astro Boy, Kimba the White Lion, Hi no Tori* (Phoenix), and *Black Jack*. It was Tezuka's prolific work in every field of cartoon art—infants' picture books, children's comic books, arty or comic romance novels for women, risqué humor for men's magazines, social satire, political cartoons, even advertising art—that helped establish comics as respectable reading for all age groups in Japan (Patten 2004, 198). Go Nagai, another prolific manga author, created more than fifty manga stories. Together, Nagai and Tezuka helped establish manga's reputation for high quality and gradually made it one of Japan's most successful mediums.

In quantitative terms, the manga industry (both magazines and books) generated annual sales of approximately US$3 billion in the middle of the 1990s, when Shogakukan (Japan's largest manga publisher) alone issued twenty million copies a month. In 2004, there were 297 comic magazine titles published in Japan, with more than one billion copies sold. In 2008, more than two billion comic books and magazines (both weekly and monthly) were sold, not counting consumption online and via cellular phones. Weekly comic magazines such as *Weekly Shonen Magazine, Weekly Shonen Jump, Shojo Comic,* and countless others are most visible on the Japanese street. An illuminating example is the paperback edition of *Bleach,* a series about a ghost-spotting teenager, which has sold some forty-six million copies in six years (in a country of 127 million people) (Pink 2007). In 1997, manga publications were estimated to make up 22 percent of all printed materials sold in Japan and one out of every three books published in 2004 (Itō 2008, 46; The Research Institute for Publications 2009).

The Japanese market for anime is enormous as well. Anime started in Japan as far back as the nineteenth century as a product of artistic interaction between Japanese, European, and American cultures combined with new printing and media technologies. The first Japanese animated work to be shown in a movie theater was *Imokawa Mukuzo, genkanban no maki* (Mukuzo Imokawa, the Doorman), which was released in 1917.[12] The first animated feature movie, *Momotarō Umino Shimpei* (Momotarō's Divine Sea Warriors), was shown in 1945. Later, the rapid spread of television gave animators a new means of delivering their work, which soon led to the introduction of the televised cartoon format. In the 1960s, anime greatly diversified into new genres and themes, and the 1970s brought a greater degree of cooperation with toy companies, record companies, publishing companies, investment sources, and distribution companies. In 1961, Tezuka Osamu established his own anime production studio, known as Mushi Production, and created Japan's first television cartoon studio. His work, coupled with prolific anime production by Toei Animation Studio (founded in 1956), turned anime into a massive mainstream industry (Hu 2010, 83–103). Commercial anime has developed greatly since Tezuka's day and has incorporated new companies and talents. Anime today is the product of creative collaboration and social energy of various people involved in the anime business—producers, image designers, sound engineers, marketing personnel, creative fans, etc., a production system anthropologist Ian Condry (2013) calls "collaborative creativity."

In the 1980s and 1990s, anime reached new peaks. A variety of products addressing a variety of themes were consumed not only via television and cinemas, but also via Internet, video games, cellular phones, and advertising billboards (Poitras 2008, 49). Anime that was originally aimed at a very young audience, such as *Poke'mon* and *Digimon,* became famous among children of all ages, while adult-oriented anime, such as *Neon Genesis Evangelion* and Miyazaki Hayao's movies, enabled adults to find intellectual depth as well as enjoyment in anime. In 2003, domestic retail sales of anime-related licensed merchandise in Japan amounted to ¥1.7 trillion. *Poke'mon* has generated ¥1 trillion in sales in Japan alone since the famous animated character was first introduced more than a decade ago.[13] If we include the sale of other media and related products, such as animated movies, anime soundtracks, and animated characters, the *Poke'mon* total sales would reach ¥2 trillion.[14]

Lastly, Japan has a large television industry that produces most of the content consumed domestically. The Japanese television industry reached a state of maturity as early as the late 1950s, when several major television stations already operated in the domestic market (NHK, NTV, Fuji TV, and NET—later to be known as Asahi TV). In the early 1960s, after importing American television programs for a decade, these broadcasters began producing many modern Japanese television programs. In the 1970s and 1980s, they began to produce a wider variety of television programs, ranging from children's programs and anime to family dramas and miniseries. The 1990s were the golden age of Japanese "trendy dramas,"[15] which gradually found an expanded audience in East Asia (Clements and Tamamuro 2003). The majority of television programs appearing on Japanese television today are produced domestically. In the past twenty-five years, domestic television production filled approximately 95 percent of the broadcasting hours in the country. In 2001, only 3,036 hours were imported, accounting for 4.9 percent of total broadcasting time (Figure 3.7; Hara 2004).

As we can see from the figures presented above, Japan has an enormous domestic market for its own popular culture, including music, movies, video games, anime, manga, and television programs. In the past two decades, Japan has also been exporting popular culture on a massive scale, and this is the trend we will explore next.

Japan's Popular Culture Goes Transnational

In the first few decades after World War II, Japan's cultural industries mainly targeted the domestic market and their development was a result of local demand. An exception was commercial animation, which from

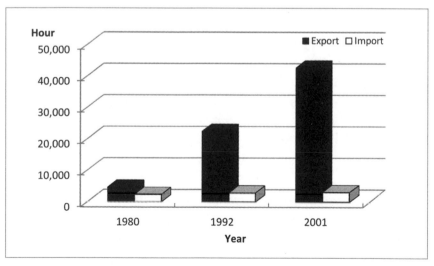

FIGURE 3.7 Import and Export Hours of Japanese Television Programs, 1980, 1992, 2002. (Source: Japan Media Communication Center 2004)

its inception was aimed at foreign markets (Hamano 2005, 7; Sugiura 2008, 133–134). In the 1980s, however, many Japanese companies started to mass market their products overseas, and Japan gradually became a major exporter of popular culture. Japanese forms of entertainment, especially manga, anime, and video games, are now highly acclaimed abroad for their extremely well-developed narratives and realistic depictions of speed in motion, attracting the attention of artists, designers, creators, and of course consumers.

The expansion of some of Japan's cultural industries abroad was in part an intentional strategy that came to fruition during a period when recession caused an already saturated domestic market to decline (S. Shiraishi 2000, 305). At first, the export of Japanese culture included only a small number of products, mostly anime, but it has since broadened and intensified, both in volume and in the range of products and spin-offs. As we shall see in chapter 5, it is not only Japanese popular culture commodities that are consumed abroad, but also Japanese popular culture formats and genres, which are imitated by cultural industries in other countries. The success of one product in the market stimulates the popularity of other products. For example, the success of Japanese anime has bolstered sales of characters, video games, and manga.

As Japanese cultural industries expanded overseas, they began to generate substantial profits. By the early 1990s, Japanese popular culture had become a huge export industry. In a 1993 white paper, METI estimated that more than 60 percent of the approximately ¥55.3 trillion that multimedia industries were expected to generate in 2015 would come from sales of software, motion pictures, artistic images and sound, television games, and broadcasting. The same white paper predicted that by 2015 culture-related industries would become the largest segment in the Japanese economy (METI 1993, 210). Another report, by JETRO, estimated that 2007 revenues from movies, games, and merchandise agreements had reached ¥20 billion (JETRO 2007, 4).

According to a broader definition of popular culture, the export value of Japanese media, copyrights, publishing, fashion, other entertainment, and fine art tripled over an eleven-year period beginning in 1993. As seen in Figure 3.8, overall cultural export value gradually increased from ¥0.5 trillion in 1992 to more than ¥1 trillion in 1997 and to almost ¥1.5 trillion in 2002, totaling as much as ¥10.5 trillion for the entire period. This rate of export growth is especially impressive given that the manufacturing sector's exports during the same period increased by only 20 percent and totaled ¥52 trillion (Sugiura 2003).

It was the export of anime that pioneered Japan's great cultural expansion overseas. A JETRO report (2005) estimated that approximately 60 percent of all animation broadcast around the world was made in Japan, with anime sales generating approximately US$4 billion a year in the United States alone. In the past two decades, animated movies such as *Ghost in the Shell* (1995), *Spirited Away* (2001), and *Tottoko Hamutaro* (2002), became the flagships of Japanese movies overseas. According to other accounts, 60 to 65 percent of the world's animated cartoon series are made in Japan, bringing in estimated annual sales of licensed goods worth US$17 billion (METI 2003, 8–9; Digital Content Association of Japan 2009).

Animated characters, a related industry, have been especially successful in foreign markets. As of June 2000, 22 million copies of *Poke'mon* game software had been sold abroad, along with 2.4 billion trading cards. The first *Poke'mon* feature movie was shown in thirty-three countries and raked in US$176 million in box office receipts.[16] According to a later report, as of March 2004 *Poke'mon* had generated US$2.3 trillion in sales (including revenues from licensed merchandise as well as box office receipts) in at least sixty-seven countries worldwide (Sugiura 2004). *Hello Kitty,* another famous character, drives an empire worth US$3 billion in global sales every year. This figure is staggering in light of the fact that

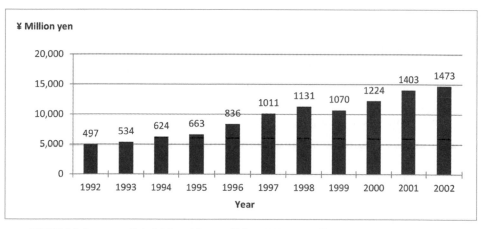

FIGURE 3.8 Japanese Global Cultural Exports Value 1992–2002. (Source: Tsutomu 2003)

the revenues of its manufacturer, Sanrio, come mainly from providing some 12,000 to 15,000 licenses a year to other companies, allowing them to use *Hello Kitty's* likeness on their products (Sanrio 2012).

The United States is the most important export market for anime. Anime started to make inroads into the American market as far back as 1963, with the successful debut of *Astro Boy,* the story of a robot's attempt to become a real boy while trying to save the world. In the 1960s and 1970s, anime series for children continued to be broadcast on American television along with Godzilla movies, which were edited and dubbed into English to suit local taste (Tsutsui 2010a, 10–11). Organized anime fandom in North America started in 1977, after the formation of the first fan club created expressly to promote anime to other American fans (Patten 2004, 22–43, 53–56). American distributors continued to import popular Japanese animated features for television through the early 1980s, but this import has since expanded in diversity and scale so that anime now offers a variety of products and genres aimed at mainstream consumers. The American anime market received its biggest boost at the end of the 1990s, amid prolonged recession in the Japanese economy, from the introduction of the famous *Poke'mon* series to American audiences, in what Anne Allison (2006, 234) called "the Poke'monization of America."

A JETRO survey estimated that the market for anime in the United States, including the sale of licensed goods, was worth US$4.36 billion in 2002, accounting for 3.5 percent of total exports from Japan to the United States. This was 3.2 times as much as the export value of Japanese steel products to the United States in the same year. In 2003, anime value reached its peak, totaling more than US$4.84 billion (JETRO 2003). U.S. anime sales have been declining since 2007, however, mainly due to illegal online downloading, the saturation of the market with low-quality anime, and shrinkage in consumer spending in the aftermath of the 2008 economic crisis (see Figure 3.9). According to JETRO, anime sales in the United States generated US$2.92 billion in 2007. In 2009, the numbers dropped again to US$2.74 billion, which included movies (US$15 million), DVDs (US$306 million), and character-related merchandise (US$2.42 billion) (JETRO 2011, 39).[17]

Overseas sales of manga have surged as well. Since the 1990s, manga has been exported on a large scale, especially to the North American market. Japan's bestselling manga weekly, *Shonen Junp,* sold more than 500,000 copies per issue per month when it was first published in the

United States in November 2002 (Sugiura 2008, 133). Sales in the United States are estimated to have increased from US$50–60 million in 2002 to US$90–110 million in 2003.[18] Manga is also extremely popular in East Asia, where it is routinely translated into various languages. While it is difficult to determine the exact extent of the circulation of translated manga, as most of it is offered in pirated versions, recent reports indicate that legitimate publishing of manga in East Asia is increasing. One source estimated that four out of every five comic books sold in South Korea in the 1990s were Japanese originals.[19] According to another estimate, nearly 80 percent of comic books available in South Korea in 2009 were translated from Japanese (Yamanaka 2010, 50).

Japan's video game industry has also never been bigger. In 2008, sales in the United States alone reached US$22 billion, while overall international video game sales rose 20 percent from a year earlier to US$32 billion. Three Japanese companies, Nintendo, Sony, and Sega, retain dominant positions in spite of Microsoft's hope that Xbox would grab a bigger share of the world's video games market, estimated at US$30 billion in sales every year (see Figure 3.10). In 2007, Nintendo captured 61.7 percent of the worldwide video games hardware market, while Sony's PlayStation

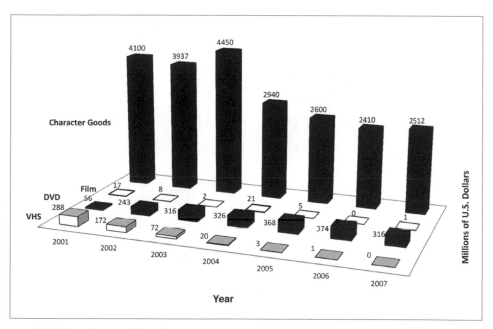

FIGURE 3.9 Estimated Size of Japanese Anime Market in the United States (Source: JETRO 2009)

captured 34.5 percent and Microsoft's Xbox only 2.3 percent (Dentsū Communication Institute 2009, 103–105). As of September 2009, Sony's second-generation game system, PlayStation 2, had sold 140 million units worldwide, more than any other system in history. In the first half of 2007, Nintendo's latest console, Wii, sold more units in the United States than Microsoft's Xbox 360 and PlayStation 3 combined. The Japanese game industry leads not only the hardware industry but software as well, boasting many of the top-selling video games in the world. Successful examples include Super Mario, Dragon Quest, Sonic, and Final Fantasy, with more than 35 million copies of these series sold abroad.[20]

When it comes to movies and music, however, Japan is a net importer. In 2003, the nation's movie exports amounted to only ¥1.1 billion, compared to ¥91 billion in imports (Nakamura 2003). There are no exact figures regarding the export of music from Japan, but statistics from Japan's Ministry of Finance indicate that music CD imports surpass exports by a wide margin. In 2003, for example, government figures show that 5.24 million music CDs were exported while fourteen times that many, or 73.77 million CDs, were imported (Figure 3.11).[21] Despite this general

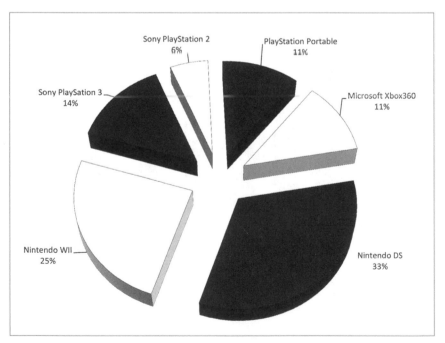

FIGURE 3.10 Worldwide Video Games Hardware Sales in 2009. (Source: VGCharts 2010).

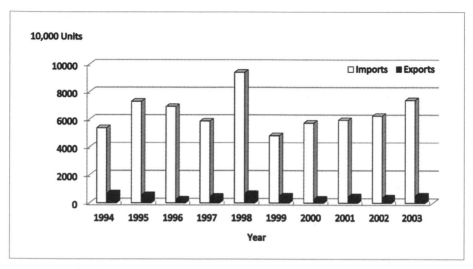

FIGURE 3.11 Music CD Imports and Exports by Units 1994–2003. (Source: Japan Ministry of Finance 2004)

trend, a few Japanese movies have become hits in overseas markets, and Japanese movie directors such as Kitano Takeshi, Yamada Yōji, Itami Jūzō, and Miyazaki Hayao have received international acclaim. Japanese music, as we shall see in the next chapter, tends to circulate less broadly, largely staying within the cultural geography of East Asia, where a few Japanese music artists have managed to establish a footing.

Government Policies and Support for Cultural Industries

The domestic success of Japanese cultural industries in the mid-1980s and 1990s and the enthusiastic acceptance of Japan's popular culture abroad caught the attention of the Japanese government.[22] The realization that cultural exports can be both economically profitable and diplomatically useful induced the government to offer support. The government has since become interested in promoting Japanese culture abroad and is constantly seeking new areas for state intervention in the promising cultural industry sector. This change of heart was supported by a domestic discourse that called on the government to make better use of its cultural resources in order to attain "soft power." Advocates emphasize the economic benefits of cultural exports and stress their potential contribution to the nation's diplomacy. Japanese media quickly took up the cause of cultural exports, rooting for the success of Japanese artists and cultural industries and expressing hopes that the sector would continue to grow.

From the end of World War II until the mid-1980s, the Japanese government did little to promote the exportation of popular culture—especially within Asia. In sharp contrast to its large investment in promoting the export of industrial products such as automobiles and electronics, the government did not treat "culture" as an object of profitable export. There was also the fear of reviving anti-Japanese sentiment or reawakening memories of colonial oppression that might cause Japan's East Asian neighbors to accuse it of "cultural imperialism." Prime Minister Tanaka Kakuei's disastrous visit to Southeast Asia in 1974 was a clear reminder of still sizzling anti-Japanese sentiments. In Thailand and Indonesia, mobs paraded outside the hotels where he stayed, screaming anti-Japanese slogans and forcing him to cut his visit short and return to Japan.

Before its defeat in the war, Japan employed culture as a strategic foreign policy tool. Japan's colonial policies in East Asia, especially in Northeast Asia, included the introduction and forceful imposition of Japanese language and culture to achieve better control of its empire and integrate other Asian peoples more closely into the Japanese empire (Heng 1999; Goodman 1991; Suzuki 2005). This aspiration only grew stronger with the 1940 proclamation of the "Greater East Asian Co-Prosperity Sphere," wherein East Asian nations were supposed to thrive under Japanese leadership.[23] Harsh cultural policies were enforced in Korea, Taiwan, and Manchukuo, the puppet state Japan installed in Manchuria in March 1932, in order to more tightly control the local populations and promote their assimilation into the Japanese empire. Toward this end, the authorities distributed Japanese movies, organized exhibitions of paintings by Japanese artists, translated Japanese books, published magazines, aired radio broadcasts in Japanese, and sent students to study in Japanese universities. At the same time, they partially or wholly banned the use of local languages, censored publications in Korean and Chinese, required locals to adopt Japanese names, and installed the Japanese language as the "national language" to be used for official purposes and in schools (Roy 2003, 41–45; Suzuki 2005, 197–199).

Cultural policies were also decreed in Southeast Asia, but these tended to be ad hoc initiatives introduced on the eve of invasion or just after establishing military control, and their implementation was more haphazard and not well planned. The conquering Japanese army commanders, who were convinced of Japanese moral and spiritual superiority, directed these policies. They consisted mainly of propaganda based on experience gained in Korea, Taiwan, Manchukuo, and other areas of China that had previously been occupied by the military. These propaganda campaigns entailed the recruitment, mobilization, and utilization of approximately three thousand Japanese *bunkajin* ("people of culture")—writers, artists, professors, and musicians—to "re-educate" the populace and "bring them docilely into Japan's cultural orbit" (Goodman 1991, 2–4).

Japan's defeat in the war and its repositioning in the postwar Asia Pacific order under American hegemony put a stop to all this. New priorities and constraints, as well as bitter memories among East Asians, mandated a passive stance toward overseas cultural exports. In fact, the Japanese government's interest in promoting the nation's culture within Asia was effectively neutralized for most of the postwar period. After the war, the term *"bunka seisaku"* (cultural policy) was first mentioned only in 1993, when the Japanese Ministry of Education, Science, and Culture called for greater cultural exchange between Japan and the rest of the world. The sort of overseas cultural promotion the government undertook then was within a wide, loose framework of "international cultural exchange" (*kokusai bunka kōryū*), which basically meant sending artists and supporting international performances to "promote and spread culture and to preserve cultural properties" (Bunkachō 2003).

In the postwar period, another form of overseas cultural promotion was undertaken by the Japan Foundation, which was established in June 1972 as part of the Japanese government's attempt to pay more attention to cultural aspects of international relations. Since its establishment, the Japan Foundation has been primarily engaged in promoting the United States' understanding of Japan's needs through cultural exchange and easing the fears of Asian neighbors regarding Japan's economic success (Kahn 1999, 69–75; Havens 1987, 335). In October 2003, the foundation became an independent administrative institution under the Incorporated Administrative Agency Japan Foundation Law. It became a de facto agency of the Japanese government with a program strategically designed to complement government objectives. Today, the Japan Foundation operates on a global scale, but the United States remains its major area of focus (Japan Foundation 2003, 8–10).

By the late 1970s and 1980s, however, improved relations with East Asian nations were creating a newly favorable climate for popular culture exports. This trend intensified with the success in the 1990s of Japanese popular culture products such as anime, TV dramas, and music, as was evidenced by the growing presence of Japanese cultural industries in the region. In North America, as previously emphasized, the rush to embrace Japanese anime and manga started even earlier, during the mid-1970s, when names such as *Sailor Moon, Tamagotchi, Hello Kitty,* and *Poke'mon* became an established part of the local popular culture market (Allison 2006). The West's new exposure to Japanese popular culture coincided with the Japanese government's changing perception of youth culture. Leisure and youth culture, once regarded as social evils, were re-evaluated and reprioritized as sources of cultural exports. Not only highbrow, traditional culture such as *ikebana* flower arrangement or *haiku* poetry— but also anime, J-pop music, and Japanese-style cooking came to be seen as legitimate cultural genres worthy of export (Linhart 2009, 216–217).

In the mid-1980s, the Japanese government finally felt free to let go of its extreme caution in promoting cultural policies overseas. In light of the success of Japan's private cultural industries, the government saw that not only had Japan's popular culture exports not generated antagonism toward the country, but that they had generated a considerable amount of profit for Japanese companies. After the government gradually adopted the view that cultural industries have the potential to both initiate industrial change and play a constructive role in the nation's diplomacy, it began looking for new ways to intervene in culture markets. This intervention involved building a new connection between industrial and cultural policies, linking culture to the amassing of national wealth by promoting the export of cultural products. From a diplomatic point of view, the export of popular culture was seen as a means of reforming the country's image abroad, in what Michal Daliot-Bul (2009) calls "Japan's Brand Strategy." She describes this strategy as a state-sponsored campaign to advance the branding of Japanese products in tandem with broader policy initiatives designed to upgrade the country's image overseas. It reflects the brand consciousness of nation-building efforts that are primarily concerned with projecting the image of the nation to a global audience.

Popular culture has thus become an object of national policy that can be managed through technological and political channels. In practice, governmental involvement focuses on supporting the infrastructure needed for the development of cultural industries. This includes supporting technology needed for delivering and consuming cultural content (especially infrastructure for accessing the Internet, cable TV, and satellite broadcasts), supporting universities and training centers that cultivate human resources with relevant knowledge and skills, and ensuring the availability of venture capital for producing movies, television programs, music albums, anime, video games, etc. These efforts also include producing optimistic reports predicting that multimedia and culture-related industries will continue to account for an increasing segment of the economy. According to Kukhee Choo's study (2012, 86–89), government proceedings dealing with the content industries have increased from 97 in the 1990s to 516 in the 2000s. Of these, anime and manga proceedings have increased almost fifteenfold and thirty-sevenfold respectively, whereas video games reports merely tripled during the same period.

The first concrete initiative of promoting Japanese contemporary culture in Asia was taken in 1988 by the Takeshita government, which advocated exporting TV programs to Asian countries. In 1991, the Ministry of Foreign Affairs (MOFA), together with the Ministry of Posts and Telecommunications (MOPT), established the Japan Media Communication Center (JAMCO) to subsidize the export of television programs to developing countries. From its establishment through March 1998, JAMCO translated 8,983 programs into English, Spanish, French, or Chinese and provided them to eighty-eight mostly Asian countries. Two other initiatives symbolize the growing commercial importance that the Japanese government has placed on the development and export of culture-related industries. The first was the establishment by the MOPT in 1997 of a committee charged with reporting on the promotion of commercial exportation of Japanese television programs. The second was the establishment by METI's Media and Contents Industry Division, in May 2001, of one of the first think tanks whose mission was to examine challenges and prospects for media and content policy, also with the aim of promoting the export of Japanese content.

At present, state support for cultural promotion overseas consists of a wide range of uncoordinated initiatives involving no fewer than thirteen governmental ministries and agencies (Zykas 2011, 155–157, 163–166; see Table 3.3). The most prominent are MOFA, the Japan Foundation, the

Agency for Cultural Affairs (under the Ministry of Education, Culture, Sports, Science and Technology, or MEXT), the Prime Minister's Cabinet (PMC), and METI. As is often the case when multiple governmental ministries and agencies address a single issue, there is competition for resources and prestige, and there is waste of time and other resources due to lack of coordination and overlapping responsibilities. The various ministries speak in different terms: MOFA advocates supporting "pop culture diplomacy," METI talks about supporting the "content indus- try" (and defines content as any cultural or artistic work with commer- cial value), and the PMC states that it wishes to promote Japanese "life culture" abroad by introducing Japanese cuisine, fashion, and Japanese brand names to foreigners.

METI and the Ministry of Internal Affairs and Communications (MIC) are both responsible for overseeing the economic portfolio of the cultural industries. They emphasize the contribution of culture to the national economy and the need to develop related infrastructure. METI's research institute (RIETI) and its think tanks have been examining ways to encourage the development and export of cultural industries, mainly by studying related literature and data. For example, a 2003 METI think tank analysis of prospects for the Japanese content industry said that in less than five years, content's share of global GDP was expected to increase (from 3.6 percent in 2002) to 6.5 percent, worth US$1.4 trillion. A 2004 JETRO report on the music industry recommended that the indus- try make the most of business opportunities in East Asian markets, espe- cially in South Korea (METI 2003, 8–9; JETRO 2004b).

Excited about the idea of linking the marketing of cultural products with that of consumer products, the Japanese government launched a "Cool Japan" campaign in October 2011 to increase the visibility of Japanese products in foreign markets. The campaign overseas was engi- neered by Japan's largest advertisement company, Dentsu Inc., which is known for its ability to communicate in a hip, pop-culture-ish style. The campaign was kicked off in Singapore and was scheduled to last for sev- eral months. According to Matsushita Tadahiro, senior vice minister of METI, the purpose of the campaign is to introduce new Japanese brands to the growing Asian consumer market and to attract new customers by appealing to non-Japanese who already have a generally positive impression of Japanese contemporary culture.[24] It introduces Japanese fashion, food, and anime and encourages travel to Japan. "Cool Japan" events were also scheduled for India, China, South Korea, France, Italy, the United States, and Brazil.

The Ministry of Education, Culture, Sports, Science, and Technology (MEXT) promotes research and education that contributes to Japanese cultural production. In June 2004, it began supporting a joint industry-university content-creation science educational program aimed at cultivating human resources for the cultural industries. The program started at the University of Tokyo and was later expanded to other schools including the Tokyo National University of Fine Arts and Music and Dōshisha University in Kyoto (Yoda 2005, 10–11). The idea is to train and qualify creative personnel, such as musicians, artistic directors, and playwrights, as well as sound engineers, designers, editors, producers, etc.—everyone whose skills are vital to the development and advancement of cultural industries.

As the government plays a bigger role in fostering the exportation of popular culture products, it has become increasingly concerned about

TABLE 3.3 Governmental Support for Cultural Industries

Cabinet Secretariat	Headquarters for IT Strategy, e-Japan Strategy, Strategic Council on Intellectual Property
Ministry of Economy, Trade, and Industry	Development of content industries • Promoting content industries' international competitiveness • Regulating intellectual property issues • Promoting broadband infrastructure • Encouraging the development of digital content • Coordinating the various layers of the industry – Providing related funds and securities – JETRO offices
Ministry of Internal Affairs and Communication	Development of content communication and broadband infrastructure • Analysis of content flows • Encouraging the use of information technology networks • Promoting broadcasting media industries
Ministry of Foreign Affairs	Introducing Japanese culture overseas • Employing cultural attachés • Issuing publications
Ministry of Education, Culture, Sports, Science, and Technology	Development of artistic and cultural work • Encouraging research regarding digital content • Conducting cultural- and media-related exhibitions and exchanges • Establishing adequate education facilities • Regulating intellectual-property-related issues – Bunkachō (Agency for Cultural Affairs)

SOURCES: Nakamura 2004; Zykas 2011

the huge losses sustained by Japanese companies as a result of illegal reproduction, mostly in Asia. According to a survey done by the Japan Patent Office, in 2000 17.6 percent of pirated Japanese products were reproduced in the Republic of Korea and 18.1 percent in Taiwan, while China's proportion was 33 percent and growing. A 2002 white paper released by JETRO recommended that the Japanese government take immediate action to tackle this problem, in part by helping Asian governments to regulate their pirate markets. In 2002, increasing recognition of the importance of competitive multimedia and culture-related industries coupled with concern over the damage caused by piracy induced the Japanese government to launch the Strategic Council on Intellectual Property within the prime minister's office. The aim of the council is to promote growth in Japanese intellectual property, including patented technologies, designs, movies, and video game software, as a means of revitalizing the economy. The council is chaired by the prime minister and includes representatives from Japan's Strategic Council on Intellectual Property, the National Police Agency, Interior Ministry, Foreign Ministry, Finance Ministry, Agency for Cultural Affairs, METI, Japan Patent Office, and Keidanren (Japan Business Federation), as well as Diet members, academics, and journalists. In its reports, the council outlined technical aspects of intellectual property protection and the need to promote creative research in universities and collaboration between companies and research institutions (Prime Minister of Japan 2008).

MOFA, together with the Japan Foundation, is charged with handling the international dimensions of cultural policy. In its publications and reports, the Japan Foundation has routinely highlighted Japan's cultural capabilities and given testimony to the popularity of Japanese culture overseas. MOFA has teamed up with various organizations to promote popular culture–related events. For example, since 2003, the Ministry of Foreign Affairs has collaborated with Nagoya-based tourism-related organizations to organize "World Cosplay Championships," where participants are judged according to their anime costumes. In 2009, contenders came from fifteen countries: Australia, Brazil, China, Denmark, Finland, France, Germany, Italy, Japan, Mexico, Singapore, South Korea, Spain, Thailand, and the United States.[25] In 2006, the ministry instituted an International Manga Prize, with the hope that it will become the "Nobel Prize" of manga. Competitors from around the world entered the first competition, and the prize was awarded to forty-three-year-old Hong Kong manga artist Lee Chi Ching, for his Sun Zi Tactics manga series.[26]

The diplomatic advantages of exporting popular culture have been personally acknowledged by recent Japanese prime ministers. In December 2004, then prime minister Koizumi Junichirō established a think tank to recommend how the government should promote the country's cultural diplomacy. In September 2005, his successor, Abe Shinzō, declared during his election campaign that "pop culture" is one of Japan's strengths. Later that year, the prime minister's foreign relations advisory panel (*gaisō shimonkikan*) recommended a "manga and animation diplomacy" approach. Specific recommendations included organizing international events to promote Japanese culture, creating a "Japan Manga Award" for outstanding foreign animators, and forming a joint study group involving bureaucrats and industry personnel. Asō Tarō, prime minister and a self-professed manga fan, has continued to support the panel's recommendations and proposed designating Japanese anime characters such as *Doraemon* and *Kitty-chan* to represent Japan as cultural ambassadors overseas.[27]

In a 2007 radio interview, then foreign minister Asō Tarō argued that promotion of Japan's cultural assets abroad is crucially important for the nation's future. Comparing the international arena to an elementary school, he likened a nation's military power to a physically strong pupil who heads a group of students, its cultural power to a smart pupil who gets high grades, and its economic power to a pupil who comes from a rich family. The first student is respected for his physical strength and the second for his achievements in class, but the rich pupil does not get much respect from his classmates. Foreign Minister Asō believes that a country that has only economic power does not gain much international recognition; it must also possess military and cultural power. Although Japan's military power has been constitutionally limited, its cultural power has been on the rise, especially thanks to manga and anime. So Asō recommends that Japan use its overseas cultural presence to upgrade its position in the world.[28]

A largely supportive domestic discourse has encouraged the government's gradual increase in involvement in cultural industries, particularly in the export of popular culture. Academics, journalists, and bureaucrats have publicly pointed out the economic benefits of popular culture exportation and emphasized its potential contribution to

Japanese diplomacy by projecting a positive image of the country abroad. Japanese liberals view the export of contemporary culture as a reflection of the country's "friendlier," peaceful side, while conservatives see the overseas success of any Japanese business as a source of national pride. Both groups hope that the enthusiasm with which East Asian consumers buy Japanese cultural products will help heal the wounds that were inflicted during Japan's imperialistic past (Iwabuchi 2002, 201).

Discussion of the impact of Japanese culture abroad is found in a wide range of academic and popular publications. For example, on the first day of 2006, the front page of one of Japan's leading newspapers, *Asahi Shinbun*, was dedicated to testimonies about the world's fascination with Japanese popular culture. The coverage included evidence of Japanese culture's commercial success in places as far-flung as Russia, China, Thailand, Europe, and North America. The newspaper emphasized the economic benefits of cultural production and export, suggesting that progress in these fields is essential if Japan is to maintain economic superiority over China and India. The second part of the article indicated that cultural exports also support diplomatic efforts by depicting Japan as a peaceful nation.[29] Another highly publicized example of acclaim for Japan's popular culture powerhouse was a 2002 article by journalist Douglas McGray, who introduced the term "Gross National Cool" (GNC) in his depiction of Japan's booming cultural innovation and life style businesses. McGray recommended that Japan put more emphasis on developing its cultural production power to boost its economy and increase its ability to influence world affairs.

An integral part of this discourse is the use of the term "soft power" in relation to the rising importance of popular culture in Japan's economy and diplomacy. As mentioned earlier, soft power is a term coined by Harvard University professor Joseph Nye to describe the growing importance of nontraditional means by which a country can wield influence over another country's wants. Soft power lies in the ability of a nation to entice, attract, and fascinate other countries and societies, so that a country "may obtain the outcomes it wants in world politics because of other countries—admiring its values, emulating its example, aspiring to its level of prosperity and openness—want to follow it" (Nye 2004a, 15). Nye first used this concept to describe America's capabilities, but he would later cite examples from Europe, Japan, India, and China (Nye 2004b).

In Japan, governmental bodies that release highly optimistic forecasts for the cultural industries routinely quote Joseph Nye's writings about "soft power" as evidence of the diplomatic advantages of popular culture. For example, the annual report issued by the Japan Foundation's International Exchange Research Committee in April 2003 underscored popular culture's potential to portray a sympathetic "national image" of Japan and to assist in achieving its diplomatic aims. The report also emphasized the increasing importance of new forms of power in today's diplomacy, characterizing them as "soft power" (Japan Foundation 2003; see other mentions of this term in Aoki 2004 and METI 2003). Although there has not been much discussion in Japan on the actual meaning of soft power (Otmazgin 2008a), and Nye himself admits that he introduced the term as a descriptive rather than an analytical concept (Nye 2008), extensive usage of the term in relation to Japan's booming popular culture no doubt provides a tailwind for greater governmental involvement in culture-related businesses.

Popular culture promotion has clearly been gaining momentum in Japan. Exportation of popular culture products was not initiated by the government, but rather was driven by market forces and entrepreneurial exploration undertaken by the cultural industries themselves. But the government has become increasingly cognizant of the potential advantages of developing Japan's cultural industries and has become involved in promoting them. Encouraged by favorable domestic discourse, governmental initiatives begun in the late 1980s have amended previous attitudes and have gradually formulated new policies that support the development of Japanese culture-related industries and export of their products.

In practical terms, the government treats the promotion of cultural industries in basically the same way it treats the country's more renowned industries, such as the automotive and electronics industries. It appoints committees that produce optimistic forecasts and recommendations and advocate investment in infrastructure. The idea behind this policy is that popular culture deserves to be added to the list of Japanese-made products that are already exported. Even if cultural product exports did not bring in outstanding profits, they are once again seen as image-boosting agents. And because there is now strong demand for Japanese popular culture overseas, the government has hope that this time around Japanese culture can help heal the wounds remaining throughout Asia as a result of Japan's imperialist past.

Conclusion

Japan is home to highly developed, highly profitable cultural industries. The figures and analysis presented in this chapter clearly indicate the existence of a large domestic popular culture market that has enormous capacity for consumption and exportation and also provides efficient mechanisms for commodifying popular culture. The Japanese domestic market is home to sophisticated systems for producing and commercializing popular culture, and these systems have a few conspicuous characteristics. Japan's popular culture production machinery is based on a special proximity between established industry and its audience. This special proximity serves to both nurture a dedicated consumer base and to cultivate new engines of creativity. We can say that popular culture production in Japan is based on active audience participation and on the industry's ongoing practice of recognizing individual creativity and co-opting it into its assembly lines. This emphasis on close reciprocity between established industry and audience is one of the main features that differentiate Japanese processes of producing and commercializing culture from what is often called the "Hollywood model."

This chapter also highlighted Japan's enormous capacity for the consumption, production, and export of popular culture. The domestic market has provided fertile ground for the nation's cultural industries to grow and has nurtured their eventual expansion abroad. Japan's huge capacity for producing and exporting popular culture suggests that the country deserves to be known not only as one of the world's biggest manufacturers of automobiles, electronics, and home appliances, but also as a cultural superpower.

The government, for its part, is now actively involved in supporting the country's cultural industries and wants exports from this sector to prove both economically profitable and diplomatically useful. Unlike in Japan's imperialist past, when the government attempted to force Japanese culture on the people of Asia, or in the years following World War II, when the government intentionally avoided exporting popular culture to Asia due to concerns about provoking anti-Japanese sentiment, today the Japanese government is actively looking for new ways to aid the export of popular culture. In practical terms, it supports technological, educational, and legal infrastructure needed for the development of Japan's cultural industries, in the hope that the success of those industries will boost Japan's economy and present a more peaceful and friendly image of the nation abroad.

The majority of studies on Japan's popular culture tend to overlook the industrial foundations of this sector and its mode of organization in favor of an ethnographic approach that concentrates on text, its representations, and its consumption by specific groups of people (for example Allen and Sakamoto 2006; Allison 2006; Craig 2000; Desser 2003; Inoue 2010; Ishii 2001; Iwabuchi 2004; Martinez 1998; Mitsui and Hosokawa 1998; Mōri 2004; Soderberg and Reader 2000; and Treat 1996). These studies provide substantial testimony to the proliferation of various popular culture confluences and contain a wealth of information and valuable analyses related to the practice and "meaning" of popular culture. In this chapter, however, my purpose was to underline the least studied aspect of the story, which is the organizational aspect of Japan's popular culture production. I have tried to show that from the very beginning, Japan's domestic marketplace constituted a fertile ground for the mass production of popular culture commodities, as well as a good springboard from which to expand into overseas markets. Put differently, in order to understand how Japanese popular culture reaches foreign markets on a massive scale, one must look first at the way popular culture is commodified and organized at home.

CHAPTER 4

////////////////

The Creation of
a Regional Market

Japanese popular culture products have been influential in East Asia as far back as the late 1970s, in both legal and pirated versions (Ching 1996; Ishii 2001). One example is the hit drama series *Oshin,* which was aired in more than thirty countries, mostly within Asia. Another example is *Doraemon,* an animated cartoon about a robot cat, which became enormously popular among young audiences in the 1980s. There are, however, important qualitative and quantitative differences between the popularity of Japanese popular culture products in the 1970s and those of the 1990s. In the 1970s, the non-Japanese audience for Japanese music and television programs was largely limited to particular groups of fans, whereas in the 1990s Japanese-produced music, television programs, anime, and manga reached a much wider, mainstream audience (Iwabuchi 2001, 55). In this later period, Japanese cultural industries have managed to export and commercialize their products on a massive scale, paving the way to reach a variety of new consumers. In fact, the 1990s and the beginning of the 2000s were golden years for Japanese popular culture in East Asia, where a wide range of products and images could be found in virtually every big city in the region in a variety and concentration unseen in any other part of the world.

The proliferation of Japanese popular culture in East Asia is especially noteworthy given Japan's imperialistic past. In spite of the suffering Japan inflicted on its neighbors in the decades leading up to the end of World War II and its attempts to use its culture as a means of controlling its colonies, its contemporary popular culture has been endorsed by the local cultural markets and affects the cultural lives of many people in East Asia, especially the young. Although people in today's East Asia may not be completely ignorant of Japan's past wrongdoings and may still be critical of the Japanese government, they continue to buy tens of millions of animation and manga products, faithfully follow Japanese-made television programs, and often listen to Japanese pop music. The result is that in many cities in East Asia, young people are constantly exposed to Japanese products and images through their consumption of popular culture.

It is important to remember that popular culture commodities do not simply appear. They are the product of organization and commercialization activities undertaken by producers, promoters, distributors, retailers, and many others who make their living from the popular culture sector. In East Asia, the expansion of Japanese popular culture has been driven by entrepreneurial ventures undertaken by companies and individuals seeking to expand in this region of emerging markets, and assisted by increasing demand from new groups of middle-class consumers. These companies and individuals have succeeded in offering their products and services to a variety of new consumers by establishing mechanisms that have overcome cultural barriers, state censorship, heterogeneity of markets in the region, and language differences.

The dissemination of Japan's popular culture has also been assisted by piracy. In East Asia, piracy (both physical and online) has been driven by continuous demand for illegally copied cultural products and has been helped by lax state enforcement of intellectual property laws. Piracy has been especially helpful in spreading Japanese popular culture, not only because it made cultural content accessible to new consumers by offering replicas at low prices, but also because it delivered content beyond the reach of government censors. Even governments in places where Japanese culture was officially banned, such as South Korea and Taiwan, have gradually come to acknowledge that they cannot completely seal off the market from the circulation of pirated popular culture commodities and that their attempts to prevent the diffusion of popular culture have been ineffective. Although piracy has certainly caused losses to Japanese copyright owners, in the long run it has been beneficial to marketers of Japanese popular culture by cultivating new groups of consumers who would not otherwise have had access to these products.

This chapter analyzes the creation of a regional market for popular culture by focusing on the spread of music and television programs. The analysis starts with a review of the macro politicoeconomic conditions that contributed to the transfer of Japanese popular culture to East Asia. This part emphasizes the notion that we should understand the dissemination of Japan's popular culture within the web of economic and societal linkages that were established between Japan and its neighbors in the decades after World War II, and especially since the 1970s.

The chapter continues with case studies of Japanese music and television companies, examining the circumstances that prompted their expansion within the region and the nature of their activities in East Asian countries other than Japan. Next, the chapter analyzes the structure, marketing, and promotional mechanisms of new markets for Japanese music and television programs, and the proliferation of Japanese music in a few major markets in East Asia. The final section focuses on how piracy has promoted the dissemination of Japanese popular culture and emphasizes its effectiveness in delivering products and content across national boundaries. This part looks at the relationship between censorship and bootleg markets and proposes a new framework for viewing the dynamism of these markets in East Asia.

To emphasize certain popular culture practices and fields, and to avoid too broad a generalization, the research in this chapter focuses on Japanese music and television programs. Although the music and television industries create products in a manner similar to the movie, comic, and video game industries, each industry has its own characteristic working environments, product development styles, tie-ups with other product categories, and methods of commercialization (Jones 2003; Berkeley 2003). A second reason to focus on music and television programs is that sounds and images are regularly presented or consumed together (as when one purchases a CD after seeing the artist perform on a television program). Japanese pop music is closely tied to its visual expression on television, as an increasing number of people listen to music performed on television (Fujie 1989, 212), and Japanese companies often promote music and television programs together in East Asia.

Setting the Scene: Japan's Return to East Asia

Japan did not return to East Asia with a suitcase full of popular culture immediately after World War II. Rather, it first built political and economic goodwill and infrastructure in the region through diplomacy, trade, investment, technical assistance, and official development assistance (ODA). It is therefore important to locate the creation of markets for popular culture products within Japan's wider economic and diplomatic involvements in the region and within the complex of economic and social initiatives that smoothed Japan's road back to East Asia after the war. These other types of connections prepared the ground for the acceptance of Japanese consumer products such as automobiles, electronics, and rice cookers, and for the transfer of popular culture commodities as well.

Broadly speaking, several key macropolitical and economic processes facilitated the expansion of Japanese cultural industries into East Asian markets. These include (a) the gradual improvement of relations between Japan and East Asian nations since the end of World War II, (b) the growing expansion of Japanese manufacturing industries into the region, especially since the second half of the 1980s, and (c) the mass movement of people (tourists, students, and businesspeople) between Japan and the rest of East Asia. These developments enhanced Japan's economic and cultural presence in the region. Let us look at these developments more closely.

The first major development was the gradual improvement of relations between Japan and other East Asian nations following World War II. The initial drive to improve relations took place under American hegemony (Asahi 1989, 8–23; T. Shiraishi 2000, 135–143). Starting as early as the 1950s, the U.S. State Department urged reluctant officials in Tokyo to provide war reparations to East Asian countries as part of the effort to forestall Chinese communist expansion (Green 2001, 168). Japan established diplomatic relations with South Korea in 1965, after thirteen years of exhausting negotiations and a Japanese economic assistance pact worth US$800 million. Diplomatic relations with the People's Republic of China were established in 1972 and further normalized after the signing of the Peace and Friendship Treaty in 1978 (Inoguchi 2002, 15–21).

World War II left fewer scars on relations between Japan and Southeast Asia than between Japan and Northeast Asia, and relations improved more swiftly with Southeast Asian countries. Kishi Nobusuke, Japan's prime minister from 1957 to 1960, cleared the way for better diplomatic and economic relations. A network of personal ties between politicians and their business associates, backed by Japanese reparations and economic aid, made it possible to forge good relations between Japan and the nations of Southeast Asia. These new relations initially meant trade and resource procurement within the framework of "economic cooperation" (Shiraishi 1997, 176–179). But during the next three decades, under the so-called Fukuda, Takeshita, and Hashimoto Doctrines, Japan further extended its relations with Southeast Asian nations, gradually establishing comprehensive diplomatic ties (Sudō 2002, 33–41).

Japan determined to improve its relations with Southeast Asia after a disastrous visit to the region by Prime Minister Tanaka Kakuei in 1974. During that visit, a mob screamed anti-Japanese slogans outside the hotel where he stayed in Thailand. In Indonesia, Prime Minister Tanaka became a virtual prisoner inside the presidential palace for three days as demonstrators outside the palace vigorously protested his visit. The Indonesian police killed eleven demonstrators, forcing Tanaka to cut his visit short and flee Jakarta early one morning by helicopter (description in Schlesinger 1997, 76). This served to alert the Japanese leadership that still-sizzling resentment and hatred toward Japan in parts of Southeast Asia could hamper Japan's further involvement in the region.

From the late 1970s onward, Japan consciously cranked up its rhetoric about regional solidarity as part of its efforts to improve relations with Southeast Asia. In 1977, then-prime minister Fukuda Takeo expounded his Fukuda Doctrine, which contained three promises: that Japan would never again pose a military threat to its neighbors; that it would build warm and friendly relations of mutual trust with Southeast Asian countries through social, cultural, and other types of exchange; and that it would work as an equal partner with ASEAN countries to help build peace and prosperity in the region (Lam 2007). As part of this move, in December 1978 the ASEAN Cultural Fund was established with five billion yen from the Japanese government to foster cultural exchange between Japan and ASEAN and within ASEAN countries themselves. Japanese diplomacy did not go so far as to advance the construction of a shared Asian identity with ASEAN at the center. Rather, Japan's relationship with ASEAN served to smooth its economic penetration into Southeast Asia (Jones and Smith 2007, 182).

To enhance economic and political relations with its East Asian neighbors, Japan also provided (and continues to provide) huge amounts of aid. Japan initiated the establishment of the Asian Development Bank (ADB) to fight poverty in Asia and has been its largest contributor since its establishment in 1966. Japan has also been the biggest donor of ODA to the region, allotting approximately two-thirds of its ODA to Asian countries. The Japanese government's resolve to continue to assist East Asia was renewed following the devastating Asian financial crisis of 1997–1998. Under the New Miyazawa Initiative announced in October 1998, Japan promised US$30 billion out of the total US$127 billion in financial assistance extended by countries and financial institutions around the world to help resolve the issues associated with the Asian financial crisis, compared to the United States' US$12 billion and the European states' US$7 billion. In the second stage of the New Miyazawa Initiative in May 1999, Japan provided additional assistance of US$30 billion (Katzenstein 2002, 22; Kishimoto 2001, 295).

A second development that substantially increased the Japanese presence in East Asia over the past three decades was the massive expansion of Japanese industries into the region's markets. For most of the postwar period, Japanese businesses traded actively in Asia, mainly by procuring and importing resources. Beginning in the 1960s and 1970s, many small Japanese firms, including labor-intensive industries such as textile companies, relocated within East Asia due to growing production costs in Japan (Ozawa 1979, 25–30). However, the Plaza Accord of 1985, which sent the yen soaring in world currency markets, spurred many major Japanese companies, notably makers of automobiles, electronic equipment, and telecommunications devices, to shift their manufacturing bases offshore to developing East Asian countries where labor was cheaper (Lincoln 1993, 139–141). New factories and ventures were soon established in South Korea, Taiwan, Hong Kong, Singapore, Malaysia, Thailand, Indonesia, and later in mainland China, drawing Japanese managerial and technical staff (Seki 1994; Yoshikawa 1991).

The regionalization of Japanese production networks connected producers, subcontractors, and distributors across sectors and national borders (Katzenstein 2005, 106). The Japanese automobile and electronics industries, in particular, built large-scale technological and production networks in East Asia, far broader than those assembled by any American, European, or Korean company (Borrus, Ernst, and Haggard 2000, 14–31). In 2002, industry estimates placed almost two-thirds of the overseas manufacturing bases of Japanese electronics manufacturers in East Asia (Ernst 2006, 166). At the same time, Japanese companies were able to preserve their control over core technologies by spreading production out among various "screwdriver factories" while keeping decision-making power centralized and maintaining their strategic core of research and development in Japanese hands (Hatch and Yamamura 1996). Since the second half of the 1980s, Japan's relations with its East Asian neighbors progressed from a basic, trade-based economic relationship to a more complex relationship wherein many East Asians felt the direct impact of the Japanese presence in their lives as they were hired by Japanese factories or their subcontractors.

In recent years, Japan has further deepened its trade relations with Southeast Asian countries by entering into free trade agreements (FTAs). Parties to these bilateral agreements agree to reduce or completely eliminate trade tariffs and quotas on each other's goods and services in order to boost trade and maximize each other's comparative advantage. Japan signed FTAs with Singapore (January 2002), Malaysia (December 2005), the Philippines (December 2006), Brunei (June 2007), Indonesia (August 2007), and Thailand (November 2007). In a more comprehensive economic partnership agreement (EPA) with ASEAN, which was ratified by the Japanese Diet on June 21, 2008, it was agreed that Japan and ASEAN's ten member states will exempt at least 90 percent of trade with each other within ten years (Scott 2008). As a result, in the past two decades Japan's economic presence in East Asia has greatly intensified, and some scholars say this has contributed to Japan's taking on an unofficial leadership position in the region, which may counter China's growing influence.[1]

A third development, which took place concurrently with the gradual improvement of relations with East Asian countries and the Japanese industrial expansion into the region, was a mass movement of people between Japan and East Asian countries. This movement began as early as the 1960s, grew in the 1970s, and reached a colossal scale after the 1985 Plaza Accord. By 1990, a total of six million Japanese tourists and businesspeople traveled to East Asia, resulting in what Brian Moeran called a "Japanese ethnoscape" (2000, 31, 25–50). In 1992, there were 93,049 reported long-term expatriate Japanese residents in Asia. This number increased to 145,498 in 1996 and reached 260,747 in 2006, accounting for approximately 25 percent of Japanese living abroad (Japan Ministry of Foreign Affairs 2006a). Together with tourists, these long-term residents encouraged the practice of peculiar Japanese activities such as playing golf and going to karaoke bars, and introduced other elements of Japanese "salaryman" culture to create an overall sense of a Japanese community.

Establishing these Japanese expatriate communities had the unintended side effect of mediating cultural interchange and transference. Since the end of the 1980s, an overseas assignment has become a more-or-less normal part of career development at many Japanese companies and practically a prerequisite for employees on an executive or technocrat track, even at medium-sized or small firms (Ben-Ari 2000, 61). Japanese employees posted overseas have exposed local workers to Japanese manufacturing organization and Japanese corporate culture. Japanese businessmen have also introduced Japanese managerial techniques overseas and cultivated them within an imported "Japanese" context (on Malaysia see Smith 2004; on Thailand see Sedgwick 2000; on Singapore see Ben-Ari 2000).

The number of students coming from within East Asia to Japan provides another indication of the increased connection between Japan and its neighbors. The attraction of Japan as a developed, modern country has lured tens of thousands of young East Asian students over the past thirty years. Since the 1980s, Japan has accepted the sixth largest number of foreign students, following the United States, the UK, Germany, France, and Australia. In 1984, approximately 12,410 foreign students studied in Japan. The number ballooned to 53,847 in 1995, to 117,302 in 2005, and to 141,774 in 2010. Many of the students and trainees who come from across East Asia to study in Japan do so at the expense of the Japanese government or Japanese corporations. No less than 93 percent of foreign students in Japan in the 1990s came from Asian countries, and the majority of them—unlike their European and American counterparts—were enrolled in long-term degree programs (Nihon Gakusei Shien Kikō 2011). While in Japan, they were exposed to various aspects of Japanese society and culture, so that when they returned to their home countries after graduating, they carried with them knowledge and ideas about Japanese culture and lifestyles.

At present, Japan enjoys a high degree of trust and appreciation in Southeast Asia. In a series of surveys conducted in six ASEAN countries (Indonesia, Malaysia, the Philippines, Singapore, Thailand, and Vietnam) in 1992, 1997, 2002, and 2008, Japan was consistently perceived in a positive light. In the 2002 survey, more than 80 percent of those questioned stated they either "trust" or "somewhat trust" Japan. In 2008, the level of trust exceeded 90 percent. In the same surveys, at least 90 percent of those questioned thought their country enjoyed a "friendly" or "somewhat friendly" relationship with Japan. Furthermore, more than 80 percent of the respondents stated that Japan, as an Asian country, "contributes" or "somewhat contributes" to the development of Asia.[2]

At the same time, however, certain difficulties remain inherent in Japan's bilateral relations with Northeast Asian countries, especially with China and South Korea. Similar surveys of Northeast Asians have not been conducted, but given their traumatic experience of Japanese occupation, it is reasonable to assume that Japan does not enjoy a similar level of trust and appreciation in China and Korea. In Northeast Asia, excluding Taiwan, Japan is publicly criticized, not only for the atrocities its military committed during the war but also for not apologizing clearly or sincerely enough. The most sensitive issues concern the representation in Japanese history textbooks of the occupation of Japan's neighbors and atrocities committed there, the mistreatment of "comfort women" who were forced to work as prostitutes for the Japanese Imperial Army, and visits by Japanese leaders to the controversial Yasukuni Shrine, which is dedicated to the spirits of Japanese soldiers and military leaders, including convicted war criminals. In addition, there are still a few sensitive territorial disputes between Japan and Korea over the island of Takeshima/Dokdo and between Japan and China and Taiwan over the Senkaku/Diaoyu islands located in the East China Sea.

Without a doubt, grievances and resentment lingering from the war and Japanese colonization persist among East Asians to this day (Shibuichi 2005, 204–205). These feelings, however, have not prevented the entry or acceptance of Japanese industries, people, or culture into the region. As reflected in the above surveys, Japan now enjoys a high degree of appreciation in Southeast Asia and is perceived as contributing to "Asia." Japan is viewed more often as an important economic partner, major employer, and source of learning than as an object of anger or resentment. Substantial political and economic relations between Japan and most of East Asia have been firmly established, and by the end of the 1980s the pathways of Japanese popular culture into East Asian markets had been firmly paved. As we shall see next, consumers have continued to buy popular culture products in spite of their being Japanese, even in places where Japanese culture was banned, including South Korea, Taiwan, and China.

Japanese Music and Television Goes Regional

Since the end of the 1980s, a few Japanese music and television companies have been diversifying their businesses by expanding to foreign markets. The expansion abroad of some of the biggest music companies was initially realized in the already prosperous markets of North America and Europe through acquisition or necessary collaboration with local companies and distributors.[3] In the 1990s, however, their expansion abroad was directed toward entering East Asia's emerging markets. Propelled by an expansion strategy and encouraged by the existence of substantial local demand, a growing number of Japanese music and television companies started to take an increasing interest in the markets of East Asia and intensified their efforts to establish a presence there.

A few specific circumstances induced the expansion of Japanese companies to enter the East Asian market in the 1990s. During most of the post–World War II years, many Japanese cultural industries were reluctant to enter markets in the region. Until the long recession hit Japan at the end of the 1980s, the Japanese market was steadily growing and was affluent enough to keep Japanese cultural industries focused on the domestic market. Overseas business growth opportunities were mostly explored in the developed markets of North America and Europe. Moreover, censorship was imposed on Japanese culture by some countries in East Asia. The Taiwanese government banned the importation of Japanese culture between 1972 and 1993, and the South Korean government only started to remove a similar ban in 1998. In Malaysia, Thailand, the Philippines, and Singapore, Japanese popular culture was occasionally banned due to its suspected "violent" nature.

But the extended economic recession in Japan on the one hand, and the rise of consumer demand in East Asian markets on the other, motivated the flow of Japanese popular culture to East Asia. At the end of the 1980s, the markets in East Asia were starting to prosper due to double-digit growth in some of the region's economies. As leisure time and disposable income increased among this region's newly emerging urban middle class, a few music and television companies started to take notice. The competition from the relatively undeveloped local industries was minimal. At the same time, Western cultural industries were less dominant in this part of the world than they were in North America and in Europe. In East Asia, American and European companies did not have the advantages of the English language and did not maintain distribution networks as extensive as they did in other parts of the world (Keane 2006). In East Asia, it was thus easier for Japanese cultural industries to enter the local popular culture market without being obliged to trample agreements with the dominant Western companies, as they would have been forced to do in the West.[4]

The entrepreneurial drive of the Japanese music and television companies was directed toward generating profit in this region's emerging markets through utilizing the knowledge and experience accumulated in Japan. In the 1990s, these companies were far more advanced than their East Asian counterparts in commodifying, producing, and marketing, and they were in a position to offer products, services, and new genres that were not available in the local popular culture markets. The expansion of these companies to East Asia initially took the form of collaboration with local companies and distributors who were more knowledgeable of the local markets. Once they obtained enough understanding of the local markets, however, they gradually assembled machineries of their own for commercializing their products and services.

Pony Canyon and Avex Trax, two of the six big Japanese music companies, are typical of the corporate mechanism that was set up to deliver Japanese music to East Asian consumers. These two companies gradually deepened their entrance into East Asian media markets by moving from licensing agreements with local companies to eventually opening local branches. In the 1980s, Pony Canyon and Avex Trax were already active in North America and Europe through their extensions in the United States and Britain. In the 1990s, they steadily established local contacts in East Asia as well, through promotions, licensing agreements, and acquisitions. Only after acquiring some market knowledge and establishing adequate contacts with local companies in East Asia did they shift to establishing a more direct presence through the opening of branches.

Pony Canyon established its own branches in Los Angeles in 1979 and in New York and London in 1985, and it engaged in various capital participation agreements with American and British media companies during the same period. It started to promote its own music and television in East Asia in the 1990s, opening branches in Malaysia in 1997 and in Hong Kong and South Korea in 1998 to market its products and seek new production opportunities. Pony Canyon's promotions included various Japanese music and television dramas, such as the music of Chage and Aska, and the successful hit dramas *Tokyo Love Story* and *101st Proposal.*

Likewise, Avex Trax made early extensions into the American and British markets and in the second half of the 1990s started to take an increased interest in entering the East Asian markets. Avex Trax established its East Asian regional base in Hong Kong in 1996. It then entered the Taiwanese market in 1997 through licensing agreements with a local company, Magic Stone, and continued a year later by replacing the licensing agreement with Magic Stone and establishing its own direct branch. In 2000, Avex Trax also established licensing and cooperation agreements with South Korea's S.M. Entertainment and went on to sign a similar agreement in Thailand. In 2002, Avex's branch in Hong Kong became the regional headquarters, in charge of managing and integrating the company's activities in East Asia.

Amuse, Rojam, JET TV, and Fuji TV are notable for their activities in the field of television. These companies became engaged in various television productions during the 1990s, often based on Japanese formats, establishing various ties with local companies and media organizations. Managed by an experienced team of Japanese producers, their goal was to recognize media-related opportunities, engage in their productions using Japanese capital, utilize management know-how and marketing strategies, and market final products back to local markets. An integral part of their work involved the use of Japanese-made popular culture production formats, such as the Japanese idol style, "trendy" television dramas, and variety shows, which were still relatively new in East Asia.

Amuse, a Japanese television company, established its own branches in Hong Kong in 1991, in China in 1995, and in South Korea in 2000 to explore new production opportunities. Its branches in East Asia were especially active in promoting joint productions with local companies and targeting the Chinese-speaking markets. The Amuse branch in Hong Kong teamed with local companies to coproduce various television programs in the 1990s. Amuse in China, together with Shanghai TV, coproduced a television documentary named *Shanghai People in Tokyo,* which was broadcast on Chinese television in 1995. The company's branch in China actively engaged in finding and producing music pop stars by holding large open auditions in big cities.

Another noteworthy case was the television production company Rojam, whose main strategy was the joint promotion of music and television. The key person in Rojam was the famous Japanese music producer, Komuro Tetsuya. Once a singer himself, Komuro is still one of Japan's leading pop music producers, considered by many to be a marketing genius who helped make the Avex Trax label one of the biggest forces in the Japanese music business. Komuro was personally responsible for the success of Japanese pop idols such as Amuro Namie, Kahara Tomomi, and Yoshida Masami. Komuro's idea was to utilize his experience in producing pop music in Asian markets, and for that he teamed with the Hong Kong–based television station TK News to establish Rojam. In the 1990s, the company produced music talent programs, where new talents were discovered and popular taste was gauged, later to be produced, packaged, and offered to a variety of new credulous consumers. The exposure in TK News of some artists produced by Komuro increased their popularity, and the singing talent competitions that were produced with Komuro's know-how were broadcast on TK News and contributed to the station's popularity. But Komuro's entrepreneurial drive did not stop there, and Rojam continued to look for new opportunities. In 1999, riding on Shanghai's growing entertainment market, Rojam opened a discotheque in the city's luxurious Nanjing-Lu district, sponsoring DJ concerts and talent competitions, which were then relatively new in China.

JET TV (Japan Entertainment Television) was another entrepreneurial attempt designed to sell Japanese musical and television content to the rising affluent middle-class audience in East Asia. JET TV was established in 1995, and until 1999 broadcast from its base in Singapore to seven destinations in the region: Taiwan, Singapore, Hong Kong, Thailand, Malaysia, Indonesia, and the Philippines. JET TV's broadcasts mainly included Japanese television dramas, variety shows, and cartoons that were also dubbed into English, Mandarin, and Thai. JET TV, however, did not stay in Japanese hands for long, as it was eventually acquired by Taiwanese- and Hong Kong–based companies in 1999 and 2002. JET TV stopped its broadcasts of Japanese programs in 2010.

Japanese companies were not always eager to enter new markets in East Asia and pursue an active expansion strategy. Iwabuchi Kōichi, who studied Japanese television dramas in Taiwan during their heyday at the end of the 1990s, offers an explanation. Based on interviews with television personnel in Japan, he argues that they calculated that it was more rewarding to focus on producing new television dramas for the domestic market (where the revenue came from local commercials and sponsorship and where the video market was high) rather than investing in expansion to new East Asian markets. This, according to Iwabuchi (1999, 188; 2001, 59), is the main reason many Japanese television companies remained aloof about East Asian markets. According to Ōta Tōru, a prominent Fuji TV producer, Fuji TV did not even develop a particular "Asian strategy," and he himself was surprised to see Fuji's television dramas become so popular in East Asia (Ōta 2004, 77–79).

Fuji TV, one of Japan's five biggest television stations, is a good example of the reluctance of some Japanese companies to expand their businesses into East Asian markets. Unlike JET TV, a company that specifically targeted the East Asian market, Fuji TV remained hesitant to market its products in East Asia although it was aware of the possibilities in expanding to this region (Hu 2004, 218). Instead, Fuji TV sold the permission to air its television dramas to local television stations without following a particular East Asia–centric strategy. Fuji TV was particularly reluctant to promote the marketing of its dramas in hardware form, such as DVDs and VCDs, due to fears of piracy. On several occasions, companies in Hong Kong asked to buy the rights to market DVD collections of Fuji TV's popular television dramas, but the company refused even though there were already pirated versions available across the city.[5] Nevertheless, Fuji TV's television dramas found receptive audiences in places such as South Korea, Taiwan, Hong Kong, Malaysia, and Singapore (Hara 2004). Fuji TV's popular television drama *Love 2000*, starring Nakayama Miho and Kaneshiro Takeshi, was simultaneously debuted in January 2000 on television channels in five locations in East Asia.[6] During the same period, Fuji TV also started exporting its television content to China, which broadcast to twenty-nine regions of the country through a Beijing-based station. In 2006, CCTV, China's biggest television station, bought twelve drama series from Fuji TV, among them *Last Christmas* and *Oku Dai Issho*. Analysts expect that the demand for Japanese television content will continue to increase as television broadcasting in China shifts to high definition.[7]

In 2001, Fuji TV made an exception when it teamed with TBS, another Japanese TV station, to collaborate with South Korea's MBC and produce the two television miniseries *Friends* and *Sonagi, an Afternoon Showers*. These dramas depicted youngsters' love stories, which exceeded national boundaries and cultural differences and difficulties. In these dramas, the Japanese heroines and Korean heroes succeeded in both their romance and work. *Friends* was a four-part miniseries coproduced by Korea's broadcasting company, MBC, and the Japanese TBS. When it was aired in February 2002 it drew great attention in the two countries, earning a 14.8 percent television rating in Japan and 17.5 percent in South Korea. *Sonagi* was simultaneously aired in Japan and Korea in November 2002 and received a 14.3 percent television rating in Japan and 13.2 percent in South Korea.[8]

These case studies show that a few of the prominent Japanese companies that entered markets in East Asia in the 1990s had already explored other markets and possessed a global reach that had started even earlier (Pony Canyon, Avex Trax, and Amuse). For others (Rojam and JET TV), expansion into East Asia was part of a regional strategy or was driven by local demand (Fuji TV). For these companies, however, East Asian markets represented new opportunities for business growth. The result, as we shall see next, was the assembly of mechanisms for exporting and distributing Japanese music and television programs and tightening cooperation between the regional branches of each company and its headquarters.

The Mechanism of Commercializing Music

The size of the companies involved in the production and marketing of commodified music in East Asia varies greatly. There is a mixture of big and small companies, all competing for a share in a highly competitive environment. There are four major companies that distribute Japanese music (Sony Music Entertainment, Universal, EMI, and Warner), in addition to ten to twenty medium-sized and small companies, which operate in each market. The big companies and some of the medium-sized ones have a more regional view of the market that enables them to promote their music by financing expensive promotional campaigns. It is the big companies that are at the center of the structure of economic power, and their regional presence gives them advantages in receiving feedback from their branches in other countries and in trading the inventories among themselves. But in order to achieve a closer familiarity with consumers and a sense of the latest popular musical styles, they need to reconfigure themselves to act like small companies. These companies have to be on constant alert for new cultural trends and preferences, find creative ways to promote their initiatives, receive feedback from the market, and react swiftly.

The small companies, on the other hand, tend to develop a more focused strategy, targeting specific audiences. They are faster to adapt to the dynamics of the popular culture market and to profit from arising opportunities, for example, by targeting specific audiences or focusing on certain musical genres and styles. A few small companies are now attempting to specifically target *otaku*—the most passionate fans of Japanese popular culture—and sell them high-quality CDs imported directly from Japan at high prices. According to Keyman Luk, the general manager of a major music distribution company in Hong Kong, in every big city in Asia there is a distinguishable group of Japanese music fans, mostly youngsters but also adults in their thirties and forties, who are willing to spend more than the average consumer on high-quality products as long as they are Japanese.[9]

Export and Local Manufacturing

At first, the Japanese music CDs and DVDs found in East Asia were imported directly from Japan. Due to the high cost of manufacturing, though, the bulk of these products since the end of the 1990s have been manufactured through licensing between Japanese and local companies and manufactured in places where the manufacturing cost is low, such as Taiwan and mainland China. The extent of this form of licensing is unknown. It is, however, estimated by JETRO that East Asia has been the bulk market for the manufacturing of Japanese music products outside Japan.[10]

Beginning in 1988, Japan's Customs and Tariff Bureau started to record the *number* of exported music items and their *value*. According to the bureau's records, between 1988 and 2005 a total of more than 218 million items, in the form of cassettes and CDs, were directly exported from Japan to East Asia.[11] The annual export sharply increased, from approximately 3 million items in 1995 to almost 21 million items in 2005.[12] The monetary value of Japanese music product exports to the nine East Asian markets has seen a steady increase as well. From 1988 to 2005, the export value rose from ¥5.5 billion in 1988 to at least ¥13 billion in 2005, totaling more than ¥250 billion over the entire period. The export value increased in six consecutive years, between 1988 and 1993; and then, for the most part, remained above ¥13 billion.

Hong Kong was the leading destination for Japan's music exports, representing 36 percent of the total value, followed by Taiwan, South Korea, and Singapore; then China, the Philippines, Malaysia, Thailand, and Indonesia (Figure 4.1). Taiwan was the second biggest export destination, representing 18 percent of the total. Hong Kong and Taiwan, however, served not only as targets of export but also as regional centers for organizing the manufacturing and distribution of CDs and DVDs to other destinations in East Asia. Japanese music companies, such as Avex Trax and Pony Canyon, often used their branches in Hong Kong and Taiwan as testing grounds for their expansion to the wider Chinese market and as distribution bases to other markets in East Asia. The cultural and geographical proximity of Hong Kong and Taiwan to mainland China was viewed as beneficial for accessing cheap manufacturing facilities and for establishing a hold in the rising Chinese market. Therefore, not all the export that went to these two destinations was consumed locally, but in some cases was re-exported to other markets in the region.

The above export figures, however, represent a conservative estimate of the size of the Japanese music market in East Asia. The figures do not include the manufacturing of Japanese music products through licensing

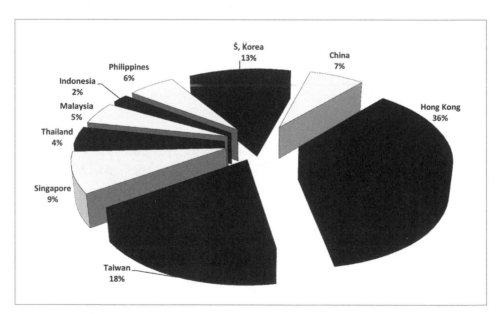

FIGURE 4.1 Export Value of Japanese Music by Destination 1988–2005. (Source: Japan Ministry of Finance 1988–2005)

agreements outside Japan, which makes up the overall majority of products sold outside Japan, as well as the wide (illegal) pirated markets for producing and distributing Japanese music products in East Asia. Taking into account the high cost of production in Japan, it was economically rational to manufacture Japanese music products in cheaper countries in Asia. Indeed, Japanese music companies, through their extensions outside Japan, locally manufactured any music CDs that were expected to sell more than five hundred to a thousand copies. Only albums whose success was doubtful were imported in small quantities from Japan for short trial periods. Otherwise, the CDs were either manufactured locally or imported from other branches of the company in East Asia. Moreover, Japanese music companies sometimes licensed other international music companies to manufacture and market their products. These figures also do not appear in Japan's Ministry of Finance's records. In addition, there is a huge piracy market for producing and distributing music products in East Asia, including Japanese music products, which is not accounted for in the figures presented here. The real figures regarding the size of the Japanese music market in East Asia are therefore much higher.

With the inclusion of the pirated music markets, Japanese music sales in Hong Kong was estimated to occupy between 15 to 20 percent of the music market during its peak period from 1996 until 1999, and between 8 to 12 percent in 2003. In 2010, however, Japanese music sales fell to about 5 to 6 percent of the market, compared to Cantonese music, which accounts for approximately 70 percent of sales, American and other Western music (20 percent), and Korean music (5 percent).[13] In Bangkok, Japanese music shares of the market were relatively low, occupying between 5 and 7 percent of the music market between 2002 and 2004. At CD Warehouse, Bangkok's biggest music shop, the sale of Japanese music in 2004 accounted for between 6 and 8 percent of sales, with American music making up approximately 45 percent, Thai music 20 percent, and jazz, classical music (including Japanese jazz and classical music), and movies making up the rest.[14] Managers of the four biggest HMV shops in Bangkok gave similar estimates.[15] In Seoul, the estimates were between 10 to 12 percent of the music market share in the first six months after the opening of the market to Japanese music in 2002, and approximately 7 to 9 percent in 2004. Average-selling albums sold between 3,000 and 5,000 copies, while the more successful albums sold more than 10,000 copies. The unsuccessful albums sold fewer than

2,000 copies. There were a few exceptions, Nakashima Mika's album *Love*, for example, sold more than 50,000 copies in the first three months of 2005, as did the albums of Utada Hikaru.[16] X Japan also had phenomenal success and is estimated to have sold 800,000 copies of its albums, plus an additional 200,000 in pirated versions. In Singapore, the share of Japanese music was more modest, occupying 8 to 10 percent of the music market between 1996 and 1998, but only 5 percent in 2003.[17]

Regional Collaboration

Collaboration between Japanese and local companies has been key for marketing Japanese music. Japanese music companies, which initially had a limited knowledge of the market, needed to rely on local agents and promoters who had an intimate familiarity with the market and who could serve as "radars" for new musical fashions and tastes. The local companies, working with Japanese companies, served as a funnel for delivering new production ideas and marketing techniques. Through this collaboration, the local companies were able to acquire new producible ideas, which could later be imitated and localized for the local market. These collaborations also made good economic sense because popular culture involves costly production and promotional campaigns, and collaborations are a way of reducing manufacturing costs and sharing the risk of bad decisions (Otmazgin and Ben-Ari 2013). To cope with the diversification of the East Asian national economies and to reduce production costs, branches of music companies shared information about the market and traded inventories. These relations created a de facto decentralized decision-making structure that could respond better to fluctuations in the market.

The Pony Canyon branch in Hong Kong, for example, is represented by a company called Forward Music, which is also responsible for the Malaysian market and frequently supplies it with information about market trends, as well as with newly released Japanese music CDs and DVDs. The same Hong Kong branch occasionally imports Japanese music CDs from Pony Canyon Taiwan in cases when inventory is out of stock or when additional merchandise is needed to supplement demand.[18] The other branches and agents of Japanese music companies in East Asia also facilitate the intraregional trade of Japanese music CDs in order to reduce production costs and avoid risk of overmanufacturing. They import only a small number of items from other branches of companies in East Asia for preliminary trial periods, as it is not worth manufacturing fewer than a thousand copies, and they sometimes buy inventories from other branches of the same company to review them.

South Korea is an exception. The majority of CDs offered in the South Korean market are manufactured locally, upon licensing from Japan. The branches of the record companies in Seoul, however, do not cooperate much with other branches of the same company in East Asia compared to their counterparts in Hong Kong and Bangkok. They do not export locally manufactured Japanese music albums to other destinations in East Asia, even in cases where they have overmanufactured an item, and only rarely import a small quantity of originals from Japan. Music industry personnel in Seoul indicated in interviews that the reason for this is that legislation in South Korea, which aims to protect local manufacturing, is making the intraregional importation of music CDs bureaucratically complicated.[19]

Interestingly in the case of music, regional trade in Japanese music products has evolved, but with minor participation from Japan in the manufacturing and distribution stages. This is due to the high cost of manufacturing in Japan, which has forced Japanese music companies to manufacture in "cheap" places in East Asia or has encouraged them to license other international music companies to manufacture and market their products abroad. The Japanese government, for its part, has consolidated the exclusion of the Japanese market in this trade. In an attempt to protect its local manufacturers, the government passed a law in 2002 prohibiting the importation of Japanese music, thus keeping the price of music products relatively high. Consumers inside Japan can now only buy Japanese music commodities that have been manufactured domestically. Since then, all Japanese music CDs sold in East Asia bear a clear warning on their cover, indicating "NOT for distribution in Japan" or "For distribution only in Korea, Indonesia, Hong Kong, Thailand, China, and Taiwan."

Some of the local branches of Japanese music companies have produced their own compilation albums, which have been made especially for the East Asian market and have not been sold in Japan. These albums are a repackaging of existing songs by different Japanese music artists and do not require the production of new material. In Japan, the production of compilation albums is extremely complicated, as the copyrights for each song are held by many agents, such as the producer, the talent agency, the sponsor, the artist himself or herself, and the artist's manager. This is all in addition to the record company, and negotiations will fail if one of these copyright owners does not agree.

Despite these difficulties, during the heyday of Japanese music in East Asia a few companies have managed to produce compilation albums featuring Japanese music artists. At JVC in Hong Kong, the local managers produced their own music collection in 2005, featuring the songs of some of the company's well-known artists. The office head revealed in an interview that this was not an easy task; they had to coordinate the interests of the different artists and their agents and go through long negotiations with the various copyright holders. He emphasized that producing this sort of album was their own idea and not a strategy initiated by the main office. Likewise, in 2004 the Avex Trax branch in Hong Kong launched *The Best of J Pop,* a music CD with a VCD included. The album stayed in the top ten of the foreign music chart in HMV shops for approximately three months. This album was not sold in Japan but from the very beginning focused on the East Asian market.[20] Following its success in Hong Kong, the album was further marketed in Malaysia, Thailand, Singapore, and Taiwan through the company's branches in these places. Other notable examples are Sony Music Entertainment and EMI, which launched their own compilation albums featuring their company's popular music artists, such as *Made in Japan* and *J Melon Pop Hits* (by Sony), and a series of albums called *Tokyo Café* (by EMI).

Sony Music Entertainment has taken it a step further by attempting to create a new musical genre through initiating ground-level album production. What is interesting about Sony's initiative is that from the very beginning its albums have been depicted as featuring "Asian" rather than Japanese music. In 2004, the company produced a two-volume pop music collection featuring Japanese, Hong Kong, Taiwanese, and South Korean music artists. The success of the album motivated the 2005 production of new volumes, which also included Thai music. Kieven Yim, a Sony Music Entertainment official responsible for the company's strategic thinking in Asia, revealed in an interview that the company was attempting to create a new, pan-Asian musical genre to be marketed to audiences from different national and linguistic boundaries in Asia. He believed that this market will develop in the long term. The company thus encourages its regional offices to produce compilation albums with an emphasis on transnational collaboration between music artists.[21]

Promotional Strategies

Like in all other entertainment fields, promotion is a central feature in the music industry. In the 1990s and 2000s, the promotion efforts of Japanese music companies in the East Asian markets were conducted with varying intensities. The larger companies, striving for broad exposure of their products through multiple means of promotion and transmission, were able to sponsor costly public relations campaigns. Their methods included promoting their products on television, radio, and street billboards, sponsoring events, inviting artists to perform and meet fans, and establishing ties with local media companies, retailers, and music journalists. Sony Music Entertainment frequently financed weekly television programs on local television stations in Hong Kong, Thailand, and, after the removal of the ban, South Korea. In addition, there were several television channels that kept local consumers informed about Japanese pop music. Channel V is noteworthy in Hong Kong and frequently showed Japanese music clips in its *Music Update* and *Karaoke Zone* shows. In South Korea in the 1990s, MTV often broadcast Japanese pop songs, M-net had a weekly thirty-minute program called *Pop Japan TV* that broadcast Sony's artists, and KMTV had a weekly one-hour program on Japanese pop. Avex Trax, as well as Sony and Universal, occasionally flies in its artists for promotional concerts in Taiwan, Hong Kong and South Korea.

The promotional strategies of smaller companies, on the other hand, was much more modest, based on the conventional methods offered through local agents, such as advertisement posters, articles in fashion and music magazines, and personal contacts with retailers. The smaller companies, however, benefited from the wider promotion campaigns of the bigger companies, which increase the overall popularity of Japanese popular culture in the market and thus cultivate further demand.

Most recently, there has been an increasing use of the Internet as a means of promotion. The music companies are relying more and more on the Internet to commercialize their music by launching their own Internet blogs or through introducing their artists across various Internet communities such as Facebook.[22] They also team up with Internet sites to allow legal downloading of music in exchange for part of the revenues. The release of a new album in stores is almost in tandem with its release online for a fee negotiated between the music company and the website/cellular company.[23] The increasing use of the Internet as a promotional tool correlates with the fact that more and more people today prefer to access music

Artist	Song	Japan Release Date	Local Release Date	China	HK	Taiwan	South Korea	Malaysia	Singapore	Indonesia	Thailand
Asian Kung-Fu Generation	Sorfa	10/20/2004	01/07/2005	•	•					•	•
Namie Amuro	Queen of HIP-POP	7/13/2005	7/13/2005	•	•	•	•	•			
Miki Imai	Dream Tour Final at BUDOKAN2004	3/16/2005	3/18/2005		•	•	•	•	•		
w-inds	ageha	06/01/2005	06/01/2005		•	•	•	•	•		
EXILE	SELECT BEST	01/01/2005	01/07/2005		•		•	•			
Ai Otsuka	LOVE JAM	11/17/2004	04/01/2005	•			•	•			
Lisa Ono	Romance Latino vol. 1	6/29/2005	6/29/2005		•	•	•	•	•		
Off Course	TWIN BEST Of Cause	9/19/1996	03/11/2005		•		•	•			
Crystal Kay	Crystal Style	03/02/2005	4/21/2005		•	•	•	•			•
GLAY	[-Ballad Best Singles~WHITE ROAD]	1/19/2005	1/20/2005		•	•	•	•			
CHEMISTRY	Kimi-ga Iru	2/23/2005	1/28/2005		•	•	•	•	•	•	
CHEMISTRY	Hot Chemistry	1/26/2005	1/28/2005		•	•	•	•	•		
Yoko Sugano	STAND ALONE COMPLEX O.S.T	2/25/2004	04/08/2005				•				
Zipcode	E-Complete A Side Singles	4/13/2005	4/15/2005		•		•		•		
Koji Tamaki	Kyo-toui KonoHi-wo Ikiteiko	2/16/2005	2/22/2005		•	•	•				
Narumi Tamaoki	Make Progress	05/11/2005	5/20/2005				•				•
D-51	ONENESS	3/16/2005	04/01/2005	•	•	•	•	•			•
Mika Nakashima	MUSIC	03/09/2005	1/20/2005		•		•	•	•		
Aumi Hamazaki	MY STORY	12/15/2004	02/07/2005	•	•	•	•	•			
Various	LOVE for NANA~only 1 Tribute~	3/16/2005	4/15/2005		•		•				
BoA	BEST OF SOUL	02/02/2005	02/04/2005		•	•	•	•		•	
Pornography	THUMPx	4/20/2005	5/23/2005				•		•		
Love Psychedelico	Early Time	02/09/2005	2/15/2005	•			•				
L'Arc-en-Ciel	Killing Me	1/13/2005	1/21/2005				•				•
LUNA SEA	MOTHER	10/26/1994	2/24/2005				•				
Hitomi Yaida	Yaiko's selection	12/01/2004	01/05/2005		•	•	•	•	•		
Chika Arisato	Good Luck To You~selected album~	3/24/2005	04/08/2005	•		•	•	•			•

SOURCE: Digital Content Association of Japan 2005.

online. In spite of the shrinking music market caused by piracy and illegal downloading, people today are exposed to music more than ever before. It is the distribution and the consumption of music that has changed, moving from traditional distribution through radio, audio recording, and live concerts, to Internet and online downloading to personal computers, cellular phones, and other accessible devices (Asai 2008b, 473–485).

Sony Music Entertainment official Keiven Yim indicated in an interview that the promotion strategies of the music companies are becoming more vigorous. As the marketplace rapidly becomes saturated with an influx of cultural consumption options, the companies need to invest more in marketing. They are coerced into spending more on "pushing" campaigns and are often forced to team up with other companies and promoters. According to the Sony official, "in order for the product to win, we need to invest in marketing and not only expect that consumers will simply access the product because it is good."[24]

Because of the relations between Japanese companies and their local agents, and thanks to their promotional campaigns, Japanese music is available in East Asia at about the same time it is released in Japan. As Table 4.1 shows, most of the music albums that were released in Japan in 2005 were released in markets in East Asia almost simultaneously. More releases took place in Hong Kong, Taiwan, South Korea, and Singapore than in Malaysia, Thailand, Indonesia, and China.

The Role of Piracy in the Creation of Markets

In addition to the formal dissemination of Japanese popular culture in East Asia via export and through the commercialization undertaken by Japanese companies, consumers were exposed to popular culture content through piracy. In fact, piracy has played a profound role in nurturing awareness of these popular culture products and delivering them to consumers.[25] Flourishing markets offering pirated versions of audio-visual products and printed materials, including music, animation, television programs, movies, and comics, have greatly invigorated the transnational transfer and trade in popular culture, including Japanese popular culture. As any visitor to East Asia's big cities in the 1990s can testify, centers for pirated popular culture products have mushroomed in all the major cities of East Asia, and pirated products were openly offered from street vendors and shops in places such as Hong Kong's Ho King and Sino Center, Bangkok's Pantip and night market, Jakarta's Senyan district, Taipei's Shihlin night market, and Seoul's Nandeamon market.

In recent years, popular culture content has also become available online, often illegally. While physical piracy was the main propeller behind the dissemination of popular culture in the 1990s, in recent years online piracy has become more prevalent. According to the International Federation of the Phonographic Industry (IFPI), for every music track bought online, twenty are downloaded illegally. Many of the music albums appear online even before their formal release at shops or on the radio. One example is the 2009 release of the new album by Taiwanese music star Sky Wu. The new album was officially launched on December 18, 2009, but was available for illegal downloading from various servers less than five hours later![26] Online piracy is also more difficult to trace. It is much more complicated for the authorities to locate the servers that allow illegal downloading, especially if those servers are located in other countries. The result is that since the early 1990s, both physical and online piracy has been a powerful engine for delivering popular culture across national boundaries, in most parts undisturbed by state regulations (Mertha 2005; Pang 2006).

Popular culture piracy in East Asia, excluding Japan, is widespread and includes the vigorously pirated music markets of China (the biggest piracy market in the world), Taiwan, Indonesia, Malaysia, and Thailand. According to the IFPI, in 2000 music piracy (as a part of the entire music market) was at least 90 percent in China, 85 percent in Indonesia, 50 percent in Taiwan, Malaysia, Thailand, and the Philippines, and 30 percent in Hong Kong, Singapore, and South Korea. In 2005, the rate was above 85 percent in China and Indonesia, and between 35 and 50 percent in Taiwan, Malaysia, Thailand, and the Philippines. According to industry estimates, in 2004 Chinese customers alone bought approximately one billion home video discs (VCDs), 95 percent of which were pirated.[27]

As discussed in chapter 2, in the 1990s East Asia's lucrative piracy markets were based on cheap manufacturing and the resilient transfer of products to a wide range of potential customers. Pirating operations of music, television programs, movies, anime, and manga publications were taken on by small- and medium-sized, guerrilla-like organizations. They were able to acquire capable labor, including workers skilled in language translation, commercial design, and VCD production, as well as in packaging, smuggling, and marketing pirated merchandise (Hu

2004, 2013). The technology that enables the transfer and spread of the products is relatively simple, at least in comparison to more technologically advanced industries such as automobiles and electronics. All that is needed is a recorder to illegally record and distribute music, animation, movies, or television programs on CD, VCD, or DVD.

The laxity of enforcement by local police in many East Asian countries has assisted the trafficking of pirated products. This is especially evident in mainland China, Thailand, Indonesia, Malaysia, the Philippines, and Vietnam, where according to an IFPI source in Bangkok, "the local police is either corrupt, or simply does not understand what is wrong with people making a living from selling pirated versions of foreign music." In the interview, he explained that it is impossible to enforce copyright violations without the help of the police, which "many times has other things to do, and is not always eager to invest in intellectual-property-related cases." When enforcement is finally applied, punishment does not serve as a deterrent in most cases (approximately four thousand popular-culture-related intellectual property cases are prosecuted in Thailand every year) and offenders are usually not asked to pay any compensation. In Hong Kong and South Korea as well, although many of the cases are regarded as criminal, music and television companies are reluctant to engage in the long and expensive process of prosecuting copyright violations in civilian courts. The problem becomes even more complicated in fighting online piracy because many of the servers and websites offering free downloads operate in other countries. There is little the music industry can do to close these websites, even if it gets the support of the authorities and the police.[28]

A personal episode demonstrates the inability of the industry to eliminate piracy. In June 2010, when I was in Hong Kong for research, I visited the office of Forward Music, a Hong Kong–based music distribution company. One of the workers came in with Chinese pop music CDs and DVDs he had just obtained. They were all pirated. He was astonished by the high quality of the CDs and DVDs, which were not only reproduced illegally but were also offered in beautifully designed packages that were not available in the original. The people who pirated these CDs and DVDs not only reproduced the content illegally, but also developed original packages of their own! Surprisingly, the people in the office did not seem to be mad about it; it was as if they had already given up fighting piracy, acknowledging that it was a war they could not win.

In the case of Japanese popular culture, piracy was critically important during the formative years of the market in the 1990s, not only because it cultivated a pool of potential consumers for Japanese products at accessible prices, but also because it facilitated the transfer of commodities and the diffusion of content into places where they were officially banned. First, piracy cultivated new markets for Japan's cultural industries by marketing illegal versions of their products to new potential audiences at accessible prices and in fact served as a way to brand and implant Japanese popular culture in the market. In this sense, piracy has served as a venue for market creation, complementing the formal marketing efforts undertaken by Japanese companies and their local agents. In many of these cases, original versions of Japanese pirated products were not even offered in the market, and the cultural content could be accessed only through buying illegally produced duplications. Many Japanese hit dramas appeared in pirated VCD and DVD versions even before they were officially broadcast on local and cable TV. Japanese television dramas such as *Tokyo Love Story, Long Vacation,* and *Yamatonadeshiko,* variety programs such as *TV Champio*n, various cooking shows, and Japanese animation such as *Doraemon, Tiger Mask,* and *Detective Conan* were sometimes available in the pirated market even before they officially appeared on public television and cable channels in Hong Kong, Singapore, Thailand, Indonesia, Malaysia, and Taiwan.

During fieldwork in Hong Kong in April 2004, I was amazed to discover the abundance of Japanese popular culture piracy. Though pirated versions of Japanese popular culture products were to be found in many shops and street vendor stalls across the city, the Sino Center on Nathan Road was especially noteworthy. In the 1990s and the beginning of the 2000s, Sino Center was the city's most notorious place for selling fake popular culture products and was also considered the Mecca for fans of Japanese popular culture and more recently of Korean popular culture. The Sino Center itself is a crowded shopping mall consisting of five floors with no less than ninety-four shops, which at the time of my survey specialized in Japanese music, anime, television dramas, magazines, manga, adult movies, video game software, and various anime-related merchandise—most of it pirated. Most visitors to the Sino Center are young people, interested in Japanese and Korean popular culture.[29]

Second, piracy has paved the way for Japan's cultural products into places where they were officially banned by the local authorities.

In Taiwan and South Korea, where Japanese culture was banned for most of the postwar period, the role of piracy is particularly noteworthy. There, piracy quickly filled the gaps created by government intervention and efficiently facilitated the dissemination of Japanese culture beyond the state's protective shield. Consumers in South Korea and Taiwan had little difficulty accessing (illegal) Japanese cultural content. The importation of Japanese culture to Taiwan was banned after Japan officially re-established diplomatic relations with the People's Republic of China in 1972, but since November 1992 it has been gradually allowed by the Kuomintang regime upon Taiwan's attempt to consolidate its relations with Japan in order to counterbalance China's influence.[30] In South Korea, Japanese culture was banned soon after South Korea regained its independence from Japan's colonization, but since 1998 it has also been gradually allowed back following the election of President Kim Dae-Jung and as part of normalizing relations with Japan (Yim 2003, 143–144). Some restrictions still remain, however, due to occasional regressions following Japanese leaders' visits to the controversial Yasukuni Shrine and the controversy over the rocky island of Takeshima/Dokdo, over which both countries claim sovereignty. Japanese music and television programs are still banned from public radio and television channels (Japan Ministry of Foreign Affairs 2006b).

Other governments in East Asia have attempted to channel the flow of culture along official lines and have imposed restrictions on the importation of Japanese popular culture. In the Philippines, Japanese manga and anime were occasionally banned because of their ostensibly violent content or because they threatened to overshadow the productions supported by the Marcos regime. For instance, young people in the Philippines never saw the final episodes of the popular anime series *Voltes V*, as it was censored in the 1980s. The official fear was that the animation, which depicts five heroes fighting against oppressive monsters, propagated revolutionary ideas against the government, but also because it was so popular that Filipino shows in the same time slot (one of which was produced by a crony of Marcos) couldn't compete with it. In Malaysia, the Home Ministry must still approve imports of comic books (most of which are Japanese) before distribution to determine their educational and political risk.[31] In 2002, the Culture Ministry in Thailand was reconstituted with the "mission to make sure we communicate with our public loudly and clearly that culture belongs to people, not organizations." The ministry regularly engages in campaigns to restrict potentially violent or vulgar pornographic cultural products.[32] In China as well, the government has been explicit in campaigning against the "spiritual pollution" brought by imported cultures. The Chinese Communist Party, with its long-standing insistence on cultural management, still tries desperately to regulate cultural production and sees the media as a powerful propaganda tool and a means of maintaining social control (Keane 2002, 121–122).

Due to piracy, however, there was little the government could do to prevent the infiltration of Japanese popular culture. In South Korea, even before the gradual removal of the ban in 1998, Japanese animation, music, video game software, and television dramas were widely present at street vendors' stalls and in markets and, later, on the Internet. In the 1990s, about 30 percent of South Korea's illegal music market was estimated to have consisted of Japanese music (METI 2002). The pirated music market made up more than 30 percent of the entire music market in the country, and illegal versions of Japanese music alone achieved as much as 10 percent of all South Korea's music market, legal and illegal combined.[33] Karaoke bars have also contributed to the popularity of Japanese music in South Korea by offering Japanese songs, both legally and illegally. The word "karaoke" itself was prohibited in public discourse in South Korea as a part of government censorship, but South Koreans were able to access Japanese music through karaoke, as it was still possible to find romanticized Japanese lyrics (Ōtake and Hosokawa 1998, 186–187; Okuno 2004, 11).

Access to Japanese popular cultural content was also available by intercepting Japanese television and radio broadcasts and using private satellite dishes. In the southern city of Busan, the exposure to contemporary Japanese culture has been immense because of the island's geographical proximity to Japan's western island of Kyushu. The residents of Busan were able to access Japanese cultural content, even before NHK started its international broadcasts in 1994, by using satellite dishes that (illegally) intercepted Japanese television and radio broadcasts. In 2001, it was estimated that as many as five million television sets in Korea received satellite broadcasts from Japan (Kim H.-M. 2004, 199, n. 14). Moreover, books about Japan were widely available in South Korea, books that provided insights into contemporary Japanese society and culture and indirectly invigorated interest in Japanese popular culture. In her study about Japanese culture in South Korea, Kanno Tomoko found that during 1993 and 1994, at least ten books about Japan were released every month. One book, titled *Boku ha Nihonbunka ga Omoshiroi* ("I Think Japanese Culture Is Interesting"), explaining the trends in contemporary Japanese culture, was released in 1998 and sold 300,000 copies, a record (Kanno 2000, 109–120).

Since the second half of the 1990s, the Internet has also played a central role in popularizing Japanese popular culture. In a survey conducted by the Korean Broadcasting Institute, 7.4 percent of the respondents stated they watch Japanese television programs via the Internet (Kim 2005). Through browsing the Internet, young Koreans can easily access, discuss, and download Japanese pop music, television dramas, and anime, using websites that specialize in Japanese popular culture. In March 2005, on Daum, the largest Internet portal in South Korea, there were more than six hundred Internet communities related to Japanese television content such as dramas, anime, and movies (including adult movies). The largest community is called Ilbon TV and has over 800,000 members (K. Lee 2008, 158).[34] Language differences are routinely overcome by using Japanese-Korean translation programs, also available from the Internet. The Internet has provided the space not only for downloading and sharing Japanese animation or movies, but also for distributing information about gathering spots for fan clubs of Japan's popular culture in Seoul (Pack 2004).

The case in Taiwan tells a similar story. In spite of a ban on the importation of Japanese culture between 1974 and 1992, Japanese popular culture was widely present due to the lucrative market of pirated items. Starting as early as the 1970s, Taiwan's pirated cable channel (the Fourth Channel) illegally broadcast Japanese television programs, among other foreign programs, and introduced Japanese television to local consumers (Iwabuchi 2002, 138–139). It is estimated that in 1985, videotapes of Japanese television programs and movies accounted for 31 percent of Taiwan's entire video rental business. According to Leo Ching (1996, 189), "despite the official ban, Japanese songs and video programs can be heard and rented in every record and video rental store; Japanese fashion and information magazines (or their Chinese versions) are readily available, even from street vendors. Today [1991], Japanese language learning has shifted from the technical to the practical, from the pedagogical to the commonplace, suggesting a better knowledge and a stronger affiliation with contemporary Japan." In the 1990s, the media in Taiwan coined a special term, *ha-ri*, to describe the extensive identification of the Taiwanese with Japanese culture and lifestyles.

A vivid example, which demonstrates how resilient entrepreneurship in popular culture can be, is the reproduction and marketing of pirated VCR cassettes of Japanese television dramas. In the 1980s, Japanese NHK morning television dramas were extremely popular in Taiwan. These television series depicting the lives of "simple" Japanese, which were broadcast on Japanese television during the morning hours, were illegally recorded and immediately translated into Chinese by Taiwanese students while still in Japan. The translated tapes were then sent with passengers' luggage on regular flights to Taiwan. They were then passed on to contact persons there, reproduced, and offered for rent in local video rental stores in Taipei in the evening of the same day! (This example is from Ishii, 2001, 26–27.)

Finally, piracy has had an impact on the regulating and institutionalizing of popular culture markets in East Asia. Piracy has been forcing local and regional organizations to cooperate in tackling copyright violations. Multinational and regional music and television companies have also been cooperating in fighting the piracy of their products. They have established local and regional federations to promote the awareness and enforcement of piracy laws and have excessively lobbied governments to articulate antipiracy measures. Piracy has also been stimulating the involvement of the Japanese government in the popular culture sector. The Japanese government has emphasized the importance of enforcing intellectual property rights and raising the issue of piracy in its FTAs with its Asian neighbors. Intellectual property officers are stationed in its JETRO offices in East Asia, and various seminars about piracy enforcement for local customs officials and judges are held. JETRO also invites delegations of judges and prosecutors from Southeast Asian countries to Japan to learn about ways to enforce intellectual property rights.[35] The issue of piracy and the need to defend intellectual property rights in the cultural industries is expected to rise in importance in the coming years, following the globalization of Japan's popular culture. The drive toward regulation is being fueled by the anticipation that slowing piracy will increase copyright holders' earnings.[36]

A framework to examine the role of piracy in enabling both the transnational and the intradomestic diffusion of Japanese cultural products in South Korea and Taiwan is illustrated in Figure 4.2. In position A, the market and the state are conceived as two conceptual spaces with different boundaries affecting each other's contours. A perfect case of a politicoeconomic relationship would be where the market and the state are interdependent and the flow of culture into the market is free. But in reality, a completely free market does not exist—it is merely an ideal. Governments intervene in all areas of commercial life by laying the foundations of laws for competition, tax, accounting, etc. Even in today's liberal democracies, in countries such as the United States, Australia, the United Kingdom, and Germany, there are extensive laws and regulations concerning ownership, competition, copyright, libel, and obscenity (Hesmondhalgh 2002, 110).

In the case of censorship, states often intervene to filter the entrance of foreign culture due to the state's policy priorities, such as when the imported culture can be destructive for the local market or offensive to the society and its values. In Taiwan and South Korea, the state has chosen to block the entrance of popular culture from Japan, giving higher priority to political considerations within the context of their historical relations with Japan. As shown in position B, however, piracy has diffused culture into the market and has avoided the state's protective shield, and it has been able to facilitate the dissemination of Japan's popular culture both into and within the market. By the time Japanese popular culture was allowed into the newly opened markets (since 1993 in Taiwan and since 1998 in South

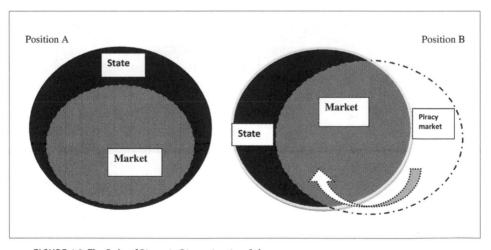

FIGURE 4.2 The Role of Piracy in Disseminating Culture

Korea), the demand for the products was already cultivated by piracy and the cultural industries were able to immediately generate sales.

Following the failure of censorship, there has been a significant relaxation of political control over the flow and consumption of popular culture in East Asia, and the restrictions on popular culture are slowly changing. Governments in this region have gradually come to acknowledge that their attempts to prevent their citizens from accessing imported popular cultures in an era of globalization are doomed to fail. Piracy, as well as information technology and the flow of people as tourists and students, make it impossible to isolate the country and stop the transmission of popular culture. Even when censorship is taking place, it is negotiated, contested, and selectively applied, due to the inability of the government to enforce its will against the illegal reproduction of cheap commodities in the form of CDs, DVDs, or VCDs (Otmazgin 2005, 514; Samuels 2012). At the beginning of the twenty-first century, only North Korea is still resisting the tide, although even there a small black market for popular culture coming mainly from South Korea operates.[37]

The established industry, as well, has started to give more attention to the problem of piracy in Asia by seeking new ways to tackle it. The response of the big companies to the infringement on their products is to lobby governments in East Asia to enforce copyright laws and to sponsor educational campaigns in schools and in the mass media warning against the damages inflicted by piracy. More recently, the big Japanese manufacturers have also been developing new technological solutions to defeat piracy. According to Yasuda Tetsuhiko, president of Sony Computer Entertainment Asia,[38] Sony has made a strategic decision to fight piracy completely. Sony's new antipiracy strategy in East Asia includes developing products that are more difficult to reproduce, such as the Sony Play Station 3 or Blu-ray discs, which are difficult to duplicate. Moreover, the company has been marketing limited editions of products to the Asian market (not including Japan), for example, a set of four discs instead of seven in Japan and tightening the connection between hardware and software, for example by developing a special chip that will be built in the hardware, recognize illegal software, and prevent it from working.

Mr. Yasuda remains optimistic about the future of fighting piracy in Asia. According to him, "when I joined Sony thirty-five years ago Japan was in a similar position with pirated music cassettes everywhere and with very little regard to copyrights. This was a real problem. However, with the combined efforts of the government and the private sector business became successful. . . . I am certain that East Asia will turn out the same." Mr Yasuda specifically raised the case of Singapore, "once a home to a prosperous pirated market, today almost no [pirated products] are available. In this respect, the political will of the government to fight piracy, with the understanding that it is the right thing to do, is crucial."

Conclusion

The dissemination of Japanese popular culture in East Asia in the 1990s and the creation of regional markets was driven by market forces, facilitated by the industry's mechanism of commodifying and distributing cultural commodities, and invigorated by piracy. Although it is impossible to estimate the exact market share of Japanese popular culture in East Asia due to the lack of data especially regarding the pirated market, it is obvious that Japanese popular culture has not been rejected. On the contrary, it has been accepted and is consistently popular in East Asian markets. In the case of music, exports from Japan and the actions and strategies employed by Japanese companies constitute the formal way Japanese popular culture commodities arrived in East Asia. Piracy, however, has been especially effective in cultivating new communities of consumers even under restrictive conditions. The moral reasoning given by governments to denounce or prohibit imported cultures, and the paternalistic measures taken by these governments, have not been effective, and censored products have routinely found their way to consumers. Stated differently, the attractiveness of imported cultures to consumers, the ability of networks to supply related products, and extensive pirating operations in East Asia have made censorship by governments in the region ineffective. Piracy has bypassed the government and encouraged the opening of markets to cultural imports. East Asia's pirated popular culture markets are just too big and too dynamic for local governments to handle.

This chapter tells the story of the creation of the Japanese popular culture market in East Asia. In many ways, this story is no different from other popular culture confluences that have entered East Asia over the past two decades from Korea, Taiwan, Hong Kong, and more recently from China. Promoters of these popular cultures have also had to overcome market impediments, government regulations, censorship, language barriers, and social-economic heterogeneity of consumers in order to generate profit. The "Japanese story," however, has a special quality that makes it noteworthy. First, Japanese popular culture was the first non-Western popular culture to break into East Asian markets on a large scale, and in this sense it opened the way to other popular cultures from the region to break beyond their immediate domestic market. This is especially true for the so-called "Korean Wave" ("Hallyu"), which started later but followed the example set by the Japanese wave. Second, as we shall see in chapter 5, the impact of Japan's popular culture goes beyond the immediate creation of a market for popular culture commodities. It has also served as an example and a model for the local cultural industries, which emulated its success. Many of today's East Asian popular culture industries are largely based on the Japanese model, especially in music, television dramas, idol fashion styles, animation, and comics.

CHAPTER 5

////////////////////////

Japan's Regional Model

The importance of Japanese cultural industries to the regionalization process in East Asia lies not only in the creation of new markets for popular culture commodities and in establishing collaboration with local companies, but also in serving as a model and in propagating a region-wide transformation of structural arrangements to commodify and commercialize popular culture. This position of Japan as a model for popular culture production was established both through Japanese companies' active introduction of cultural production formats to local markets and through the emulation of the Japanese example by local cultural industries. The result is that much of today's popular culture production in East Asia is based on Japanese formats, especially in music, television dramas, idol fashion styles, comic publications, and animation. In East Asia, popular culture products might dovetail locally and use internationally drawn motifs and languages, even if the format is Japanese. The impact of the Japanese cultural industries thus should not be evaluated only by the dissemination of their products and sales records per se, but also by the processes they entail, their conspicuous adaptation by local cultural industries, and their overall regional influence. The news about the death of the "learn from Japan" campaign is too early. This learning is still taking place in the field of popular culture.

The adaptation and emulation of Japanese formats does not, however, mean that East Asia's popular culture has completely become Japanese or that the Japanese model has been blindly imitated by the local cultural industries. First, the process of adaptation and emulation entails a wide degree of localization and appropriation that necessarily changes the original form. The internalization and reproduction of imported formats, especially in the field of popular culture, is inherently flexible and contingent and is open to various interpretations. As we shall see regarding the Korean cultural industries, although they initially emulated Japanese formats, they eventually developed their own recognizable features. Second, I would argue that the transformation of Japanese popular culture production formats and know-how actually propagates a variety of local productions and heterogeneous practices, which are able to express their own particular content using these imported formats. The result is the diversification of popular cultures rather than the domination of Japanese popular culture.

What is a "Japanese" format and, more basically, what constitutes "Japanese popular culture"? One thing we need to remember is that the Japanese model itself is not original in the sense that it was constructed through heavy borrowing from foreign cultures. According to cultural studies scholar Iwabuchi Kōichi (1998, 169), Japanese popular culture is the result of successful learning from America: "Since World War II, Japanese popular culture has been deeply influenced by American media. There has been no policy of imposing any quota on foreign popular culture in the audio-visual market since the war. Japan quickly localized these influences by imitating and partly appropriating the original, rather than being dominated by American products and 'colonized' by America." Similarly, Tsunoyama Sakae (1995, 98–114, 191) argues that Japan has not only internalized American influences but has also acted as a mediator, a substation in the flow of modernity from the West to Asia. In his view, commodities and influences coming from the West have been successfully transformed and refashioned to suit the consumers' tastes in Asia: "Filtration through a Japanese prism has made American popular culture something more familiar to people in Asia . . . the universal appeal of Japanese popular culture in Asia is based upon its erasure of any nationality from popular culture of American origin."

The construction of "Japanese popular culture" is thus not an "authentic" creation but the skilled incorporation of imported cultures, especially from the West. The "Japanese model" was not derived entirely from Japanese ancient traditions and culture or from the country's premodern visual art. Rather, it is the result of combining internal cultural and artistic traditions and skills with external influences. At the same time, however, Japanese popular culture has its own unique stamp. It is not a mere emulation of foreign influences or "Japanese facelessness," in the sense that it represents a recognizable line of products associated with Japan. While the Japanese model for popular culture production is the product of mimicking, borrowing, and experimenting at different periods of time, in a few popular culture fields (*kawaii* idols, television productions, pop music, manga, and anime) this model has been consolidated and is being recognized in Asia as Japanese. Indeed, there is nothing Japanese in animated characters such as *Hello Kitty, Doraemon,* or *Poke'mon,* and Japanese television and music shows do not necessarily embody subliminal cultural messages that resonate with Asian consumers, beyond perhaps the similar physical appearance of Japanese and Asian music and television idols. Nevertheless, a Japanese flavor lies in the formation of a specific genre explicitly and implicitly associated with Japan.

Take anime, for example. It is possible to recognize Japanese-style anime and distinguish it from Disney's animation even as it becomes steeped in different cultures through translation. Disney's format typically contains clear-cut good-versus-evil story elements, strong handdrawn graphics, and fluid animated moments, including a cast of supporting animal characters who often accompany the hero and heroine (Hu 2010, 143). In contrast, Japanese anime has a more sophisticated graphic quality, a wider thematic diversity, and an inclination to reject the Western convention of happy endings and sunny optimism in favor of darker, more complex, and morally ambiguous narratives (Tsutsui 2010, 53). Manga tells a similar story. According to Nadav Rotchild's study (2011, 33), a few important contextual and esthetical elements differentiate manga from Western-made comics:

> Manga sometimes contains adult themes, and caters to adults as well as children, in contrast with the Western notion that comics are meant for kids. Manga story arcs are very long, at times stretching for thousands of pages, while Western comics tend to be short and self-contained. Manga's drawing style is built upon the mimicking of notion, emotion, and action, whereas Western comics are much more text heavy and rely very little on the fluidity of motions or emotions. The icons, shapes, and signs used to express emotions in manga (such as the appearance of three small rectangles on the forehead to show anger, or a bead of sweat

that signifies an awkward situation) hold no meaning for Western readers. Comics are drawn from left to right and in full color in the West, but from right to left and only in black and white in Japan.

As we shall see later, cultural industry personnel in East Asia are able to recognize the Japanese model even when it is incorporated into other popular culture confluences available in the market.

This chapter makes a distinction between "content" and "format" in popular culture and focuses on the externalization, adaptation, and reproduction of Japanese formats for popular culture production in East Asia. The first part of the chapter recognizes and examines some of the prominent Japanese production formats that have been adopted and emulated in East Asia since the 1990s. The second part looks closely at the transformation of Japanese formats where it is most obvious and most extensive: the emerging Korean cultural industries. At the same time, this part also emphasizes that although many Japanese popular culture production formats have been adopted and internalized in South Korea, the Korean cultural industries have greatly advanced and at present stand on their own and maintain their own recognizable features. The last part discusses the appreciation given to the Japanese cultural industries, both to their products and their formats, by popular culture industry personnel in East Asia. The major purpose here is to analyze the reasons for the success of Japanese popular culture and its impact on the local cultural industries, based on the knowledge and expertise of specialists in the field. This part is based on in-depth interviews conducted between 2004 and 2010 with sixty-eight individuals from local cultural industries in Hong Kong, Singapore, Shanghai, Bangkok, and Seoul. This group includes personnel from prominent music and television companies, as well as government officials, officials from affiliated organizations, academics, media specialists, promoters, and people from media-related organizations.

Regionalizing Popular Culture Production Formats

As part of marketing popular culture products and initiating new productions, Japanese cultural industries needed to collaborate with local companies and organizations, which had a better understanding of the local markets. As discussed in chapter 4, starting from the end of the

1980s, a few Japanese music and TV companies estimated that substantial business potential existed in the markets of East Asia. But they needed to obtain adequate knowledge of the local markets and gain the ability to conduct expansionary activities such as advertising, local packaging of products, public relations, and the creation of distribution routes. In addition, they needed to recruit capable personnel who were familiar with the local popular culture market and spoke the language. In the manga and anime industries, Japanese companies also needed to use local subcontractors to reduce production costs and maintain profitability. For these purposes, collaboration with local companies was imperative. The expansion of Japanese companies therefore initially included teaming up with local companies and agents to gauge expansion possibilities, establishing manufacturing and marketing contacts, and carrying out promotions.

Collaborations with local companies, however, were not one-way relationships. Through these collaborations, local companies and promoters were able to learn new Japanese popular culture production formats and acquire experience. The collaborations between Japanese and local companies were therefore instrumental in spreading popular culture production formats. The exposure to production formats previously developed and tried in Japan was essential to the process of local learning. In the animation industry, for example, many animators in the region first gained their experience in animation while working for companies that collaborated with Japan as subcontractors. Local workers hired for this purpose subsequently came to view the Japanese productions as the model and as a standard to be achieved (Hu 2010, 144–145). This later gave rise to various new local productions based on Japanese formats and eventually led to these formats playing a central role in everyday popular culture innovation, commodification, and production in East Asia. In this way, the Japanese cultural industries gradually turned from being content providers to becoming format providers as well.

Before we examine some of the Japanese formats that were transferred to East Asia through collaboration, it is important to define the terms "collaboration" and "format" used in this study. By "collaboration" I refer to any activity that entails working jointly with others in ways that cross national boundaries. I purposely cast a wide net over the products I refer to since the processes involved in their production and consumption overlap, interlink, and resonate with each other (for a discussion that elaborates on collaboration in popular culture see Otmazgin and Ben-Ari 2013). The collaboration between Japanese and local companies in East Asia should thus be seen not only as cooperation for economic purposes (to reduce production costs, access consumers more efficiently, etc.) but also more broadly as a social process involving interaction and the cumulative exchange of ideas. In our case, this collaboration not only assisted in commercializing Japanese popular culture, but it also facilitated the transformation of production formats that have been adopted and emulated by the indigenous industries.

"Format," in the context of this book, is regarded not only as the variable elements needed for production, but also the wider technologies, capital, and marketing that surround the production. The transformation of formats thus is seen as not only the license to remake certain products (television programs, movies, animation, etc.) in another territory, but also the active adaptation and development of the format together with the knowledge and resources that will help ensure its adaptation and acceptance. In television, for example, the format package is a kind of recipe that comes with accessories and tips for the program's reproduction elsewhere, or it makes available a certain mold that assists the production team in other markets in making and marketing their own version of the program. What is marketed is not a complete program but rather a body of knowledge and accompanying resources that help in the remaking of a program (Moran 2008, 461–462).

One of the major advantages of formats, which make their adaptation much easier, is that they can easily be customized to suit local tastes and expectations. Formats provide a basic platform that has already proven to be successful in another place. At the same time, formats enable the insertion of local content (local languages, narratives, costumes, accessories, etc.). In this way, local producers can use these formats to express their own creative interest and add their own nuances. A second major advantage of formats is that they are not necessarily attached to a certain language. In our case, Japan's linguistic isolation from the rest of East Asia has been bridged by reformatting content and producing content that does not necessarily encode Japanese linguistic characteristics. Nevertheless, it is also important to remember that Japan's popular culture products, especially in their written forms such as manga, have an advantage in the Chinese-speaking world: the use of Chinese characters.

The use of Chinese characters in Japanese writing makes popular culture products more acceptable in the region, especially in Taiwan, Hong Kong, Singapore, and mainland China.

The Production of Idols

One famous Japanese format is the production of idols. Japanese-style idols are young, usually between the ages of fourteen and twenty-four, and are supposed to be more than "mere" music artists. Japanese-style idols usually appear in certain configurations, such as in three-girl bands or five-boy singing groups with remarkable dancing abilities, or as a lead female singer accompanied by five male band members. Singing ability and extraordinary physical attributes are less important than that idols are expected to maintain close contact with their audiences and represent the notion that "anyone can be a star." These performers almost never make or play their own music; their songs are written and produced by professional songwriters. Idols' hit songs are accompanied by, and synchronized with, dance choreography that operates with remarkable precision. Much of the fame of these idols is achieved through frequent appearances on television programs and commercials. Females are usually supposed to strike "coy" poses that reflect sweetness and purity, while the males adopt a more stylish or "cool" appearance. They are often "life-sized," meaning they are depicted as fairly standard, just like "the girl or boy next door" (Ugaya 2005, 97–98). This is contrary to Western idols, who often possess outstanding physical or personal attributes.

Japan's idol industry is a formidable mechanism consisting of record companies, talent production agencies, and electronic media that cooperatively ensure the availability, production, and commercialization of packaged commodities (Ching 1996, 178). Take live performances, for example. Live performances by Japanese music idols are highly orchestrated. In addition to the meticulous planning of the costumes, choreography, and structure of the performance, the audience is expected to take an active role in the show. While on stage, the idol or a member of his or her staff gives precise instructions to the crowd, like clapping hands at specific moments or repeating the lyrics of a tune. Sometimes the crowd is even divided into subgroups that are expected to perform different duties at different moments. The production level of the show is high in terms of sound, lights, multimedia effects, and accessories used, and the live performances are impressively commercialized. There are strict rules regarding copyright. Personal cameras are not allowed into the performance area, and taking pictures is usually prohibited. A variety of merchandise depicting the idol, such as T-shirts, scarves, posters, and pictures, is routinely offered in the performance area in addition to the idol's music CDs, and registration forms are necessary to join the fan club.

The Japanese female duet Puffy is perhaps the best example of Japan's idol production. The two young female singers were recruited and debuted under strict guidelines established by their producer Okuda Tamio and their record label Sony Music Entertainment Inc. From the very beginning, Puffy were not produced to be only music artists. Rather, they were expected to be multitalented performers, frequently appearing in advertisements, television programs, and commercial campaigns, as well as serving as models to a heavily industrialized set of fashions and accessories. Puffy have had a few successful music hits, including *Ajia no Junshin* (Asia's Innocence) and *Kore ga Watashi no Ikirumichi* (This Is My Way of Life), but they were as popular for their daily appearances on magazine covers, advertisement posters, and in commercials for various companies ranging from Honda to Shiseido as for their musical hits (Ugaya 2005, 96–99).

Puffy frequently appeared at live concerts and in commercials in East Asian cities, especially in Hong Kong and Taiwan, where they were not only extremely popular but were also imitated by local music artists (for example, the Hong Kong–based girl group Twins). Puffy later attempted to break into the North American market. In 2001, their first album, *Spike,* was released in the United States followed by a concert tour the next year. In 2004, their characters appeared in an animated series under the label the *Puffy Amy Yumi Show,* which ran for three seasons, and in 2006, they appeared in the "Japan cool campaign" organized by the Japanese government to attract tourists to Japan. Much of Puffy's success has been carefully orchestrated by their producer and their music label Sony Music Entertainment Inc., but even they did not imagine that Puffy's success would go this far. According to Tanaka Akira, former director of international marketing at Sony Music Entertainment Inc., and in charge of the Asian market, "no one at Sony sat down and calculated what would be the revenues from Puffy's success five or ten years later.[1]

The girl band AKB48 (short for Akehabara) is another example of Japan's formidable idol-production system, which in recent years has also reached out to Asian consumers. Created by famous producer Akimoto Yasushi in 2005, approximately sixty fairly "average" teenage girls, with a meticulously orchestrated line of clothing and accessories, appear in a variety of publicized events, including music concerts, café openings, fashion gatherings, meetings with fans, commercials, and television programs. Between one event and another, AKB48's girls also record their own pop music albums, singles, and video clips, which by January 2012 had sold more than eleven million copies in CDs alone. AKB48's music is offered for sale together with a huge variety of derivative products such as fashion accessories, posters, picture books, T-shirts, toys, magazines, playing cards, and the like. The girls in the band compete in a sort of general election where fans vote on which members of the band will participate in recording AKB48's next album. Only fans who purchase AKB48's albums or licensed accessories are allowed to vote—the more you buy, the more voting right you receive. Riding on the wave of success, AKB48's production team created several sister groups in Japan: SKE48, based in the Sakae area of Nagoya, NMB48, based in the Namba district of Osaka, HKT48 in Hakata, Fukuoka, and SDN48 (short for Saturday Night 48), which is intended to include more mature idols. AKB48's girls occasionally go to concerts and meet fans in Asian countries, and in June 2011 an official "AKB48 café" was opened in Singapore to serve as a hub for fans and as an audition center for girls with potential to become next-generation idols. In 2011, an Indonesian version of the band, called JKT48 (short for Jakarta) was created,[2] following the same promotional methods used by the other sister bands, and in 2012 there were preparations to debut similar sister groups in Shanghai (SNH48) and Taipei (TPE48).

Kawaii as a Commodity

The Japanese idol style draws heavily on the Japanese notion of *kawaii*, usually translated into English as "cuteness" or "lovability." The word "*kawaii*" in Japanese is made up of two *kanji* (Chinese) characters that signify "able" 「可」 and "love" 「愛」. The Japanese culture of *kawaii* is vaguely defined as the primal innocence of childhood, epitomized by playful designs in "ice cream cherry-blossom pink and tea green colors" (Faiola 2003). According to another description, *kawaii* is "attractive by reason of daintiness or picturesqueness in manners or appearance as a child or a small animal" (Richie 2003, 53). Japan's *kawaii* culture was initially driven by teenagers and young women but in recent years has spread to other segments of Japanese society. The development of the *kawaii* culture, as a few observers have argued, reflects the transformation from classical aesthetics, which depict ideas about work, marriage, future, etc., especially among young women and men, to an economic growth machine that has spread its commercial goods both domestically and globally (Yomota 2006, 134–152).

The *kawaii* notion is difficult to measure as a commodity, but it is widely visible in everyday life throughout Japan and in East Asia, where the making and selling of *kawaii* products is an enormous industry. The rise of *kawaii* as a commercial culture has spread widely since the 1970s, first in the form of stationery but then quickly in the form of a huge variety of products, from accessories and cellular phones to food and clothing. The cute fad continued into the 1980s and saturated mainstream media through popular idol singers who spread *kawaii* through their "innocent babe dresses, childish talk, pastel-colored fashion, and their love of cute stationery goods and fluffy animals" (Satō 2009, 39). In the 1990s, the rest of the industry caught up and the *kawaii* notion became represented in anime, games, and manga, which increased the acceptance of *kawaii* in wider segments of the population. The saturation of products sold has now reached an enormous scale. Take any successful Japanese animated character, be it *Hello Kitty, Anpan-man,* or *Peko-chan:* each is a source for a trajectory of products and images available for sale, including stationery, toys, clothes, accessories, playing cards, posters, cups, cookies, and videos on demand, to name but a few.

At present, the cute craze has spread throughout the world—interestingly enough, in spite of Japan's stagnant economy and aging population. *Hello Kitty,* an emblem of cute merchandizing, drives an empire worth no less than a billion dollars in global sales every year! Other successful features that have become widely familiar among children and youngsters across the globe include *Pok'emon, Doreamon,* and *Tamaguchi* (a hand-held digital pet). Even outside of Japan, young people up to their thirties are now influenced by the Japanese concept of "cuteness," as represented in a genre of products and fashion styles, as an alternative to the American notions of "coolness" or "sexiness" (Yomota 2006, 172–187). According to one vivid observation (Yano 2009, 681), "from the trinket-laden sidewalks of Harajuku to the traffic-clogged streets of Bangkok to the catwalks of New York, Japanese cute, as exemplified by *Hello Kitty,* inhabits a prime space of visibility. The eyes of many parts of the industrial world, it seems, have turned to Japan as a source of cute." As we shall see later, in East Asia there is a conscious attempt to imitate Japan's *kawaii* as part of the promotion of popular culture commodities.

J-Pop

Japanese pop music, often referred to as "J-pop," represents another production format constructed in Japan through the processes of borrowing, mimicking, and hybridizing American pop and rock music. The result is a highly constructed set of catchy melodies with an international image, packaged to suit Japanese consumers' tastes and lifestyles (Iwabuchi 2002, 85–129; Mōri 2009). Indeed, the progress of many Japanese music artists has been enabled through absorbing heavy influences from American music and indigenizing it into its own form. Since the end of the 1980s, though, J-pop has been considered to be at the same level of production as American pop music (Ugaya 2005, 7, 64).

The J-pop format embodies a few recognizable characteristics. First, it is overwhelmingly idol-driven. It is not listening to the music per se that is important, but rather the practice of being a fan of the artist that has become indispensable. Second, diverse means of communication are utilized as part of the promotion. In contrast to American or European pop stars, Japanese-style pop music artists are supposed to be multitalented. They are expected to not only master singing and dancing, but also be very fashionable, frequently appear on television shows and commercials, take part in various advertising campaigns and events, and sometimes appear in television dramas. In Japan, even when their singing careers have come to an end, they might still be regarded as *talento* (talents) and employed as guests on television shows. Third, Japanese pop music was the first in this region to include casual English lyrics in songs—catchy phrases that are repeated in the stanza. Japanese pop music initially included English lyrics to add an international appeal to the songs and not necessarily to interest foreign listeners. But English lyrics also opened a way for J-pop to have greater popularity in East Asia. There, non-Japanese-speaking listeners can recognize and repeat some of the English lyrics without necessarily mastering Japanese. The practice of including English in pop songs has been gradually imitated in pop music throughout East Asia. Many Korean, Mandarin, Cantonese, Thai, and Indonesian pop songs now include the repetition of English lyrics in a stanza.

Lastly, J-pop songs are heavily tied to other forms of media, both as a means of promotion as well as to generate revenues from multiple circuits of information and communication. Many of the songs become hits only after appearing in television dramas, commercials, movies, or animated series (Fujie 1989, 212). According to Asai Sumiko (2008a), tying songs to other forms of media can greatly determine their popularity. In a focused survey of Japanese popular music chart hits in 1990 and 2004, Asai found that not only the fame of the artist or the band determines the song's popularity but also its ties with other forms of media expressions and its appearance on compilation albums featuring songs by different artists. In other words, good songs cannot make it on their own; to become popular they need the promotional operation of the established industry, which diversifies its exposure to new listeners.

If we take Japanese diva Hamasaki Ayumi, one of the most successful Japanese female music artists in the 1990s and 2000s, all but two of her singles have been tied to either a commercial or television program.[3] Other examples include the song *Oh! Yeah!* by Oda Kazumasa, which was the title song of the famous television drama *Tokyo Love Story* (Fuji TV, 1991), the song *Love Love Love* by the famous band Dreams Come True, which appeared in the drama *Say You Love Me* (TBS, 1995), and the song *My Graduation* by the girl band *Speed*, which was used for a food manufacturing campaign.

Tie-Up Strategy

"Tie-up" is the common name given to the strategy that Japanese companies have used to popularize their music since the 1980s, first in Japan and later in other parts of the world, but especially in East Asia. The tie-up system is basically a marketing strategy that promotes sound and image conjointly for mutual benefit. This includes the intermixing of music with various visual forms, such as the production of special karaoke tracks and tailor-made video clips. The initial aim of the tie-up strategy was to serve as a commercializing device through the use of various media (for example, by featuring a musical show on television). But tie-up strategies also create a potentially profitable afterlife for a product in new commercial outlets, most commonly by designating a popular song to be reused in a commercial advertisement.

Tie-up is also common in the form of combining software and hardware. Several major record companies in Japan, such as Sony Music Entertainment Inc. and Victor Entertainment Inc. are subsidiaries of companies that manufacture audio equipment. In this way, they can control the production and distribution chain of the final product by tightening the relations between hardware and content (Asai 2008b, 474). For example, EMI used to promote the sales of company-produced music CDs, together with the promotion of Toshiba's CD players. In the field of karaoke, the tie-up strategy is essential—Japanese companies have benefited from the marketing of karaoke machines in East Asia, which has automatically generated the promotion of requisite music necessary to enjoy the machines (Otake and Hosokawa 1998).

The tie-up between music and television is typically the strongest, combining television programs and commercials featuring hit songs. Ugaya Hiromichi (2005, 74–78) has estimated that in the second half of the 1980s, about half of the fifty most popular songs each year in Japan were tied to either television dramas or commercials. In the 1990s, this trend grew even further and approximately half of all J-pop songs were tied up to other forms of media. Music then was increasingly used for commercial messages on television and as signature tunes in television dramas and movies when the audio recordings were released. As explained by Asai Sumiko (2008b, 477), "Record companies may reasonably expect an increase in audio recording sales and a reduction in management risk by adopting the tie-up system, since information on the music is speedily diffused to the public through the mass media." According to her study, from 1990 to 2004, 80 percent of the top-selling singles, especially the biggest hits, sold through tie-ups.

This way of commercializing music is sharply different from the way the music industry typically works in North America, where associating music with commercial campaigns is seen as derogatory. There, the common view is that music is being devaluated and loses its status as art if overly repackaged for mass consumption (Ugaya 2005, 94). In Japan and later in East Asia, the attitude is generally different. Japanese, as well as Korean, Mandarin, Cantonese, and Thai pop music, are widely promoted through tie-up, sometimes so much that it is difficult to distinguish between the song and the commercial.

Auditioning Stars

Star-search programs and talent competitions represent another format that has been successful in Japan and later exported to East Asia. The idea is similar to the U.S. *American Idol* and British *Pop Idol* television programs: produce music talent programs where new talent can be discovered and popular taste gauged, later to be produced, packaged, and offered to a variety of new consumers. In between, the producers try to create a media buzz to draw attention to both the TV station that broadcasts the show and the production agency that will handle the newly discovered stars. In the Japanese case, Johnny Entertainment is the best-known example in this field. Since the 1980s, the company has been using venture companies to produce successful lines of music artists and bands, taking advantage of the encounter between music and commercial ventures. The company is also known for meticulously crafting every aspect of their music artists' lives—from their music to the clothes they wear, the events they participate in, the people they meet, and their exposure to the media (Stocker 2001, 225).

Japanese companies sought to utilize their experience in producing to cash in on stars in East Asia's emerging media markets. As we read in chapter 4, a few Japanese companies did so quite successfully. The unintended consequences of the activities of these Japanese companies, however, were that their productions greatly influenced the local cultural industries, which soon started organizing their own music competitions. Local producers continued to rely on the formats and organizational methods they previously learned from the Japanese, but this time they did not need the help of Japanese partners. The most well-known example is *Suta Tanjo* (A Star Is Born, NTV, 1971–1983), a Japanese popular star-search program, which in the 1990s found its way to East Asia as a similar program called *Asia Bagus!* In Japan, *Suta Tanjo* auditioned applicants through singing competitions, which were recorded and broadcast live from public halls. The auditions and televised contents took place in many locations across the country. The adolescent winners, selected by executives from top record companies and artists' management agencies, sometimes became professional music artists and star idols. They include famous names such as Yamaguchi Momoe, Mori Masako, Sakurada Junko, Iwasaki Hiromi, Nakamori Akina, Matsuda Seiko, Koizumi Kyoko, and Pink Lady, among many others. Throughout the 1970s, the popularity of *Suta Tanjo* in Japan skyrocketed.

In East Asia, Fuji TV produced *Asia Bagus!* as a star-search program, together with local companies in Singapore, Malaysia, Indonesia, Taiwan, and South Korea. The idea was basically to repeat the Japanese success and generate profit not only from the sale of content but more broadly from externalizing the Japanese experience. Initially, the production and direction was mainly in the hands of Japanese staff. *Asia Bagus!* was broadcast in prime time in five East Asian countries and became influential in shaping young consumers' sense of fashion and lifestyles, in addition to their musical tastes (for a detailed discussion on *Suta Tanjo* see Stevens and Hosokawa 2001; for *Asia Bagus!* see Iwabuchi 2002, 100–106).

Asian Beat is another example of a Japanese-led regional entrepreneurship in this field. Inaugurated in 1998 and sponsored by Yamaha, it is considered one of the biggest amateur band contests held in East Asia. It started out from early qualifying rounds in nine different locations (Japan, Taiwan, Hong Kong, Thailand, Singapore, Malaysia, Indonesia, mainland China, and Korea). The finalists gather in Tokyo for the Grand Final to perform in front of world-renowned music artists who serve as the judges. The profit for the Japanese organizers is twofold. Young promising artists from across the region are gathered and gauged, and the winning artist is later produced and commercialized. For the sponsor, Yamaha, the highly publicized competitions carried out in Japan and the other locations increases its image penetration and helps to enhance its brand power in the region.[4]

Hori Production further developed methods for recruiting singers. In 1993, it established branches in Hong Kong and Beijing to trace and produce music pop stars. In cooperation with the Beijing City Department of Culture, it launched a talent-scout caravan and conducted live television broadcast auditions. Amazingly, 400,000 would-be Chinese singers auditioned, including Dai Rao, who later became an idol. In Vietnam, Hori Production held another idol audition in 1995, in cooperation with the Vietnamese government, drawing 1,800 local applicants (Aoyagi 2000). Although this figure seems much less impressive than the figure from China, it is significant for Vietnam, which is a much smaller country with a less developed media market.

Many big-name idols have been produced by following the Japanese exported formats. In China, collaboration between Japan's talent agency Yoshimoto Kogyo and Sony Music Entertainment Inc. created the Shanghai Performance Doll, a band of four young women that debuted in 1990 as a Chinese version of Japan's Tokyo Performance Doll (ibid). Other Japanese-produced idols in the 1990s, likely known by any pop music fan in East Asia, include Jie Liu of China, Soteji-Wa-Idol, Susie Kang and BoA of South Korea, Andy Lau, Vivian Chow, and Sammy Chen of Hong Kong, Maribeth of the Philippines, and Emile Chow, Vivian Hsu, and Tarsy Su of Taiwan.

Television Productions

Japanese television programs also tremendously impacted the television industry in East Asia, in many cases setting the regional standard. As rising local demands were stimulating the growth of the region's television industries, the Japanese television industries were in a key position to introduce high-quality and innovative programs that had been previously nurtured and gauged in the Japanese market. At the same time, the local television channels in East Asia, which started to develop only later, still needed to upgrade and diversify their programming. Initially, they did not have enough experience, knowledge, or capable personnel to meet the audiences' rising demands. The inundation and emulation of Japanese television programs in East Asian markets thus came exactly at the time when many regional television industries were attempting to develop an identity of their own. In this context, the ability of the Japanese television companies to finance, produce, and market high-quality television programs propelled them to positions of leadership in the field and made them a source of imitation by local companies.

Take Thailand, for example. There, Japan's television programs have not only provided content for the local television and cable stations but have also served as a model for the local television industries. Animated television programs were broadcast on Thai television in the early 1980s, followed by dramas, variety shows, and movies. The development of Thailand's television market over the past two decades, however, has created demand for both imported television content and television production know-how. Panadda Thanasatit, then president of Kantana, Thailand's biggest television production company, admitted in an interview that when they were planning and carrying out many of their productions, such as dramas, animation, and especially variety shows, they always looked toward Japan as a possible model. She emphasized that there was still a shortage of qualified Thai personnel for Thailand's growing media industry.[5] In the case of news, however, the president of the production company said that the dynamic (American) CNN model was preferred over the slow-paced Japanese style.

Others in the industry pointed out that Thai attempts to develop comic and animation industries were clearly based on imitating Japanese-style comics and not the American Walt Disney model (which is available in the Thai market but not as popular).[6] Other interviews with television personnel further emphasized that good production quality and the swift narrative pace were also factors that contributed to why young viewers enjoyed Japanese series. They emphasized that they were trying to learn from Japan on how to produce commercially successful television programs, but they admitted that high production costs still impeded many of their attempts.[7]

The production of popular "trendy" television dramas exemplifies the extent of Japanese influence. These productions started in Japan at the end of the 1980s and have been successfully broadcast on television channels across East Asia since the end of the 1990s (Clements and Tamamuro 2003, xxvii). The idea behind the production of Japanese trendy television dramas was to produce a story that did not deal with a serious theme or any social issue. Rather, it targeted younger audiences by featuring fashion, music, and trendy urban environments. According to the famous Japanese television producer Ōta Tōru[8] (2004, 70), these trendy dramas are mere "package" dramas, in which setting, cast, and music weigh more heavily than the content of the drama.

Starting with the popular television dramas *Tokyo Love Story* and *Long Vacation*, Japanese television dramas swept through the markets of Hong Kong, Taiwan, South Korea, China, Singapore, and Thailand, creating the so-called "Japanese wave" (Leung 2004). In Hong Kong, Japanese television dramas had an especially strong impact on local television productions. According to Benjamin Ng (2004), in the late 1990s there were more than twenty Hong Kong dramas that closely emulated the story lines, plots, music, photography, and dialogue of Japanese dramas, even to the point of plagiarism.[9] Similarly, in her study of trendy Korean dramas, Lee Dong-Hoo (2004) showed how producers substantially borrowed formats and ideas from Japanese originals. According to her study, the dramas that were broadcast in the 1990s borrowed heavily from the popular Japanese dramas of the late 1980s and the beginning of the 1990s, but then gradually took on a shape of their own. Trendy Korean dramas such as *Jealousy* (KBS, 1992), *Lovers* (KBS, 1993), *Pilot*

(MBC, 1993), *The Final Game* (MBC, 1994), and *Love in Your Heart* (MBC, 1994) indeed created a new genre of popular drama that differentiated from old-style traditional dramas, but excessively used popular Japanese dramas as a model. One Korean drama (*Konnani*) was even accused of plagiarizing Japan's famous drama *Oshin*.

It should be emphasized that although Japanese television dramas were widely emulated in East Asia, they were also localized to suit the local audience and eventually developed their own nuances. Compared with Japanese dramas, Hong Kong dramas have longer and more complicated story lines. Hong Kong dramas are also less idol-driven and last longer, a series of at least twenty episodes as opposed to Japan's traditional twelve-episode series. In Korea, as we shall see later in this chapter, the themes of the dramas are more family oriented and display a more materialistic affluence, but they are not as sexually liberal.

Commodifying Asian-ness

Some recent initiatives by Japanese companies imply that they are trying to create a sense of Asian-ness in the form of a commodity in order to reach a wider pool of consumers. These are commercially driven attempts to invent new cultural products and cultural genres by intentionally attaching to them certain images, motifs, and feelings associated with "Asia" (Otmazgin 2011a). These attempts make good economic sense: by producing something that is not only Japanese but also "Asian," the target audience immediately increases. At the same time, however, there is also some amount of risk. There is no certainty that consumers will prefer to buy something vaguely defined as "Asian," rather than something closer to them, such as popular culture that is defined as Thai, Indonesian, Korean, or Chinese.

The production of the movies *Asia Beat* and *Southern Winds* in the early 1990s was one of the earliest postwar Japanese attempts to create an "Asian-ness" in the form of a commodity. These Tokyo-led collaborations connected different media forms and content to reveal a new "Asian" media culture across big cities in East Asia. *Southern Winds* (1992) included four episodes produced in collaboration with established moviemakers in Japan, the Philippines, Thailand, and Indonesia, and displayed a series of hectic urban scenes in Indonesia, Manila, Bangkok, and Tokyo. *Asia Beat* consisted of six full-length movies, promoted as a "multi-country collection," involving emerging directors and creative staff from Japan, Taiwan, Hong Kong, the Philippines, Singapore, Malaysia, and Thailand. The first episode began in Tokyo and featured the Japanese star Nagase Masatoshi as a Japanese man traveling through Asia to look for the people who killed his parents. The next episodes were set across Hong Kong, Indonesia, the Philippines, and Thailand and were seen from the perspective of these different locations.

Collaboration between Japanese and Korean companies to produce and market music and television programs provides another example of these kinds of initiatives. Since the end of the 1990s, a few such collaborations have taken place, though high production costs still keep these attempts at an embryonic stage. The mere existence of Japanese-Korean collaborations is especially noteworthy given the contentious historical and political relations between these two countries. The case of the talented female singer BoA is perhaps the most successful example of a Japanese-Korean collaboration and demonstrates the potential of cross-border cultural productions. In the 2000s, BoA was one of the most famous pop stars both in Japan and South Korea. The young star, who is often referred to as "Korea's Britney Spears," was born in South Korea but with the help of the management of a Japanese company, Avex Trax, debuted in Japan at the age of thirteen. Her phenomenal success in the Japanese market—the second biggest market in the world—was repeated in South Korea under the management of South Korea's S.M. Entertainment, one of the country's leading music companies. In 2002, the star was the first non-Japanese Asian singer to top a million copies of sales in Japan, and since then she has released an album at a rate of almost one per year, all sung in Japanese and all charting high and in tandem with releases in South Korea (*The Japan Times,* January 1, 2009).

BoA's transnational appeal is not an entirely new trend. Japanese companies and promoters, recognizing the marketing potential of Japanese music in East Asia, have been promoting Japanese music artists as "Asian" idols for some time. The success of Hamasaki Ayumi, the bestselling Japanese music artist in East Asia and considered by many as an Asian diva, illustrates this strategy. Apart from commercializing her music, she frequently appeared in commercials and advertising campaigns throughout the region. As part of a strategy to popularize her music in East Asia, she occasionally performed in promotional concerts. At the MTV 2002 award ceremony in Singapore, she performed in front a live audience of 7,000 and 150 million home viewers across Asia, dressed in a kimono bearing the Chinese characters for "love," "peace," and "future." Following her publicized tour to Southeast Asia, her manager revealed that the singer's strategy was to gain an even larger following in Asian markets (*Time Asia*, March 25, 2002). Other prominent Japanese music companies have attempted to market their artists as "Asian" in order to achieve better-selling records in East Asia. Artists such as Nakamori Akina, Amuro Namie, Hirai Ken, the duet Chemistry, and the boy bands Wind and SMAP have attained superstar and cultural idol status that has exceeded their status as mere singers, and they have often become fashion models for young East Asians.

In television, Japanese-Korean coproductions have had lesser success. Their importance, however, lies not only in the productions themselves but also in tightening cooperation and providing a substantial framework for future collaborative projects. Relatively successful coproductions include television dramas such as *Friends* (2002), *Sonagi, an Afternoon Showers* (2002), and *Star's Echo* (2004). These dramas depicted youngsters' love stories that transcended national boundaries and cultural differences and difficulties. In these dramas, the Japanese heroines and Korean heroes succeeded in both their romance and work. *Friends* is a four-part miniseries coproduced by Korea's broadcasting company, MBC, and the Japanese TBS. When it was aired in February 2002 it attracted much attention in the two countries, earning a 14.8 percent television rating in Japan and 17.5 percent in South Korea. *Sonagi, an Afternoon Showers* was simultaneously aired in Japan and Korea in November 2002 and received a 14.3 percent television rating in Japan and 13.2 percent in South Korea. *Star's Echo*, a two-part mini series that aired in January 2004 in Japan and South Korea, received a rating of 9.1 percent.[10]

It is, however, still too early to tell if this sort of "Asian popular culture" will lead the way for the industry in the future. Pan-Asian productions cost a lot and they seem to work better in movies than in television programs or music. The language still presents a barrier for the marketing of popular culture across countries. Tanaka Akira, the former director of international marketing at Sony Music Entertainment Inc. and in charge of developing the Asian market, thinks that pursuing an only "Asian" popular culture will result in great losses for the industry. According to him, "Asia" is too big and too diverse to be minimized into a single commodity that can resonate with different audiences from different ethnicities in the region—unless you market in the United

States as an (invented) "Asian" commodity. But he thinks there is still a place for collaborations between companies and entrepreneurs from different countries to explore business opportunities along ethnic and linguistic lines. An example would be to market music from Okinawa in Indonesia, or Indonesian music, performed by artists from Okinawa, in Japan, or to produce music albums and performances by Chinese, Malay, and Indonesian artists.[11]

The Japanese Origins of the "Korean Wave"

In no other place did Japanese cultural industries have a bigger influence than in South Korea. Over the past three decades, Korean popular culture productions have extensively emulated their Japanese counterparts both domestically and in their expansion to new markets abroad, especially in pop music, television productions, and manga, and more recently in animation and fashion. As we saw in chapter 4, in spite of the contentious historical and political relations between the two countries, the Korean government could not prevent entirely the transfer and acceptance of Japanese popular culture. This was partly due to piracy, but also because when it came to popular culture, young Koreans did not always listen to their government. In the case of delivering formats, the acceptance was easier since it was not the Japanese content that was being allowed but the organizational arrangements for producing it. The Korean cultural industries could adopt Japanese formats and fill them with their own content without attracting too much criticism.

At the same time, however, it is important to note that Korean popular culture has developed its own identity and in many cases has ceased to be only an imitator of Japan's popular culture. Korean cultural industries now produce their own material and market it both domestically and abroad on a massive scale, at times exceeding the Japanese cultural industries in popularity. Japan itself has, in recent years, become a diligent importer of Korean popular culture. In a survey conducted in Japan in 2005, a quarter of the respondents said they were interested in Korean movies and television dramas and almost half in Korean food. The broadcast of the hit television drama *Winter Sonata* during 2004, and the popularity of its star Bae Yong Joon (or "Yon-sama" as he is known among fans in Japan), encouraged more than 300,000 Japanese tourists to visit the ski resort north of Seoul where the drama was filmed.[12]

As was the case in other markets in the region, the extended emulation of Japan's cultural industries came at a point when the Korean cultural industries were starting to rise. Indeed, Japan's popular culture was accepted in South Korea as far back as the 1960s and 1970s, even though it was officially banned. Translations of Japanese manga were conducted on a large scale (Yamanaka 2010) and some Japanese melodies were also reportedly popular, readily available through the radio or in karaoke bars in Seoul and Busan (Ōtake and Hosokawa 1998, 186–187). Those with high antennas and satellite dishes could also receive television broadcasts from Japan (Kim H.-M. 2004, 199). But the heavy, industrially driven emulation of Japanese formats, including music, television, manga, and animation, took place in the second half of the 1980s, at a time when the Korean cultural industries started to grow rapidly.

The media liberalization in the 1980s led to the opening of the Korean cultural market and invigorated an extensive production of movies, television programs, pop music, and animation. According to the Korea International Trade Association, in 2004 Korean cultural exports generated KRW 1.4 billion in added value, responsible for raising Korea's gross domestic product by 0.2 percent, and it accounted for the majority of the tourists from Japan and Southeast Asia visiting Korea (Lee 2008, 178). According to the Korea Creative Content Agency, export of broadcasting content from South Korea in 2009 amounted to US$183.5 million, up 1.9 percent from 2008, especially to Asia.[13] Korean television dramas, which have always been the centerpiece of television watching among the Korean audience, started getting exposure abroad in the 1990s, first in China and soon reaching audiences in Japan, Hong Kong, Taiwan, Vietnam, and Singapore. The export of Korean television dramas has increased dramatically. According to Lee Miji's study (2010, 267–269), in 2001 Korea started to export more television programs than it imported, and in 2007 it exported nine times more than it imported (US$20 million compared to US$180 million). In 2009, almost 98 percent of the export was television dramas going to Asia. The level of exported cinema has also soared. In 2004, 193 Korean movies were exported to 62 countries earning US$58 million, in comparison to only 15 movies in 1995 (Shim 2008, 21–27).

The so-called "Korean Wave," or Hallyu as it is known among fans, is a glaring manifestation of the rapid progress the Korean cultural industries have achieved. In less than a decade, South Korean television dramas, movies, music, and fashion have gained immense popularity throughout East Asia and beyond.[14] Korean idols have become phenomenally popular. Won Bin and Song Seung-hun are widely known to young East Asians through their parts in the hit television drama *Autumn Fairy Tale* (2000). Other well-known South Korean idols include Jang Dong-gun (*Friends*), Cha Tae-hyun (*My Sassy Girl*), Lee Jung-jae (*Il Mare*), Kyon Sang-woo (*My Tutor Friend*), and Bae Yong Jun (*Winter Sonata*).

The "Korean Wave" did not stop in Asia. In the mid-2000s, a few Korean stars started to appear in Hollywood movies and popular American television shows, including Rain (also known as Bi) who appeared in the Wachowski brothers' *Speed Racer* (2008) and *Ninja Assassin* (2009), Byung-Hun Lee, who appeared in the Hollywood blockbuster *The Rise of Cobra* (2009), and Yoon-Jin Kim, who appeared in ABC's popular hit series *Lost*. These idols, labeled by the Korean media as "world stars," have managed to draw the attention of wider audiences in America and Europe in addition to Korea and Asia.

The rise of Korean popular culture production and marketing is invigorated by the prediction that the cultural industries are expected to generate meaningful revenues for the economy and assist the marketing abroad of Korean consumer products, such as automobiles, cellular phones, and cosmetics. The Korean government, for its part, has started to take an increasing interest in developing this sector. Following the growth of the country's cultural industries and the success of Korean popular culture abroad, the government's cultural policy has shifted from focusing on cultural heritage and traditional arts during the 1970s and 1980s to popular culture since the 1990s (Shim 2008, 30; Yim 2002, 42–47). At present, the government actively intervenes to foster the growth of what it calls the "creative industries" (music, movies, television content, etc.) and to promote Korean pop culture as an export industry. It provides various incentives for creators, supports research in the field, and has established two quasi-governmental agencies—the Korea Culture and Content Agency (KOCCA) and the Korea Foundation for Asian Cultural Exchange (KOFACE)—to further nurture the growth of this sector.

Where does Japan's popular culture come in? Manga is one of the fields where Japanese influence is most traceable. Japanese manga gradually entered Korea, first as a cheap commodity but later as an established field of art and a source of inspiration. Yamanaka Chie (2010) divides the entrance of manga into Korea into three main periods. The first period was the translation of Japanese manga into Hangul in the 1970s and 1980s, when Japanese culture was still banned from entering Korea. In this period, Korean fans illegally translated manga books and journals and did not aspire to create stories of their own. In the 1990s, however, Korean manga artists started to develop their own stories, but Japanese manga continued to be the starting point. Korean manga artists continued to mimic the same story lines, characters, and narratives found in Japanese manga, but they created their own side stories, invented new scenes, or added new twists to the original story. In this second period, the localization of Japanese manga also took place, with Korean artists adjusting manga to local tastes and translating the Japanese Kanji, Hiragana, and Katakana into Hangul. (Translating manga, it should be noted, is more complicated than translating novels and requires much creativity. In manga, the translator must translate not only the story but also must adjust it correctly to the picture.) More recently, Korea entered a third stage, where Koreans invent their own manga stories, using the expertise and experience they acquired while translating and developing Japanese manga. The surrounding images, story line, and packaging, however, continue to resemble Japanese manga, much more than they resemble American or European comics.[15]

South Korean television dramas provide another traceable example of productions that were initially based on Japanese formats. According to Kim Hyun-Mee (2004, 262), the Japanese dramas were the first to successfully incorporate the idea of consumer culture—a highly appealing narrative for Asia's younger generation—and thus provided a model for the Korean television dramas to emulate. A report issued by the Korean Broadcasting Institute in August 1999 indicated that Japanese programs were a role model for Korean television productions in terms of technical narratives and a reference index. In this process, as Korean Television specialist Kim Yung Duk (2005, 262) remarks that "Japanese dramas, which first successfully incorporated consumer culture in their narratives in Asia, directly or indirectly, provided a model for emulation." In some cases, Korean companies went beyond emulation to simply plagiarize Japanese programs. As a result, a few entertainment programs on Korean television were canceled.

In an interview in Seoul, a producer working with the Korean Broadcasting Service (KBS) explained how this emulation system worked.[16] At the end of the 1990s, Korean television productions were deeply "inspired," according to him, by Japanese television productions. This was true in a variety of television programs, ranging from animation, dramas, variety shows, and even documentaries. This "inspiration" mechanism worked as follows: at first KBS-affiliated personnel in Japan would scan television programs, record them, and send samples of those they thought would be interesting in South Korea. In Seoul, producers would view these programs, learn from them, and evaluate whether or not they could succeed in Korea. Selected programs were sometimes sent to a pilot audience to see how they were accepted. At the end of this screening process, the Korean producers would judge and decide if they wanted to produce similar programs. In the past few years, KBS has been interested in producing documentaries about Asia (the KBS slogan for 2006 was "Window to Asia"). For that, the KBS producer indicated, they have been extensively watching and learning from documentaries produced by NHK.

In television dramas, Korean producers borrowed heavily from the popular Japanese dramas of the late 1980s and early 1990s. Korean television productions have gradually developed, however, and are no longer emulating Japanese productions. Korean television productions have incorporated locally drawn motifs, becoming even more popular than Japanese productions in Asia (Lin and Kim 2005). As Hong Jung-Ui, a KOCCA official, remarked proudly, "South Korean companies no longer imitate Japanese productions or are no longer being used as sub-contractors for Japanese television productions. . . . South Korean television productions have greatly developed in recent years, and the relations with Japanese companies are under the framework of collaboration."[17]

In a focused contextual analysis of the Korean drama *Jealousy* (1992) and the Japanese drama *Tokyo Love Story* (1991), Lee Dong-Hoo (2004) analyzed common similarities and differences between the Japanese and the Korean productions. According to her study, the Korean drama used many motifs taken from the Japanese original. Some of these are that the plot always takes place in an urban environment, mostly in Tokyo and Seoul; the heroine and hero are always young, successful, and cosmopolitan; there is dynamic camera work that captures in detail the feelings of the heroes; the title songs play an important part in the storytelling as well as in the drama's publicity; there is a fast story tempo with dynamic plot twists; there is no obvious villain who badly twists the lovers' fortune; and a consumerist appetite is reflected throughout the story, manifested in excessive shopping, extended leisure time, traveling, and going to trendy cafés. There are, however, a few differences, which emanate from the localization and social conditions in Korea. For example, in the Korean dramas material affluence is much more obviously manifested; family relations play an indispensable part of the plot; marriage is the ultimate romantic goal of the plot; and sexual purity is maintained—lovers hug and kiss but never go to bed.

In pop music as well, it is possible to trace some tenacious Japanese roots, especially in the joint promotion of pop music and idol culture. South Korean singers and bands, like their Japanese counterparts, are promoted as more than merely music artists; they appear as idols and fashion leaders and frequently appear in fashion magazines, commercials, and television dramas. The use of English lyrics in Korean pop songs, as in Japanese pop songs, is also prevalent. In an interview in Seoul, a promotions manager of S.M. Entertainment, one of South Korea's largest music companies, unwittingly admitted that in the 1990s South Korean music companies were widely imitating their Japanese counterparts.[18] The interviewee mentioned that S.M. Entertainment, which had a strategic cooperation agreement with Japan's Avex Trax, was itself a diligent learner of Japanese musical production formats. The interviewee gave as an example the company's famous female music artist BoA, a singer who has found success in both Japan and South Korea. Another noteworthy example of the Korean emulation of Japanese musical production formats is the Korean girl band SES, which debuted in the late 1990s and emulated the casualness in style and appearance of the Japanese girl band Morning Musume. A last example she raised was the boy band Tohoshiki, which is very similar to the famous Japanese boy band SMAP in the composition of the group, their music, and even their fashion style.

Siriyuvasak and Shin's study of Korean culture in Thailand (2007) found that the Korean cultural industries not only imitated the themes and genres used by Japan's popular culture but also the marketing methods developed by Japanese companies. One of the interesting cases they analyzed was the collaboration between the Korean girl band Baby V.O.X. and GMM Grammy, Thailand's biggest music company. Like the promotion of Japanese idols, Baby V.O.X.'s promotional strategy included marketing special karaoke albums and tailor-made short video clips. Another example was the Korean male music idol Rain, who became popular in Thailand through the production of localized tracks of his song *I Do* and a duet with the famous Thai female singer Panadda Ruangwut. Rain's participation in the popular Korean television drama *Full House* also contributed to his popularity in Thailand, where the series was broadcast.

Siriyuvasak and Shin's evidence also suggests, however, that the Korean music industry has done more to localize their products to appeal to consumers in each market. The companies that promote Korean music artists have invested more in producing local cover songs and in bringing the artists to Thailand for promotional tours and concerts. Indeed, music personnel in Hong Kong, Singapore, and Bangkok emphasized in interviews that South Korean companies have been investing more than their Japanese counterparts in integrating their activities in East Asia.[19] According to these personnel, South Korean companies, in their expansion into new markets, have been more willing to cooperate in finding solutions to overcome copyright impediments. Keyman Luk, general manager of a music distribution company in Hong Kong, revealed that compared to Japanese companies, South Korean companies "are much easier to do business with. They ask for a reasonable price, they are more willing to let us use posters and other pictures of the artist—that are essential for the promotional campaign—and it is much easier to work out promotional tour schedules."[20]

Keyman Luk also mentioned one case of negotiation with Fuji TV about marketing Japanese television dramas in DVD format in Hong Kong. Fuji TV was strict on minor copyright issues, even though many of the dramas had already appeared in pirated versions in the city. The negotiations ended unsuccessfully, and the only DVDs of Fuji TV's television dramas found in Hong Kong today are pirated ones. Another promotions manager of a large music company in Bangkok complained that even after he succeeds in bringing famous Japanese idols for promotional visits, his Japanese counterparts strictly limit the idols' exposure to fans and mass media. Liu Xia, a distributor of television dramas in China for Hong Kong's TVB, made similar allegations regarding the inflexibility of dealing with Japanese companies: "Compared to their peers in the region, Japanese distributors want to control too much of their products, such as the contract period, the broadcasting channels, the broadcasting time. . . . As if it is not difficult enough to get Japanese dramas on Chinese television, due to censorship and regulations prohibiting international dramas on Chinese television before 10 p.m. I don't think their business strategy fits the Chinese market."[21]

Remarkably, all the other interviewees agreed that it was much easier to obtain a South Korean company's approval to use pictures of the artist for promotional purposes. In the Japanese case, they have to go through a long and meticulous approval process, which often slows an idol's momentum or exposure in a market and leads to the failure of promotional sales. When these personnel were asked why they think doing business with South Korean companies is easier than with Japanese companies, they gave three possible reasons. A few thought that Japanese business practices or the "Japanese culture of making business," as they called it, is too long and meticulous and gives an advantage to the South Koreans. Others pointed out that South Korean companies are more eager to enter markets in East Asia because they do not have as big a domestic market as their Japanese counterparts and expansion abroad is their only way to significantly grow, while for the Japanese the domestic market remains the first priority. Another point emphasized was that the cost of Japanese cultural content and its production is higher than that of South Korea, which gives the South Korean products some advantage. All the interviewees, however, agreed that in recent years Korean companies have been doing much more than Japanese companies to popularize their products.

Curiously, many retailers in East Asia tend to place Japanese and Korean popular cultures in the same category. Trendy Japanese and Korean dramas and music, for example, are seen as representing the same genre and are offered for sale in the same sections of the store. In music shops throughout Hong Kong, Singapore, Bangkok, and Shanghai (but not in Seoul or Tokyo), Korean music is offered alongside Japanese music, and sometimes integrated into it. Magazines that deal with Japanese popular culture (such as *J Spy* and *J Teen* in Bangkok) have started to cover Korean culture as well, following the success of the "Korean Wave." Many youngsters in East Asia have indicated that they see Japanese and Korean popular cultures as being a part of the same genre.

What Is Special about Japan's Popular Culture? Interviews with Cultural Industry Personnel in East Asia

What is special about Japan's popular culture and why has it been successful? I posed these questions to sixty-eight individuals from the local cultural industries in Hong Kong, Singapore, Shanghai, Bangkok, and

Seoul. They include executives working in music and television, as well as government officials, academics, media specialists, promoters, and officials from media-related organizations. I thought these were the best people to ask these questions given their knowledge and specialties in the field. The interviews themselves included four types of questions: (1) general questions regarding the local popular culture markets, especially regarding music, television, and the piracy of products; (2) more specifically, questions regarding the popularity, appreciation, and capacity of Japan's popular culture in comparison to other popular cultures available in the market; (3) questions regarding their promotional efforts and cooperation with other companies and agents in commodifying and marketing popular culture; and (4) questions concerning their views on various aspects of contemporary culture, society, globalization, and politics in East Asia. What follows is an analysis of the appreciation of Japan's popular culture and the reasons for its success, as reflected in these interviews.

One recurring central point in the interviews was that a major reason for the success of Japanese popular culture in East Asia lies in providing high-quality products that consumers want to buy. It is an accepted fact in the industry that Japan's popular culture products are highly innovative and well produced. The interviewees all agreed that the level of Japanese popular culture productions is very high. They were fascinated with the way Japanese popular culture has managed to capture many receptive consumers in East Asia since the 1990s, but they could not always explain precisely what was so interesting and attractive about it. Most of them, however, emphasized that Japanese popular culture products, such as music, television dramas and variety shows, and manga and anime, were far better produced in terms of sound, image, and fashion than any other local products, be it Chinese, Thai, Singaporean, or Korean.

When I asked them how we could evaluate "quality" in culture, especially popular culture, and how we could appreciate the high "quality" of Japan's popular culture, their terminology became very technical. They all thought that the cultural industries in East Asia were still inferior to those of Japan in terms of the level of production, sophistication, and the costs invested. They emphasized that Japanese productions were better in terms of sound engineering, camera operation, image editing, floor management, and design, and that the Japanese culture industries were more experienced in mediating between the project and the wider cultural and economic surrounding (funding, market demands, distribution network, etc.). A manager in charge of the acquisition of animated television programs at ITV, a large television station in Thailand, pointed out that the station planned to broadcast Thai-made animated programs "as soon as local production reaches an adequate standard." In the meantime, they would continue to broadcast only Japanese animation because "it has the highest production quality and a swift pace in the narratives that make young viewers enjoy the Japanese series."[22] Another promoter of animation in Hong Kong admitted that "although we aspire to produce [Japanese] anime-like quality, our local productions have yet to attain the same level . . . we are still basically mimicking the Japanese. Economically too, we are not as successful. Take the Hong Kong–made animated feature *A Chinese Ghost Story* (1997). It completely failed at the box office."[23]

A few of the interviewees compared the success of Japanese culture to the success of Japanese cars and electronics in the world market, pointing out their qualitative advantage in technology and human design. A regional marketing strategist for Sony Music Entertainment Inc. based in Hong Kong explained that Japanese media products are successful because they are "much more artistically developed, aesthetically designed and sophisticatedly marketed than any other products in the [East Asian] market . . . it is the same successful way in which Japan has made the rest of the world buy their cars instead of American cars."[24] This point, that Japan is the source of a variety of high-quality products, ranging from manufacturing and consumer products to culture, was repeatedly raised in the interviews.

In another interview, a high official from KOCCA, a governmental agency in charge of promoting the country's cultural industries, insisted that the key to success for cultural products is quality.[25] According to him, Japanese, and recently Korean, cultural products are successful because of their quality, which corresponds to the needs of today's consumers. In this regard, "a television drama, for example, is just like a cellular telephone . . . if the quality of the drama is high, in terms of story line, casting, costumes, and editing, consumers will appreciate it." For the purpose of promoting Korean popular culture and "creative industries," he sees his job as directing the country's cultural industries to produce high-quality products that can be marketed domestically and abroad. Interestingly, he gave Japanese examples to explain his strategy for developing Korean cultural industries (other interviewees in Seoul and Bangkok often did so as well). For instance, he mentioned the success of the famous Japanese horror movie series *The Ring* as a model worth following in paving the way for Korean movies into foreign markets.

Some of the music and television personnel interviewed emphasized that the Japanese cultural industries have the advantage of a high number of trained and creative personnel. According to them, qualified personnel are essential in developing export-oriented music and television industries.[26] These qualified personnel include (a) creative personnel, such as musicians, directors, composers, and script writers; (b) technical personnel who can perform technically oriented tasks such as sound engineering and mixing, camera operations, image editing, floor management, and design; and (c) experienced managers, editors, and producers to mediate between the project and the wider cultural and economic surrounding (funding, market demands, distribution network, etc.) and accordingly make executive decisions. In this sense, the interviewees estimated that Japan is at least a decade ahead of other cultural industries in East Asia.

Others indicated that the experience and knowledge accumulated in the Japanese affluent domestic market is an important factor in the success of Japan's popular culture abroad. This experience and knowledge includes not only the production know-how itself, but also using the right promotional means and the commercial development of the final product toward a profitable end. According to a marketing director of a big record company in Seoul, "it is not only the product or the production itself, but also the knowledge of how to develop it commercially. . . . *Doraemon* or Hamasaki Ayumi, for example, are not only an animated character and a female music artist. They are also the source of two huge industries that cater around them . . . but the development of the product is not an easy thing to do. You need to be very creative to finally cash in on your product. You also need to have the right experience of how to negotiate through various forms of media and communication and make your product sell."[27]

The majority of interviewees also emphasized the point that the overall appreciation of Japanese popular culture products and their early availability in East Asia play an important role in the success of their marketing. Since Japanese culture has already been represented in this region through earlier versions of its popular culture, especially anime, the acceptance of new popular culture commodities is easier. Thai television personnel indicated that the availability of Japanese manga and anime in the market conjointly promotes them both. She emphasized that "if a Thai kid liked reading Japanese comic[s] he would most likely enjoy watching Japanese animation on television."[28] According to her, the station (Channel 9) tried to broadcast American animation in the past to gauge the tastes of audiences. The ratings, however, were low and it became clear to the station's managers that the Thai audience overwhelmingly preferred Japanese animation. But the station hoped to broadcast Thai animated programs "as soon as local production gets to an adequate standard." Others thought that idol culture drives many youngsters to become fans of Japanese pop music. In this sense, music artists are not liked only for their music, but also for their look, fashion, behavior, and media coverage. One manager in a music company even thought that some of the most obsessive fans "do not even care about the music," but rather enjoy being exposed to the singer's appearance or the band's fashion sense.[29]

About a third of the interviewees thought that the physical appearance of the Japanese idols (music artists and actors), such as hairstyle, eye color, height, etc., made it easier for similar-looking East Asian consumers to appreciate them. Eight of the interviewees thought that "cultural proximity" played "some role" in attracting East Asian consumers. They maintained that Japanese cultural products contained an "Asian fragrance," which made local consumers sympathetic to Japanese products. Only two of them (out of sixty-eight interviewees) suggested that the success of Japanese culture primarily emanated from the products' embodiment of an "Asian cultural substance," which resonated with local consumers. When asked to define this "Asian cultural substance" and "Asian fragrance," physical similarities (eyes, hair, body size, and familiar behavioral expressions such as shyness and child-like excitement) were the only reasons given for the ostensible cultural sameness between Japanese and other East Asians. A Bangkok-based managing director of a music distribution company explained: "There must be something appealing in the way a young Japanese pop diva dresses like a child and not as an American sexy superstar . . . maybe it is because she has a [sic] typical Asian hair and shrill voice."[30]

Another important point raised in the interviews was that the overall positive image of Japanese consumer products greatly assists the acceptance of popular culture as well. Approximately two-thirds of the interviewees thought there was a correlation between the proliferation of Japanese cultural products and the general appreciation of the "made in Japan" label in East Asia, that Japanese cultural products enjoy the same positive image that Japanese manufacturing and consumer products have in East Asia. In this way, for example, the success of Japanese automobiles, rice cookers, cameras, and many other consumer products invigorates the popularity of popular culture as well. As explained by a promotions manager for a music company in Hong Kong: "Japanese products are everywhere: cameras, cars, motorbikes, cosmetics, accessories, computers, fashion, etc. They are all associated with good quality and are considered to be very advanced. . . . Japanese popular culture products are not much different. When youngsters buy a Japanese music CD or a Japanese animation DVD, they knows [sic] they got something good."[31] He advised me to go for a walk at night around Hong Kong to take note of all the Japanese brand names that dominate the huge neon-lit billboards across the city.

The "made in Japan" label is highly appreciated, considered to be of high value and technologically superior, and eventually assists the marketing of Japan's popular culture. This also relates to the point that East Asians are exposed to wider aspects of Japanese society and culture through the proliferation of Japanese consumer products (Chua 2000). This is in contrast to the unidirectional representations of Japan in the West. A survey conducted in 2002 by NHK's Broadcasting Culture Research Institute demonstrates this tendency. The survey examined the way Japan is presented on television in a few selected countries, including the United States, the United Kingdom, China, South Korea, and Taiwan. The results showed that Japan is depicted indirectly and stereotypical images are used in television productions in Europe and America. In East Asia, on the other hand, the portrayal of Japan is direct and much more diverse, delivering a multidirectional view of Japan (Hara 2004, 87).

Looking toward the Hong Kong island business district, one cannot avoid seeing all the huge neon lights attached to skyscrapers depicting the names of famous Japanese companies such as Nikon, Hitachi, Canon, Panasonic, Sanyo, Sony, Sharp, and Sogo department store. There are many renowned Japanese brand names with a global appeal, most of which are automobile and electronics companies.[32] Indeed, while companies such as Toyota, Honda, Sony, Nintendo, Canon, and Panasonic are known worldwide, many other Japanese brand names have a more conspicuous regional presence. Japanese department stores for example, such as Mitsukoshi, Takashimaya, and ISETAN, have been extensively operating in the region's big cities, merchandizing a wide variety of consumer products, according to consumer taste shaped in Japan.[33] Moreover, design and clothing companies, such as MUJI, Uniqlo, and Mizuno, cosmetic makers such as Shiseido and Kanebo, and food chains such as Yoshinoya and Family Mart, are highly visible in urban areas in East Asia, to a degree that is unseen in other parts of the world. Japanese popular culture has also become a ubiquitous sight in East Asia's urban landscape. Japanese pop music, anime, manga, television programs, fashion magazines, and movies have been endorsed by the local popular culture markets and they now constitute an integral part of the cultural lives of many people who live in the region.

Conclusion

While the export of the Japanese-style management system has greatly declined since its heyday in the 1980s, in the 1990s and 2000s it was still taking place in the field of popular culture. In East Asia, Japanese formats for popular culture production have been adopted and emulated, considered as a model by many in the region's cultural industries. The position of Japan as a model is not much different from the "learn-from-Japan" campaign in the 1980s, when Japanese management and production techniques were emulated and reproduced abroad. As we saw, in East Asia today Japan is still a major source of learning on how to make and handle commodified culture toward a potentially profitable end. In this sense, the importance of the Japanese cultural industries to the regionalization process in East Asia has not only been in creating new markets for popular culture, but also in having an impact on the way this region's cultural industries operate.

 This chapter has analyzed the circulation of Japanese popular culture production formats in East Asia and their integration within the local popular culture markets. In chapter 4, we saw that in entering new markets in East Asia, Japanese companies have utilized their know-how in media gauging, scouting, producing, and marketing popular culture. Chapter 5, on the other hand, has shown that the Japanese cultural industries are highly appreciated and have become something to be imitated, which has served to upgrade East Asia's popular culture production standards as well. This was especially apparent in the "Korean Wave," where Japanese music and television production formats were extensively emulated and viewed as a means of advancing local cultural production. Moreover, as reflected in the interviews with local cultural industry personnel, in East Asia Japanese cultural products and formats are highly appreciated due to the quality of their products and productions and have been assisted by the overall positive image that Japanese brand names enjoy. The majority of the cultural industry personnel interviewed also thought that ostensible cultural similarities between Japanese and East Asians do not play a significant role in the success of Japanese cultural products. Only two of the sixty-eight interviewees thought that the primary reason for the success of Japanese culture in East Asia emanates from an "Asian cultural substance" that resonates with local consumers.

The trade in formats plays an important role in the transformation of the cultural industries of East Asia and beyond. For the cultural industries that buy or emulate these formats, it is a way to upgrade their own productions and diversify their activities. In recent years, the practice of licensing formats has been increasingly regarded as a potentially profitable source of income for the copyright holders, especially in the television industry (Keane 2006, 845; Moran 2008, 459). According to Jean Chalaby (2012, 36–37), the trade in television formats started in the early 1950s in a few Western countries, especially in the United States, United Kingdom, France, Spain, and Italy. This trade, however, was transformed in the late 1990s with a few successful formats (*Who Wants to Be a Millionaire?*, *Survivor*, *Big Brother*, and *Idols*), which placed it at the heart of the television industry. It is now a thriving global industry worth an estimated 3.1 billion euros per year.

A few Japanese television companies have found that format sales is a convenient way to make money without fear of their concept or star performer being lost in translation. Successful Japanese remakes include Fuji Television Network's cooking competition *Ryōri no Tetsujin* (Iron Chef) and NTV's *Money no Tora* (Money Tigers), in which would-be entrepreneurs seek investment from venture capitalists, a show that was sold in about twenty countries worldwide.[34] But problems are still embedded since the concept of "format rights" carries relatively little legal weight and the law is not as strict regarding program setups and ideas as it is in cases of copying a finished work. A few Japanese companies filed copyright infringement suits against foreign TV networks and are still hesitant in expanding to the East Asian market. Nevertheless, I believe that better law enforcement in many parts of East Asia and the increasing awareness of intellectual property rights violations opens a way to Japan's cultural industries becoming even more involved in East Asia's popular culture market.

CHAPTER 6

//////////////////////

Conclusion

Japanese Popular Culture
and the Making of East Asia

Let me paint for you ten pictures: first, youngsters in Hong Kong sharing the latest anime series, which they just downloaded from the Internet; second, a Taiwanese housewife watching a trendy Japanese drama on cable television; third, a Japanese female vocalist singing in front of an excited crowd at the Pattaya International Music Festival in Thailand; fourth, a group of Chinese fans translating a Japanese comic book into Mandarin; fifth, a young Indonesian girl showing her friends the Japanese fashion magazine she just bought from a street vendor in Jakarta; sixth, young Malaysians, inspired by their fascination with Japanese video games, learning Japanese at a local language school; seventh, Kitty-Chan chopsticks for sale in a Singapore shop; eighth, a young Korean amateur manga illustrator flying to Tokyo's Akehabara district in search of inspiration for his work; ninth, suited METI officials exchanging business cards with representatives of major TV channels at a "cool Japan" event at the luxurious ION Orchard Building in Singapore; and tenth, Japanese foreign minister Komura Masahiko at an official inauguration ceremony in Tokyo, appointing Doraemon, one of Japan's most famous anime characters, as a special cultural ambassador to the world.

What kinds of organizations are behind these popular culture products and productions? Who are the agents that produce them and how do they get commercialized and distributed? What kind of cross-border

161

collaborations do they entail? What sort of impact do these cultural commodities have on state politics? And how do these products, agents, and industries contribute to the regionalization of East Asia? This book endeavors to answer these questions by focusing on the character, dynamics, and wider implications of recently emerging regional systems that produce, disseminate, and market popular culture in East Asia. Specifically, this book examines the role of popular culture and its various mechanisms and trajectories in the construction of the East Asian region by focusing on the expansion of Japanese cultural industries into East Asian markets since the late 1980s.

As discussed in chapter 1, in spite of dramatic changes in East Asia's popular culture markets in the past two decades, little attention has been paid to the economic and industrial aspects of cultural production. The available literature on the presence and acceptance of Japanese popular culture in East Asia has typically taken an ethnographic and interpretive approach, focusing on contextual analysis or on the process of consumption. Especially noteworthy is Kōichi Iwabuchi's pioneering work, *Recentering Globalization* (2002). In this book, Iwabuchi positions the rise of Japanese cultural power within a broader, global-level phenomenon and argues that the expansion of Japanese culture within Asia in the 1990s correlates with the decentralizing forces of global-local relations (other examples include Allen and Sakamoto 2006; Berry, Liscutin, and Mackintosh 2009; Craig 2000; Desser 2003; Inoue 2010; Ishii 2001; Martinez 1998; Mitsui and Hosokawa 1998; Mōri 2004; Soderberg and Reader 2000; Treat 1996). These works no doubt provide rich information and analysis related to the images reflected by popular culture products, to the ideas and messages they encapsulate, and to the practice of Japanese popular culture abroad.

On the other hand, studies on regionalization in East Asia have paid little attention to popular culture. Because they do not regard the "culture industry" as a viable object of analysis, they generally overlook the regional implications of mass commodification and export of popular culture. Although regionalization and regional formation are dealt with in depth in political economical spheres (recent examples include Ba 2009; Beeson 2007; Calder and Fukuyama 2008; Frost 2008; Lincoln 2004; Shambauch and Yahuda 2008), popular culture is not.

Interesting as these studies are, for the purposes of this book three major issues are missing from the existing literature. First, not enough information is given about the organizational aspects of Japanese popular culture in East Asia, especially regarding the dynamics of production and distribution, nor about the initial advantages that Japanese cultural industries had over local cultural industries, which enabled them to exert strong influence in local popular culture markets. Second, literature on Japanese popular culture in East Asia typically endorses globalization and the dynamics of global-local relations as the only possible frameworks for analysis, overlooking the importance of the "region." Most scholars view the expansion of Japanese popular culture overseas as part of a global process and overlook the specificities of Japanese popular culture's acceptance and conspicuous impact within the cultural geography of East Asia (Otmazgin 2008b). Third, the available studies do not systematically analyze the regional transformations brought about by Japanese cultural industries or explicitly investigate their contribution to the regionalization process in East Asia.

This book addresses the above lacunae and looks into the hitherto overlooked relations between the organization of popular culture and the process of regionalization. It focuses on the big picture and aims to provide a comprehensive, empirically grounded study of the production, market expansion and circulation, and reception of Japanese cultural industries in East Asia. The investigation started by examining the process of cultural commodification in Japan, the scale of the domestic market there, and the Japanese government's responses to the industry's development (chapter 3). It then analyzed the creation of regional markets for Japanese music and television programs, the impact of Japanese cultural industries on local cultural markets in East Asia, and the appreciation for Japanese cultural products and formats expressed by personnel from the local cultural industries (chapters 4 and 5).

The book is theoretically driven rather than simply descriptive. It argues that the experience of Japanese cultural industries in East Asia provides new insights into the relationship between the organization of cultural production and the notion of regionalization. This experience shows that the organization of popular culture can affect the dynamics of regional formation by supporting the construction of transnational markets for cultural commodities in geographically proximate economies and by stimulating collaboration among companies, networks, and individuals involved in the commodification, manufacturing, and marketing of popular culture. These processes, it is argued, spark a regionwide transformation of structural arrangements and cognitive frameworks used to commodify and commercialize culture.

Of course, this does not suggest that the organization of popular culture is the single most important determinant of regionalization. But this book does argue that the politics and economics of regionalization necessitate an examination of cultural industries and that the transformations engendered by the regionalization process cannot be fully understood until regional developments in the organization and appropriation of popular culture are better grasped and contextualized.

In what follows, I discuss in greater detail why Japanese popular culture has been successful in East Asia and how that success has affected popular culture markets and governments in the region. I will then discuss how expansion of Japanese cultural industries is likely to affect the regionalization process in East Asia in both the short and long terms, and I offer some analytical and theoretical insights into the relationship between popular culture and the process of regional formation.

How Did Japan's Popular Culture Succeed in East Asia?

Given the proliferation of Japanese cultural commodities in East Asia, it is important to address this question: How did Japan's popular culture become an integral part of East Asia's cultural market and come to exert such wide influence over local cultural industries? The question raises fundamental concerns regarding the way culture and economy interact in a free-market system. This study endeavors to show that it is possible to understand the expansion of Japan's popular culture in East Asia by looking at the mechanisms by which the industry works, rather than focusing solely on the content of the products or on the narratives and images they reflect. What Philip Napoli (2009, 161) points out about media industries is relevant to our discussion of cultural industries as well:

> As much as media industries are cultural and political entities, they also are economic entities, and the understanding of the economic constraints and incentives under which they operate, and the basic economic characteristics of the products in which they deal, can provide valuable insights into a wide range of dimensions of media industry behavior . . . given that an increasing proportion of the media sector around the world is becoming privatized and commercialized . . . understanding

the economic dynamics underlying the buying, producing, and selling of media audiences, can lead to more well-grounded research on media industries, regardless of its disciplinary point of origin.

The investigation in this book thus offers a dialectical look at organizational aspects of cultural diversity, focusing on the dynamics of production, distribution, and regulation of Japanese popular culture.

As we saw in chapter 3, a key factor in the success of Japanese popular culture has been the nation's domestic market, which developed rapidly in the second half of the twentieth century. From the late 1960s, Japan's domestic popular culture market was already far more dynamic and rich in terms of cultural commodification, production, and consumption than that of any of its East Asian neighbors. This head start provided adequate ground for development in such fields as music, television, manga, and anime, at a time when most other markets in East Asia were still struggling to supply basic needs to local people who lived in poverty. It is therefore not surprising that Japan—Asia's first industrialized nation, with the region's most advanced economy—was also the first in the region to develop an advanced popular culture industry. By the end of the 1980s, with roughly a twenty-year head start on their neighbors, Japanese cultural industries were mature enough to expand into overseas markets and offer their products and experience to local cultural industries in other parts of East Asia.

Another reason for the success of Japan's cultural industries is the highly efficient "Japanese way" of commodifying and commercializing culture based on facilitating broad audience participation, actively extracting creativity from the market, and transforming that creativity into a set of standardized, accessible products. As we saw in chapter 3, unlike the so-called "Hollywood model" wherein a small group of professionals are responsible for the majority of creative work, Japanese-style cultural production involves a wide range of participants and thrives on close reciprocity between the established industry and its audience. Amateur artists and the *otaku* sector play an especially helpful role in the creative process by constantly providing new ideas to be aggressively co-opted, commodified, and commercialized by the established industry. I do not mean to say that the Japanese model is necessarily "better" than the Hollywood model, but I simply point out that a different and highly efficient system of commodifying and producing popular culture has evolved in Japan.

A third factor in the Japanese cultural industries' growth in East Asia has been their success in working with local agents and promoters to create effective machinery for commercializing products and services. As we saw in chapter 4, Japanese music and television companies have assembled effective systems for exporting and distributing Japanese music and television programs and have tightened cooperation between branches within the region. As a result, a variety of Japanese popular culture products can now be found in all big cities across the region. In this context, chapter 4 described the creation of pan-Asian markets for Japan's popular culture commodities, especially music and television programs.

In addition to lawful dissemination of popular culture products in East Asia via exports or commercialization by established cultural industries, black markets for pirated products served as a powerful engine for the dissemination of Japanese popular culture, especially during the formative years of the regional market in the 1990s. Flourishing markets offering pirated versions of audio-visual products and printed matter gave a big boost to regional trade in popular culture by introducing cheap reproductions of the hottest cultural products to groups of consumers who could not afford the genuine versions. This underground channel was especially important in places where Japanese culture was officially banned, whether due to historical and political considerations (South Korea, Taiwan, mainland China) or because of its "violent" content (Singapore, Malaysia, the Philippines). In this sense, "informal" strategies for crossing borders and bypassing regulations of nation-states were no less important to the formation of markets for popular culture than the formal mechanisms employed by companies and institutions.

It is important to note that in spite of their regionwide presence, Japanese cultural industries do not maintain a dominant position in East Asia, and non-Japanese companies have built competing local and regional production systems. In recent years, Korean movie and television drama productions have overtaken their Japanese counterparts in popularity in most of East Asia (Chua and Iwabuchi 2008). As discussed in chapter 2, other East Asia–based popular culture confluences, notably Chinese and Korean, have been diffused throughout the region, and various waves of popular culture have been extensively disseminated and consumed in many parts of urban East Asia, which points toward diversification rather than homogenization of the region's popular culture market. Although Japanese cultural industries have a comparative advantage over other cultural industries in East Asia and have established a foothold in the cultural markets of the region, they have not assumed a dominant position or prevented local cultural industries from developing.

A comparison between Japan's cultural industries and its automobile and electronics industries, which have achieved far greater dominance in East Asia, reveals why the cultural industries were not able to hold on to their competitive advantage in East Asia for a longer period. In automobiles and electronics, Japanese industrial expansion led to the creation of regional production networks that tie together producers, subcontractors, and distributors across sectors and national borders (Katzenstein 2005, 106). These industries have constructed sophisticated technological and production networks in East Asia that are far deeper and broader than those built by American, European, or Korean companies (Borrus, Ernst, and Haggard 2000, 14–31). At the same time, the Japanese automobile and electronics industries have maintained control over core technologies by dispersing production to various "screwdriver factories" while maintaining centralized decision-making power and keeping research and development in Japanese hands (Hatch and Yamamura 1996).

In the cultural industries, however, it has been impossible to protect the Japanese advantage by maintaining centralized control over the distribution of popular culture commodities and formats. For one thing, rampant piracy and lax enforcement of copyright violations in East Asia have taken a big part of the production and distribution of Japanese popular culture products out of the hands of the established industry. Accessible reproduction devices, such as recorders and CD and DVD players, and more recently the Internet, make culture pirates' work easier than ever. As we saw in chapter 4, pirated replicas account for a big part of the market for Japanese popular culture products in East Asia.

The Korean manga market provides a good example. Korean manga (*manhwa*) got its start in the 1970s and 1980s, based on illegal translation and copycatting of Japanese manga. During that period, Korean manga artists took their first steps into the industry and Korean audiences were exposed to large quantities of manga. Only later did the Korean manga industry begin to develop original stories and gradually develop its own original character. As Yamanaka Chie's (2010) study concludes, if not for bootleggers operating unhindered by copyright laws, the Korean manga industry could not have developed as it has.

Even without pirates, Japanese cultural industries could not have kept their know-how from leaking to indigenous producers because their production formats are highly transferable. Producing a music album or a television program is, after all, technologically much easier to achieve than manufacturing a car or a plasma television, and it requires a much smaller investment of capital and equipment compared to the startup of an automobile or steel products factory. As I emphasized in chapter 1, because human creativity is at the core of a cultural product's value, it is relatively easy and cheap to commodify and reproduce such products. Affordable digital equipment, including cameras, musical instruments, and video editing equipment, makes it possible for just about anyone to commodify their everyday creativity and reproduce products relatively cheaply, while the Internet can facilitate the low-cost marketing of packaged cultural content.

In the popular culture business, there is also considerable freedom for entrepreneurs to facilitate change, in contrast to traditional factory production, which tends to be based on fundamentally rigid, rational, systematic, and highly organized processes (Negus 1992, 46). The business of illegally reproducing and distributing popular culture commodities exemplifies this difference. As we saw in chapter 4, the technology that enables these operations to manufacture and transfer fake products is relatively simple, at least in comparison to technologies required for entry into more advanced industries such as automobiles and electronics. The same accessible technologies and low level of funding that enables local producers to copy Japanese culture products also enables them to commodify their own original cultural content.

Another factor that has kept Japanese cultural industries from dominating the East Asian region is their own lack of enthusiasm about breaking into the regional market. Japanese automobile, electronics, and other manufacturing industries saw expansion into East Asia as unavoidable due to the sharp appreciation of the yen in the aftermath of the Plaza Accord (Seki 1994, 8–9, 85–86). During most of the postwar period until the burst of Japan's economic bubble at the end of the 1980s, however, the domestic market was affluent enough to keep the vast majority of Japanese cultural industries focused on operations at home. Even today, after prolonged economic recession, the Japanese market remains profitable and is seen as the first marketing priority for cultural industries (chapter 3). Expanding into new markets requires a good deal of capital and knowledge even for a cultural industry, and it entails a greater degree of risk than operating at home. These considerations still discourage Japanese cultural industries from making fresh attempts at overseas expansion. This is true for other Japanese service industries. Although many Japanese companies understand the benefits of globalization, as Orr, Salsberg, and Iwatani (2011, 153) point out, they prefer to remain focused on the domestic market because they lack the ambition required for initiating an aggressive global expansion strategy.

In a 2005 interview, Yamada Yasuhide, vice president of JETRO Bangkok, repeatedly complained that in spite of his efforts to convince Japanese media companies to expand their operations into Southeast Asia, only a few were willing to do so. Their reluctance was mainly due to fear of copyright violations and a sense of insecurity about entering markets they do not know well. Nevertheless, Mr. Yamada insisted that East Asia's markets present vast opportunities for Japanese cultural exports that outweigh the challenges. According to him, "East Asia's markets are too important to ignore and Japanese companies should look for ways to facilitate the export of Japanese popular culture to East Asia, and to profit from it despite the persistence of piracy. . . . If offered the same opportunity, American companies would have already grabbed it and taken over the market. We [the Japanese government] should try to talk Japanese companies into making the most of their position, even if we have to use a whip."[1]

One more factor that has prevented Japanese cultural industries from expanding more aggressively in East Asia is that until very recently, there was little governmental support for cultural exports. As we saw in chapter 3, throughout most of the post–World War II period the Japanese government did little to encourage the expansion of its cultural industries into East Asia due to fears of resurrecting old grievances and due to a lack of confidence that "culture" could possibly be economically profitable. This stance contrasted sharply with the government's wholehearted support for the expansion of the country's heavier industries, such as automobiles, electronics, and telecommunications.[2] The Japanese government has yet to even provide comprehensive official statistics about the economic output of the nation's cultural industries sector; related information is published in vague and overlapping categories such as art, leisure, culture, media, sport, "content," and the like.

Just how clueless can government statisticians be about the economic value of culture? When I first approached Japan's Customs and Tariff

Bureau for information about music exports, I was shocked to learn that until 1985, Japanese music exports had been measured by weight! The government actually recorded how many kilograms of music had been exported each month! Only after 1985 did the bureau begin to report exports of Japanese music in terms of its monetary value.

Of course, governmental involvement would not necessarily have paved the way for Japanese cultural industries to prevail in East Asian markets. It could, however, have helped. Governments can support cultural industries and stimulate cultural production through a wide variety of measures such as tax relief, subsidies, loans, and relocation support. They can also provide necessary physical infrastructure for communication, publicity, research and development, etc., as well as educational infrastructure (e.g., training sound engineers, artistic editors, producers, etc.) and legal infrastructure (e.g., laws that protect copyright). I think it is fair to say that for most of the postwar period, the expansion of Japanese cultural industries within East Asia took place without the kind of active support that Japan's government extended to many other industries.

Although Japan's cultural industries maintain a considerable advantage over the cultural industries of other countries in East Asia, mainly due to their prodigious domestic market and well-developed mechanisms for commodifying culture, they have not maintained the kind of wide lead enjoyed by Japan's more technology-based industries, such as automobiles and electronics. Unlike what happened in the 1970s and 1980s, when Japan provided the technology, capital, components, and strategic management for burgeoning regional manufacturing networks in East Asia (Katzenstein 2006, 25), Japanese cultural industries were never able to dominate outside their home markets by providing popular culture commodities and formats, but rather from the very beginning of their overseas expansion they became integrated into a regional market fabric that offered a variety of popular culture products.

The Regional Impact of Popular Culture

The regionwide presence of cultural industries invokes both quantitative changes (e.g., denser circulation of popular culture and more transnational collaboration in the production and marketing of popular culture) and a qualitative shift toward a regional production system that is no longer based upon separate national economies, but instead adjusts the location of production, distribution, and consumption of goods according to regionwide considerations. The emergence of regional popular culture markets not only encourages cooperation among all those involved in commodifying and commercializing culture, including innovators, producers, promoters, distributors, entrepreneurs, etc., but also causes different people in different places to share the same set of cultural commodities and perhaps also attendant lifestyles and ideas.

Denser (and many times uncontrolled) circulation of popular culture in East Asia has the potential to weaken individual states' control over the inflow of culture and hamper their efforts to utilize culture for their own purposes, such as nation building. As we saw in chapter 2, in the past, the involvement of the state in arts and culture in East Asia was typically directed toward the dissemination of specific values and traditions it chose to promote to construct a national community based on shared symbols and narratives, or in some cases as a control tool to mobilize people by emphasizing their cultural similarities. Placing a large quantity of cultural commodities outside the reach of state guidance weakens the state's ability to influence mass opinion by implementing its own (politically motivated) cultural policy.

On the other hand, popular culture can invoke changes in official cultural policy. As we saw earlier, private-sector success prompted governments (Japan's in chapter 3 and South Korea's in chapter 5) to redirect their inward-looking cultural policies in favor of policies that encourage export-oriented cultural industries, which have the potential to gain "soft power." In these cases, the state does not disappear from the scene but rather adapts to new, unavoidable circumstances and looks for new ways to intervene and build a new basis for legitimacy.

The following paragraphs look more closely at three aspects of Japanese popular culture's impact on East Asia: the creation of regional markets for Japanese popular culture commodities, the export of cultural production formats and their emulation and adaptation by local cultural industries, and changes in state policy as governments increasingly come to view cultural exports as an integral part of market activity worthy of governmental intervention.

The Creation of Regional Markets

As we saw in chapter 4, Japan's popular culture has managed to establish a solid footing in East Asia, especially in urban areas. Encouraged by the evolution of mass markets for standardized cultural goods, Japanese cultural industries have expanded into East Asian markets and created efficient, regionwide mechanisms for producing their wares and distributing them to mainstream audiences. In virtually every big media shop in every East Asian urban area it is possible to find a variety of Japanese music and television products. Japanese fashion magazines and manga are also readily available in every major bookstore, in Japanese or translated into a local language. Japanese anime and video games have been embraced so fully by local popular culture markets that they now constitute an integral part of the cultural lives of many young East Asians.

Interestingly, Japanese cultural industries have managed to overcome daunting language barriers and popularize their products among a variety of audiences that do not understand Japanese. In spite of the existence of what Sinclair, Jacka, and Cunningham (1996, 11–14) call "geolinguistic regions," where cultural commodities are circulated between groups of countries that share a common linguistic background, Japanese culture has managed to break into different "linguistic regions." Moreover, the successful expansion of Japanese cultural industries within East Asia and the wide distribution of Japanese products are especially astonishing given Japan's history as a colonizer. Despite the suffering that imperialist Japan inflicted on its neighbors in the decades leading up to the end of World War II, Japanese culture has become firmly established as an integral part of the regional cultural scene, even providing an alternative to Western popular culture products.

Indeed, there is still no shortage of resentment toward Japan in East Asia. Reminders of enduring anger at imperialist Japan are occasionally displayed in anti-Japanese demonstrations in Korea and China, often following reports of a Japanese leader paying respects at Yasukuni Shrine (which commemorates soldiers, but also enshrines the spirits of convicted Japanese war criminals), or the publication of new Japanese history textbooks, or a skirmish over the sovereignty of rocky islets[3] off the coast of Japan or in the East China Sea (Kohari 2005; Kumagai 2006). Nevertheless, as was shown in chapter 4, Japan's popular culture has managed to overcome these feelings and find broad acceptance among audiences in East Asia. By embracing Japanese culture, consumers in South Korea and Taiwan simultaneously reject the official interpretations of Japanese culture offered by their governments.

In the new East Asian popular culture, different types of consumers in different locations are able to access the same assortment of products.

Japan is thus widely represented in East Asia by its cultural products and innovations, rather than being recognized only for its economy, industrial power, and managerial techniques—all of which seem to be in decline. The scope and impact of Japanese cultural industries is eminently regional. That is to say, although Japan's popular culture possesses global marketing appeal and many of its products have been successful in other parts of the world (especially anime in North America), it has found a special degree of regional acceptance in East Asia that is reflected both in the broad spectrum of products offered and in their high concentration, as well as in the active way they are embraced. In East Asia, Japanese culture products are not simply consumed on a massive scale, but they are also actively emulated, developed, and incorporated into local productions. It is therefore appropriate to emphasize the influence of Japanese cultural industries on local markets in East Asia and to describe their activities as complimentary to the regionalization process, rather than to talk only about their global expansion or to label their overseas success as just another manifestation of globalization.

At the same time, it is important to emphasize that not all markets in East Asia are equally exposed to popular culture, nor do all East Asian communities participate equally in the consumption of Japanese popular culture. The presence of Japanese music culture and television, for example, varies from one market to another and is generally most visible in urban centers where a certain modicum of consumer culture has evolved. According to the findings examined in this book, Japanese culture has a stronger presence in Hong Kong and Seoul than it does in Bangkok. In this sense, the "region" that Japan's popular culture inhabits does not consist of nation-states in their entirety but instead encompasses middle classes from various parts of urban East Asia.

Formats for Dissemination

Not only have Japanese popular culture products been disseminated in the markets of East Asia, but Japanese cultural production formats themselves have also been regionalized. In this sense, Japanese cultural industries have evolved from being just content providers to being also format providers. As we saw in chapter 5, Japanese formats for musical and television productions have been extensively imitated in East Asian markets. These production formats were either actively introduced by Japanese companies or adopted unilaterally by local cultural industries. Japanese pop music, idol creation, talent competitions, and various types of television programs are the examples analyzed in this study. The adoption of Japanese production formats by indigenous cultural industries in East Asia is especially noticeable in the case of South Korea, where companies faithfully imitated the production and promotional strategies used for making Japanese pop music shows and television dramas.

Both Japanese cultural products and cultural production formats have gained a high level of appreciation in local markets. Most of the cultural industry personnel interviewed in this study (chapter 5) said that the main reasons for the success of Japanese cultural productions were their high quality and the positive image that Japanese brand names enjoy in East Asia. The interviewees noted that many of their own productions were based on Japanese cultural industries' models for the construction of an advanced cultural industry that produces high-quality popular culture.

That it is Japanese formats that are being emulated may raise concerns in some quarters about Japanese cultural imperialism and the imposition of Japanese values. Proponents of the cultural imperialism argument fear that the intrusion of cultural industries into less developed countries, especially from the West, has led to the imposition of Western cultural norms on these societies at the expense of and ultimately leading to the destruction of indigenous traditions (for example, Dorfman and Mattelart 1984; Fajes 1981; Frith 1991; Hamelink 1983; Robertson 1991; Schiller 1976; Tomlinson 1991). Others suggest that certain popular culture products and forms are setting a unified agenda by controlling the agents of cultural production and imposing a sort of collective will (Herman and McChesney 1997, 9; Hesmondhalgh 2002, 174; Hu 2010, 138). This book cautions against these sorts of allegations of a Tokyo-sponsored movement to construct a Japanese-dominated regional identity. My purpose is to show that local cultural industries in East Asia were able to emulate Japanese formats without directly absorbing their content. In fact, the adoption of Japanese production formats and know-how does exactly the opposite of what cultural imperialism theorists would expect: it actually propagates a variety of local productions and heterogeneous practices that can all express their particular content through these adopted formats. The Japanese formats serve as vehicles for preserving and transmitting a diversity of local cultures rather than for imposing domination by Japanese culture.

Japanese cultural industries in East Asia have supplied production formats that have become deeply entrenched in the everyday local production of popular culture. Japanese popular culture production has been seen as an adaptable model suitable for application to the advancement of local production. Even smaller countries with less-developed cultural industries can adopt these formats and use them for local production and export by targeting niche markets outside the domestic market. A good example is the export of Thai popular culture to neighboring Cambodia, Laos, and Myanmar, both through legal avenues (official broadcasting of Thai television programs) and illegal distribution networks (bootleg CDs and DVDs).

As a result, much of today's East Asian cultural production—especially of music, television dramas, idol-inspired fashions, comic books, and animation products—is largely based on Japanese production models. Despite the use of Japanese formats, locally made cultural products often blend local languages and motifs with international ones. Although it is difficult to gauge, the impact of Japanese cultural industries in East Asia should not be evaluated only according to how many Japanese-made products are sold, but also according to the degree of adoption of Japanese-style production processes and their overall influence on the development of the region's cultural industries.

The Growing Involvement of the State

The success of Japan's popular culture in East Asia and growing interest in the culture business have attracted the attention of the Japanese government to the point that it has placed cultural production and exportation on the national agenda. As we saw in chapter 3, the cultural industries in Japan are no longer considered a marginalized sector of the economy, but are increasingly regarded as an important part of market activity. Popular culture is given credit for helping to heal the wounds inflicted during Japan's imperialist past and, more generally, for its potential to boost the country's image abroad.

The emergence of popular culture in its new role as an important diplomatic tool quickly sparked public debate in Japan. As we saw in chapter 3, academics and journalists have been emphasizing the growing importance of commodified culture in the country's future and encouraging the government to actively support it. The "soft power" argument has also grown fashionable in recent years in response to the success of Japan's popular culture abroad, and it is now incorporated into the state's exploration for new arenas of potential intervention.

Encouraged by the domestic discourse, the Japanese government has started to take popular culture more seriously and is currently pursuing an active role in its industrial development. Despite imperfect coordination between the various ministries and some remaining holes in the legal infrastructure designed to support the sector (Kozuka 2008, 15–84), the government has taken steps to aid Japan's culture industries, primarily by providing support for the infrastructure needed for the industries' development (Otmazgin 2011a). This includes supporting technology needed for delivering and consuming cultural content (infrastructure for the Internet, cable TV, and satellite broadcasts), nurturing human resources for the industry by supporting universities and training centers, and ensuring the availability of venture capital for producing movies, television programs, music albums, anime, video games, etc. Government ministries and agencies also routinely produce highly optimistic forecasts for the cultural industries, prompting more governmental involvement.

In October 2011, the Japanese government launched a "Cool Japan" campaign in several countries across the globe (Singapore, India, China, South Korea, France, Italy, the United States, and Brazil). The aim of "Cool Japan" was to brand Japan as a culturally exciting country and, no less important, to facilitate economic gains by boosting sales of both popular culture and general consumer products. Toward this end, METI, the ministry in charge of the campaign, set up a "Cool Japan Strategy Promotion Program" within its Creative Industries Division and hired Dentsu Inc., Japan's leading advertising company, to publicize the campaign. METI senior vice minister Matsushita Tadahiro remarked that the purpose of the campaign was to introduce Japanese brands to foreign consumers who had already been exposed to images of Japanese contemporary culture.[4] "Cool Japan" is a refreshing attempt to invigorate the stagnant Japanese economy, and it might prove successful in increasing foreign consumers' awareness of Japanese products. But there is a danger that excessive government intervention can actually end up killing the cool. As Christopher Graves (2011, 412) put it, "one cannot pronounce oneself 'cool.'" When a government agency like METI calls itself cool, says Graves, it runs the risk of looking every bit as uncool as a middle-aged father who tries to impress his teenage daughter's friends and ends up mangling their slang.

As the business of commodifying and exporting culture gains momentum, other East Asian countries are also placing cultural industry development on their national agendas. A few governments in the region are particularly fascinated by Japanese cultural exports and hope to replicate Japan's success. As governments in East Asia gradually take note of the potential advantages of developing exports from their own cultural industries, they start to think about developing industries related to television, music, animation, etc. Some have recently taken active measures to develop domestic cultural industries with export capabilities.

South Korea, the most conspicuous of these governments, has taken a deep interest in the connection between industry and culture. Since the 1990s, Seoul has dramatically changed the focus of its cultural promotion activities, shifting from an emphasis on the traditional arts that it supported in the 1970s and 1980s to the pop culture it pushes today (Shin 2008, 30; Yim 2002, 42–47). The South Korean government began strongly supporting the development of its "creative industries" (music, movies, television content, etc.) and promoting Korean popular culture as an export industry. In 1998, former President Kim Dae Jung announced that the promotion of cultural industries was strategically important for the nation's future.

The Ministry of Culture and Tourism's Cultural Industries Bureau is in charge of designing South Korea's cultural policy, while the Ministry of Information and Communication supports the technological infrastructure required by the country's cultural industries. The Ministry of Culture and Tourism has been holding international fairs to introduce Korean popular culture to possible buyers and has been encouraging Korean companies to cooperate in the production and marketing of cultural commodities. In 2005, the ministry announced that it would work with local universities to create a graduate school specializing in culture-related technologies and an undergraduate program to foster expertise in the field of cultural industries (K. Lee 2008, 179).

The government's establishment of the Korea Creative Content Agency (KOCCA) in 2001 and the Korea Foundation for Asian Cultural Exchange (KOFACE) is a good indication of how seriously the Korean government takes the establishment of its own export-oriented cultural industries. These two government-supported agencies are charged with nurturing the competitiveness of the country's cultural industries abroad, and they serve as mediators between the government and the private sector. Both organizations maintain offices in the United States, the United Kingdom, and Japan. KOCCA is more export-oriented and focuses on securing the infrastructure, technology, and financial resources needed for the growth of the cultural industries. KOFACE works to stimulate the growth of Korea's cultural industries through the exchange of information with the private sector and by facilitating international cooperation with institutions and governments around the world.

In recent years, Thailand's Ministry of Information and Technology has also been supporting the development of the country's animation and movie industries, not only for domestic consumption but also for export. The former Thaksin administration provided tax incentives and sponsored related events to encourage the local industry to produce and export more movies every year. Thailand also sent a delegation to the Japan Chamber of Commerce to discuss sending a study team to Japan.[5] The government supports the efforts of Kantana, Thailand's biggest television production company, aimed at making the country a regional media production hub. Kantana has begun training workers for the industry in collaboration with local universities and is gearing up to be able to provide all the production and postproduction tools a television or movie company would need to come and produce their projects in relatively low-cost Thailand.[6] The government is helping by investing in infrastructure to make Thailand a base for the shooting of foreign movies, allowing Thai companies to supply the production teams with a variety of services.[7] The government also provides tax breaks to encourage exportation of movies to neighboring Southeast Asian countries and to the growing Chinese-language markets in mainland China, Taiwan, and Hong Kong, in order to revive the Thai movie industry, whose overall production plunged from about two hundred movies a year in the 1980s to about half a dozen in 2004. In 2003, the Tourism Authority of Thailand began sponsoring an annual Bangkok International Film Festival, where "Best ASEAN Film" awards are presented in elaborate, Oscar-style ceremonies. Thai authorities also support the Pattaya International Music Festival, which has taken place every summer since 2004, with participation by musicians from across East Asia along with local music artists.

In Hong Kong as well, the government has been working on restructuring the local movie industry since the late 1990s. In 1998, following the 1997 Asian financial crisis, the Hong Kong movie industry's box office receipts declined by 6.2 percent from the previous year, and again in 1999 by 7.8 percent (U.S. Department of Commerce 2004). In an effort to halt this decline, the Hong Kong government formulated initiatives to combat piracy and to support the long-term development of the movie industry. In April 1998, it established the Film Services Office (FSO) to facilitate movie production in Hong Kong and to organize film festivals in various cities outside Hong Kong to promote Hong Kong movies internationally. In addition, from April 1999 until March 2004, the Hong Kong government operated the Film Development Fund, which approved a total of US$49 million for seventy-two projects in support of moviemakers and moviemaking infrastructure. And as of January 2004, because of the Mainland and Hong Kong Closer Economic Partnership Arrangement (CEPA), Chinese-language products made by Hong Kong companies were no longer subject to import quotas imposed by mainland China, and from January 2005 they were exempt from all import tariffs (Film Industry of Hong Kong 2006).

Although China's enormous domestic market absorbs most of the nation's cultural production, in recent years China too has reshaped its cultural policies to focus on stimulating exports (Keane 2006, 847). At the seventh annual Beijing science and technology expo, held in May 2004, a nonprofit organization named Creative China Industrial Alliance (CCIA) made its first public display of intent to promote "the concept of creative industries." CCIA-sponsored discourse on "creative industries" (*chuangyi chanye*) continued in Beijing and Shanghai through a series of discussions attended by both Chinese and non-Chinese participants. Meeting organizers cited international models such as South Korea, which has been exporting an increasing amount of popular cultural products to China, to make the case that China needs to invest in the development of its own culture industries. The term previously used for "cultural industries" (*wenhua chanye*) was soon revised to "creative economy" (*chuangyichanye*), a new term that emerged in the years following the initiation of these discussions. Other catchphrases that became fashionable in policy documents concerning cultural production include "new economy," "service economy," "knowledge-based economy," "cultural economy," and "experience economy" (Keane 2007, 78, 140). CCIA has even negotiated compromises over state censorship, allowing movie and television creators greater freedom than has ever been known in China, as another way to support the development of the creative sector (Samuels 2012; also see Dimitrov 2009).

Concurrent with their growing awareness of the importance of industrialized culture, governments in East Asia are becoming more active in clamping down on piracy. They have come to see the economic damage piracy causes and the need to cooperate on improving enforcement of copyright laws. The Japanese government has been emphasizing the importance of enforcing intellectual property rights by repeatedly raising the issue in free trade agreement talks with Singapore and Thailand and by repeatedly warning against piracy of Japanese products in Asia (JETRO 2001, 2002). Japan is also undertaking a major overhaul of its related legislation to better protect the intellectual property rights of Japanese media companies in this age of globalization (Kozuka 2008). Multinational and regional music and television companies have also been active in fighting piracy of their products, by establishing local and regional federations to promote awareness and enforcement of antipiracy laws, and by lobbying hard to convince governments to put sharper teeth on their antipiracy measures.[8]

Implications for the Regionalization of East Asia

The central argument of this study is that the activities of cultural industries underpin regionalization in East Asia. As explained in chapter 2, regionalization through popular culture is essentially a bottom-up, market-led process that induces collaborations and cooperation in the creation of markets for cultural commodities and encourages international coproduction of popular culture products. It includes a variety of capitalistically motivated activities undertaken by nonstate actors who commodify, manufacture, and commercialize culture in three or more geographically proximate and interdependent economies. This kind of regionalization is not the result of actions taken by governments or their representatives. Rather, it evolves spontaneously in the course of normal business and cultural activities, out of the reach of state guidance and at times in spite of it.

Several developments described in this study have important consequences for the regionalization of East Asia. The first is the emergence of regional markets for popular culture products offered to individuals. Throughout urban centers in East Asia, Japanese cultural commodities are routinely circulated and widely available, adding to the variety of other Japanese consumer products present in the market, such as electric appliances, cars, clothing, and cosmetics, and integrated within a confluence of other imported and local popular cultures. Curiously, the spread of Japan's popular culture in the 1990s did not appear to have been hampered by history, national boundaries, or geo-politics; it has managed to reach audiences even in places where it is forbidden or where there is animosity toward the producing country. Since the spread of Japanese cultural products is driven by the will of consumers, there is little a government can do to control it in a market economy. While the reach of Japanese culture into new markets is rarely impeded by national borders, there is nevertheless a visible boundary that limits its spread: Japanese popular culture products ultimately reach only those who can afford them, i.e., mostly middle-class youngsters who live in urban areas. In rural areas, there is far less consumer interest, or at least far less actual trade.

Of course, popular culture can also be used to incite conflict and hate. For example, the controversy over the scale and historical meaning of the Nanjing Massacre has become a common theme of Chinese television programs, documentaries, and movies. More than thirty television series on Japan's wartime aggression were produced in China to commemorate the sixtieth anniversary of the end of World War II (Lo 2012, 177). On the Japanese side, there are some manga series, such as *Intro to China* (*Manga Chūgokunyūmon*) and *Hating the Korean Wave* (*Manga Kenkanryū*), that portray Chinese and Koreans as enemies of the state and urge readers to refute "masochist" versions of Japan's modern history. But these are the exceptions. While tension between regionalism and national identity remains high at the state-to-state level in East Asia, popular culture overwhelmingly manages to mediate this tension. As I showed in chapter 4 regarding the acceptance of Japanese popular culture in South Korea, China, and Southeast Asia, consumers remain highly politicized regarding issues related to wartime history and state-to-state politics, and occasionally they even participate in skirmishes over historical accounts. Nevertheless, when it comes to popular culture, they seem willing to circumvent government censors, reject official interpretations provided by the state, and set aside resentments and suspicions.

An unintended consequence of the creation of regional markets is the regionalization of taste that has resulted from different people in different places experiencing the same cultural products. Regionalizing Japanese popular culture entails more than just selling anime, manga, and fashion magazines in neighboring countries; it also involves harmonizing peoples' cultural sensibilities and creating shared experiences. The creation of regional markets enables different people in different places to access the same set of products, to share similar cultural preferences, and consequently to appropriate similar lifestyles, practices, thoughts, etc. The intention of the industries that deliver culture is to generate profit, not to spread cultural messages throughout East Asia. Nevertheless, cultural industries do end up serving as cultural emissaries. They build platforms upon which people from different urban communities can share the same cultural experience. This may well help people in East Asia to start seeing themselves as inhabiting a single region and to develop a common language made of shared sounds, images, and texts. People in different countries, who speak different languages, can grow up watching the same cartoon shows on television as children and dancing to the same music as teenagers. If, for example, Indonesian, Taiwanese, and Thai people listen to the same music and play the same video games at the same time, they will have a much better chance of understanding each other and relating to each other than they would if they did not share these products and experiences.

This same idea applies at the regional level: the concentrated dissemination of cultural commodities and images in East Asia may cause people to see themselves as members of a wider region defined by appreciation of the same popular culture. After all, regions are not defined only by governmental policies, economic relations, history, or geopolitics. As argued by Berry, Liscutin, and Mackintosh (2009, 22), the East Asian region is being constructed discursively and normatively as a cultural entity. Not only do popular culture productions arise from local narratives and tastes, but they also have the potential to change the way people perceive those local narratives and tastes, whether the people consider them to be their own or not. Cultural industry operations have brought different people in different locations in East Asia under the umbrella of the region, suggesting that the various places in the region share a common temporality.

The second way that the internationalization of popular culture is contributing to region building in East Asia is through the impact that the emergence of regional markets for Japanese popular culture products has on businesses and other institutions involved in the production and transfer of culture products. The emergence of regionwide markets encourages creators and promoters to seek opportunities outside their immediate domestic market and prompts adjustments in corporate strategies. For example, companies may need to find new ways to access transnational audiences and to receive feedback from multiple local markets. As we saw in chapters 4 and 5, Japanese companies have teamed up for this purpose with indigenous promoters and organizations, and the resulting regionwide collaborations and alliances are having far-reaching effects on the East Asian cultural market.

The expansion of Japanese cultural industries within East Asia has also influenced the development of indigenous industries. The Japanese cultural industries have introduced new systems of commodifying, producing, commercializing, and managing culture and have served as models of how to implement those systems. They disseminate new forms of industrial organization and propagate new ideas about how to treat and commodify "culture." In this way, Japanese cultural industries' expansion gives rise to regionwide culture production based on formats adopted from the Japanese. People who work in local cultural industries continue to recognize these formats as Japanese even after they have been used to produce native content. In a certain sense, however, they have become the common property of cultural producers throughout the region and are no longer only Japanese.

The third way Japanese cultural industries have impacted regionalization is through their influence on cultural and diplomatic policies formulated by East Asian governments and on the way the governments view the role of popular culture in the political and economic life of the state. As described earlier, the dissemination of popular culture and consumer practices was going on in cities before governments started to take notice and attempted to capitalize on these flows. But now that some private companies have already been so successful, governments in East Asia have become keenly aware of the potential for realizing economic gain through the commodification of culture, and they have begun to search out new ways to intervene. In recent years the Japanese, South Korean, Thai, Chinese, and Hong Kong governments have each taken active steps to support the development of their own country's export-oriented cultural industries.

The transnational activities of cultural industries have the potential to effect major, regionwide changes in governmental priorities and allocation of resources. As we saw in chapter 3 regarding Japan, seeing the potential of cultural exports woke up the government to the desirability of allocating resources as part of a new cultural policy. The rising scale and importance of cultural production may bring some governments to question whether their country needs a television industry, a music industry, or an animation industry. Do they need these industries any more than they need automotive or computer industries? And what is the proper balance between economic and political profit or loss that should result from cultural investment? In this context, for countries that seek to diversify their domestic markets and develop new economic sectors, cultural industries represent one possible avenue for market transformation. For Japan, as well as for South Korea, Thailand, and China, the East Asian region is a convenient and potentially profitable destination for cultural exports.

In this study I have endeavored to show that region making can be an unintended result of the dissemination of popular culture, brought about by industries and agents that commodify, produce, and commercialize cultural commodities across the borders of nation-states. In the long term, the developments described in this book regarding Japanese cultural industries may come to exemplify the difference between *regionalization* and *regionalism*. This is because in addition to facilitating cooperation among individuals and companies involved in the commodification and commercialization of culture, cultural industries also disseminate ideas, sensibilities, and images as a side effect of their commercial activities.

Given the number of hours that many people in East Asia spend every day in front of their television screens, going to movies, listening to music, or playing video games, as well as the large amounts of money they are willing to spend on these types of cultural consumption, is it unreasonable to suppose that these activities have a significant impact on their lives and perceptions? Isn't it likely that they introduce new images and options and create new social and symbolic references? If we can think of economy or security as factors that define a region, why shouldn't we be able to think of popular culture in the same way?

NOTES

////////////

Introduction

1 In this study, *East Asia* refers to both Northeast and Southeast Asia. As will be made evident in chapters 2 and 4, it is impossible to separate Southeast Asia from the broader East Asian region as flows of trade, finance, migration, and culture connect the entire East Asian region. More importantly for the purposes of this book, circulation of Japanese popular culture is particularly widespread around large cities in East Asia.

2 Figures for a younger age group would likely be significantly higher, as teenagers appear to be the most enthusiastic consumers of Japan's popular culture (*Yomiuri Shinbun*, September 10, 2006).

3 Estimates were given to the author between April 2004 and May 2005 by fourteen promotional managers of Japanese music companies with branches in Hong Kong, Singapore, Thailand, and South Korea. The figures include estimates of pirated music sold in these cities. In reaction to the Japanese occupation of the Korean Peninsula before and during World War II, the sale of Japanese cultural products was banned in South Korea for more than fifty years.

4 The survey was conducted among fifteen- to twenty-four-year-olds, offering multiple choice answers. See Hakuhōdō News 2003.

5 In this study, "commodification" is understood as a series of active relationships dedicated to the transformation and commercialization of artistic or cultural materials into mass-marketed cultural commodities.

6 The interviews were non-schedule-structured and focused on the subjective experiences of the interviewees regarding particular situations or phenomena that had been previously studied and analyzed to a certain extent by the interviewer. The questions were designed to advance the research hypothesis. Although interview meetings were structured, interviewees were given opportunities to define and express their opinions regarding the subjects addressed by the interview.

Chapter 1: The Political Economy of Popular Culture

1 For example, Caldwell 2008; Baker and Hesmondhalgh 2010; and Mayer, Banks, and Caldwell 2009.

2 There are a few good studies that have attempted to integrate the two divided research traditions based on materialism. These include Babe 2009 and Peck 2006.

3 The term "culturalized" is from du Gay and Pryke 2002.

4 One of the most comprehensive studies of cultural industries is Hesmondhalgh 2002. Although it is entirely focused on the Euro-American experience, it meticulously follows the various cycles of cultural production and views them in the context of the internationalization of cultural industries. Other recommended works that touch on the subject of cultural industries are Caldwell 2009; an edited volume by John Hartley (2005) and one by Power and Scott (2004).

Chapter 2: Popular Culture and the East Asian Region

1 This chapter contains extracts from "Cultural Commodities and Region-alization in East Asia," which appeared in *Contemporary Southeast Asia* 27, no. 3 (December 2005): 499–513, published by the Institute of Southeast Asian Studies.

2 Such as the efforts of imperialist Japan to promote "Asian solidarity" under the Japanese-led "Great East Asia Co-Prosperity Sphere," or since the formation of the Association of Southeast Asian Nations (ASEAN) in August 1967.

3 For introductory literature about regional formation theories, see Fawcett and Hurrell 1995; Hass 1973; Kahler 1995; and Mansfield and Milner 1997. For realist theories, see Betts 1994; Crone 1993; Gibb and Michalak 1994; and Grieco 1997. For institutional theories, see Haggard 1997; Milner 1998; and Solingen 1996. For identity-related aspects of regional formation see Acharya 2000; Mayall 1995; Nabers 2003; and Wendt 1994.

4 This study looked at sixteen economies in East Asia: Brunei, Cambodia, the People's Republic of China, Hong Kong, India, Indonesia, Japan, South Korea, Laos, Malaysia, Myanmar, the Philippines, Singapore, Taiwan, Thailand, and Vietnam.

5 It should be noted that essentializing differences between coast and hinterland in China may be tricky since a few "inner" cities, such as Chengdu or Xi'an, can adopt cultural and cosmopolitan appearances similar to Shanghai. Also, the fact that around two hundred million rural residents commute to work in cities may in the long term ameliorate the rural-urban gap, especially in cultural terms. I thank Yuri Pines for raising this point.

6 Here I adopt Simon Frith's definition of "consumerism" as a symbolic practice whereby social identity is articulated and the organization of taste is shaped by the aesthetic choices people make. See Frith 1997, 116–117.

7 The study looked at Brunei, Cambodia, the People's Republic of China, Hong Kong, India, Indonesia, Japan, South Korea, Laos, Malaysia, Myanmar, the Philippines, Singapore, Taiwan, Thailand, and Vietnam.

8 "North Korea Eases Open the Door to Harry Potter, Britney Spears—If Only for a Select Few," *Mainichi Daily News,* November 3, 2005.

9 Regarding the global spread of America's popular culture, one might see Hamano 2003; International Federation of Phonogram and Videogram Producers 2000–2002. For American movies, see U.S. Department of Commerce (available at http://www.statuse.gov); *Hakuhodō News* (available at http://www.hakuhodo.co.jp).

10 Varangkana Trivittayakhum, general manager, EMI Thailand, interview with the author, Bangkok, February 7, 2005.

11 The "Korean Wave," also known as "Hallyu," refers to the rapid spread of the popularity of South Korean movies, television dramas, pop music, fashion, accessories, and food culture throughout East Asian markets since the end of the 1990s. See Shin 2007.

12 Figures from Korea Broadcasting Institute, April 2005; BBC Asia, December 22, 2004.

13 Bollywood, it should be noted, does not refer only to the Mumbai-based movie industry; it also includes a broader set of cultural phenomena including music, dance, fashion, and other cultural products and activities. See Gopal and Moorti 2010, 4.

14 General manager, JVC Hong Kong, interview with the author, Hong Kong, April 15, 2004.

15 Keiven Yim, senior director, Sony Music Entertainment, interview with the author, Hong Kong, June 21, 2005, and Tanaka Akira, interview with the author, Tokyo, September 18, 2010.

16 Author interviews with personnel from television companies in Hong Kong, Singapore, and Thailand during April–July 2004 and January–February 2005.

17 For global and regional views of piracy levels, see International Federation of Phonogram and Videogram Producers, *Music Piracy Report* 2002, available at http://www.ifpi.org.

18 Completed in March 2008, the study entailed 5,741 online interviews with urban individuals aged fifteen to thirty-four in mainland China, Hong Kong, India, Indonesia, South Korea, Malaysia, the Philippines, Singapore, Taiwan, Thailand, Australia, and Vietnam. See The Asia Pacific Music Forum 2008.

19 Salamander Davoudi, "Pirates on Parade," *Financial Times,* July 22, 2009, 7.

20 Author interviews with IFPI officers in Hong Kong, Singapore, and Thailand, April–July 2004 and January–February 2005.

Chapter 3: Japan's Popular Culture Powerhouse

1   In the 1970s and 1980s, Japanese animation and cartoons were known in the United States as "Japanese animation" or "Japanimation," but since the late 1980s these terms have been replaced by the word "anime."

2   Formerly called the Ministry of International Trade and Industry (MITI), for many years it was considered to be the most important and powerful government ministry because of its close ties to major Japanese corporations and its decisive influence over the country's international trade policies. The classic study on MITI is by Johnson 1982.

3   In Japanese, the word manga 「漫画」 stands for both comics in general and Japanese comics in particular.

4   "What Lies Behind the Global Success of Manga?" *Japan Spotlight,* May / June 2005, 15.

5   "Soft power" is a term coined by Joseph Nye to describe nontraditional and increasingly important means, such as a country's culture or ideals, that can be employed to influence another country's desires. See Nye 2004a. For recent works on soft power and its critics see Watanabe and McConnell 2008; Otmazgin and Ben-Ari 2012, 15–17.

6   As of 2005, these were Toshiba-EMI, Sony-BMG, Universal, Avex Trax, EPIC, Victor Entertainment, Warner Music, and Pony Canyon.

7   For example, in recent years Tokyo-based Japan Digital Contents Trust, Inc., has been campaigning to attract investors to fund specific entertainment ventures. In 2003, the company raised enough capital to finance the careers of five emerging female entertainers, offering 10 to 12 percent of sales as profit for investors. "Investors Sought for Wannabe Stars," *The Daily Yomiuri,* November 27, 2003, 2.

8   A survey by *Nikkei Shinbun,* January 24, 2005, 25.

9   *Business Week Online,* June 10, 2002.

10   Herman, Leonard, Jer Horwitz, and Skyler Miller, "The History of Video Games." Gamespot. CBS, 2002, October 2, 2010.

11   Some trace the origin of manga even earlier to caricatures ("*fūshi*" in Japanese) and picture scrolls found in temples in Japan as far back as the seventh century. For a historical account of the evolution of manga in Japan, see Itō 2008.

12   On the beginning of anime in Japan see http://litten.de/fulltext/nipper.pdf, accessed January 4, 2013.

13   *Japan Spotlight,* Data for Content Business, May/June 2005, 26.

14   *Nikkei Shinbun,* January 13, 2004, 29.

15   "Trendy dramas" refer to TV dramas produced since the late 1980s, which target young audiences and feature popular actors. They are always formatted as twelve-week series and address contemporary issues of particular

interest to young people, such as the lifestyles of career women, love affairs, and the modern urban experience.

16 *Shūkan Toyo Keizai* [Weekly Toyo Keizai], August 30, 2003.

17 This data does not include merchandising for the highly popular *Hello Kitty*, *Domo-kun*, *Power Rangers*, and *Transformers*.

18 "What Lies Behind the Global Success of Manga?" *Japan Spotlight,* May/June 2005, 15.

19 *Time. Com Asia,* March 5, 1999, 1.

20 See Final Fantasy online, available at http://www.ffonline.com. Details about sale of Japanese video games are available at http://www.mcvuk.com/features/403/JAPANESE-2008-MARKET-REPORT.

21 These estimates do not include overseas production of Japanese music under license from Japanese companies nor pirated versions of Japanese music. Thus the circulation of Japanese music outside Japan, as we will see in chapter 4, must be higher than the figures presented.

22 This part contains extracts from Otmazgin 2011a.

23 "Greater East Asia Co-Prosperity Sphere" (*Dai tōa kyōeiken*) was a plan promoted by leaders of the Empire of Japan around 1940 to form an autonomous region under Japanese leadership. Although the exact limits of "Greater East Asia" were never clearly defined, the term usually included Japan and areas where it had taken control, including Korea, Manchukuo, and other parts of China, and parts of Southeast Asia. Sometimes the term designated a wider area that included India, Australia, Hawai'i, New Zealand, Outer Mongolia, and Eastern Siberia, which were not "yet" under Japanese control. See documents of Yabe Tei, Matsuoka Yosuke, and Tōjō Hideki, in Lebra 1975. For a broader perspective of Japan-centered regionalism during the 1930s, see Mitani 2004.

24 Matsushita Tadahiro, interview with the author, October 6, 2011, ION Orchard Building, Singapore.

25 "Japanese Win Cosplay World Title," *Japan Times* online, August 3, 2009, available at http://search.japantimes.co.jp/cgi-bin/nn20090803a5.htm.

26 http://www.animenewsnetwork.com/news/2007-06-30/hong-kong-artist-wins-japan's-1st-manga-nobel-prize.

27 Asahi.com, April 10, 2005; *Yomiuri Shinbun,* November 11, 2005.

28 Asō Tarō, interview in *Nikkei Business Online,* December 6, 2007. Available at mhtml:https://mail-attachment.googleusercontent.com/attachment?ui=2&ik=303ae7b2ce&view=att&th=126fcca7fa6ab9bb&attid=0.1&disp=safe&realattid=f_g6182vr30&zfe=windows-1252:en&zw&saduie=AG9B_P-f6rTjVgAg1IR7pIyv_aMO&sadet=1328439721265&sads=zr40Xw41HhDSHh_KgmB31C4wqwk&sadssc=1. I thank Nadav Rotchild for bringing this interview to my attention.

29 *Asahi Shinbun,* January 1, 2006, 1–3.

Chapter 4: The Creation of a Regional Market

1   A viewpoint that positions Japan's leadership role in Asia within a set
of various multilateral and global arrangements, and complementary to
American leadership, is found in Berger, Mochizuki and Tsuchiyama 2007;
Cowhey 1993; Inoguchi 2002; and Katzenstein and Shiraishi 2006. A perspective that depicts Japan's leadership in Asia in a more independent and
ambitious light is Blechinger and Legewie 2000; Hatch and Yamamura 1996;
and Pyle 2007.

2   The polls sampled 800 to 895 adults in each country; they are available at
Japan's Ministry of Foreign Affairs 2002. Available at http://www.mofa
.go.jp/mofaj/area/asean/yoron.html. For a summary of the 2008 survey
results see http://www.mofa.go.jp/region/asia-paci/asean/survey/
summary0803.pdf.

3   For example, Sony acquired CBS records in 1988 and Columbia Pictures in
the following year; Matsushita purchased MCA-Universal in 1990 and in
the same year invested US$600 million in Walt Disney Corporation.

4   For comparison, in the American market, the concentration of cultural
industry corporations is enormous. In music, the five largest music groups
account for more than 87 percent of the U.S. market. In 1997, the six largest
movie studios had more than 90 percent of the U.S. box office revenues and
produced 132 of the 148 movies that received wide distribution. None of
this Western domination existed in East Asia in the beginning of the 1990s.
See McChesney 1999, 17–18; Shita 1995, 297.

5   Keyman Luk, Forward Music, interview with the author, Wanchai, Hong
Kong, June 14, 2004.

6   Tatiana Kampempool, interview with the author, Bangkok, January 17,
2005.

7   "Fuji TV no Rendora Chugoku no Hōsōkyaku Kōnyu" [Chinese
Broadcastings Purchase Dramas from Fuji TV], *Yomiuri Yukan,* June 12, 2005,
14. Most of the television broadcasting in China is still analog, while in
Japan most filming and broadcasting has already moved to high definition.

8   *Friends* tells a romantic story between Jihoon (Korean idol Won Bin), son to
a conservative Korean family, and Tomoko (Kyoko Fukada), a Japanese girl,
who together overcome all differences and difficulties. *Sonagi, an Afternoon
Showers* is a two-part romantic thriller, starring Ryoko Yonekura and
Ji Jinhee. *Star's Echo,* starring Noriko Nakagoshi and Cho Hyun-Jae, features transnational love relations between a Japanese heroine and a Korean
hero. For a contextual analysis of these dramas, see Lee 2004.

9   Interview with the author, Wanchai, Hong Kong, June 22, 2010.

10 See report in Industrial Reports 2004.

11 The information provided here is based on export figures obtained from Japan's Ministry of Finance. This information addresses nine major markets for Japanese music: Hong Kong, Taiwan, South Korea, Singapore, Thailand, China, Malaysia, Indonesia, and the Philippines. The information in this study does not include the export of Japanese music to other markets in East Asia, such as Vietnam, Myanmar, Cambodia, Macao, and Brunei, because exports to those markets are relatively small. It should be noted, however, that such exports do exist and that Japanese popular culture has a presence in those markets as well.

12 The bureau's definition of "Japanese music products" includes all kinds of music and any hardware medium that contains musical sound that is produced or manufactured by a Japanese company in Japan. Therefore, Japanese music exported products referred to in this research mainly consists of CDs, cassettes, and records, which, under Japan's Ministry of Finance's Customs and Tariff Bureau, are categorized as hardware that contains sounds, with or without images.

13 Keyman Luk, Forward Music assistant general manager, interview with the author, Wanchai, Hong Kong, June 14, 2004; Billy Leung, EMI promotions manager, interview with the author, Tsimshatsui, Hong Kong, June 15, 2004; Candic Chan, JVC promotions manager, interview with the author, Tsimshatsui, Hong Kong, June 18, 2004; Jennifer Lau, Universal Music marketing manager, interview with the author, Tsimshatsui, Hong Kong, June 18, 2004; Kieven Yim, Sony-BMG senior director, interview with the author, Admiralty, Hong Kong, June 21, 2005.

14 Estimates given to the author by the shop manager, Bangkok, January 21, 2005. It should be noted, however, that the building is located in an area where many long-term Japanese residents live, so they might be responsible for a part of the Japanese music consumption.

15 Estimates given to the author, Bangkok, January–February 2005.

16 Compounded estimates given to the author in interviews with the personnel of five record companies and managers of twelve music shops in Seoul, March–April 2005. Utada Hikaru's first album *Automatic* is estimated to have sold more than 100,000 pirated versions, so when the market opened it (legally) sold only about 17,000 copies.

17 These figures are the author's estimates compounded from export statistics, shop surveys, and information given by music companies' personnel and shop managers in these cities.

18 Keyman Luk, Forward Music general manager, interview with the author, Wanchai, Hong Kong, June 22, 2010.

19 Anonymous by request, interview with the author, Seoul, April 12, 2005; Lee Jon, interview with the author, Seoul, May 2006.

20 General manager of JVC Hong Kong, interview with the author, Tsimshatsui, Hong Kong, April 15, 2004; HMV marketing managers, interviews with the author, Hong Kong, April 17, 2004.

21 Senior director, Sony Music Entertainment, interview with the author, Hong Kong, June 21, 2005.

22 Tanaka Akira, interview with the author, Tokyo, September 18, 2010.

23 Keyman Luk, Forward Music general manager, interview with the author, Wanchai, Hong Kong, June 22, 2010.

24 Keiven Yim, interview with the author, Admiralty, Hong Kong, June 21, 2005.

25 I use "piracy" in the sense of what Laikwan Pang (2006, 4) called "direct product copying," referring to the production, circulation, and reception of creative works as fixed products. This is different from "idea copying," which refers to the copying of themes, styles, ideas, characters, plots, etc.

26 Keyman Luk, interview with the author, Hong Kong, June 22, 2010.

27 Because of the secretive and irregular nature of the pirating business, it is difficult to provide comprehensive information regarding the number and nature of the companies involved in pirating and the capacity of their production. Nevertheless, the figures presented here clearly indicate that pirated operations in East Asia are still huge. For a world and regional view of piracy levels, see International Federation of Phonogram and Videogram Producers 2002. Available at http://www.ifpi.org. Accessed October 2004. A more recent report is available at http://www.ifpi.org/content/library/piracy-report2006.pdf.

28 Ricky Fung, chief executive of IFPI Hong Kong, interview with the author, Wanchai, Hong Kong, June 4, 2004; Piset Chiyasak, managing director of Phonorights Thailand, interview with the author, Huaykwang, Bangkok, January 21, 2005.

29 This information is based on my fieldwork in Hong Kong during April to June 2004. As part of this fieldwork, I conducted a sample survey among sixty-three shops selling music, movies, television programs, and anime series. In this survey, I examined the number of titles of Japanese popular culture products offered in each store in relation to American products and locally manufactured products. During the survey, the shops' managers or workers were also asked about the popularity of Japanese contemporary culture, and about the general preferences of consumers who visit the shops.

30 Some forms of censorship started even earlier, as part of anticolonial measures. In the 1950s, the Kuomintang government in Taiwan prohibited speaking Japanese on television and only a few Japanese movies were allowed in, subject to annual quotas (Lee M. 2004, 131).

31 In Malaysia, interestingly, any software that deals with science and technology can be legally copied but any entertainment CDs / VCDs cannot. The rationale of the government is that if you copy something to learn from it, it should then be legal; if you copy something for fun, you should pay for it.

32 *The Straits Times* (Singapore), July 1, 2004, A1.

33 Japanese jazz and instrumental music was allowed into South Korea, as it does not contain Japanese lyrics. According to the author's calculations, based on data obtained from Japan's Ministry of Finance Customs and Tariff Bureau, music exports from Japan to South Korea between the years 1988 and 2002 accounted for at least ¥29 billion.

34 Other famous Japanese-related web pages in South Korea include www .ddnnzi.com, www.ruliweb.com, and www.dcinside.com.

35 Matsuo Junichi, intellectual property officer in Japan's Embassy to Thailand, interview with the author, Bangkok, January 27, 2005.

36 For example, Bandai Visual's determination to secure lost overseas revenues is expected to increase its profit from overseas sales from ¥700 million to 2 billion in three years. See Norris 2009, 259.

37 "North Korea Eases Open the Door to Harry Potter, Britney Spears—If Only for Select Few," *Mainichi Daily News*, November 3, 2005.

38 Yasuda Tetsuhiko, interview with the author, Orchard Hotel, Singapore, July 24, 2009.

Chapter 5: Japan's Regional Model

1 Tanaka Akira, interview with the author, Tokyo, September 17, 2010.

2 See http:/ / www.jkt48.com / index-jp.html#jkt48.

3 "Empress of Pop," *Time Asia*, March 25, 2002, 48–55.

4 See http:/ / asianbeat-yamaha.typepad.com/.

5 Panadda Thanasatit, interview with the author, Bangkok, February 8, 2005.

6 In 2005, the Thai government was even planning to send a formal study delegation to Japan. Matsumoto Keisuke, secretary general of the Japanese Chamber of Commerce in Bangkok, interview with the author, January 25, 2005.

7 Author interviews with six television personnel from five major television stations, Bangkok, January–February 2005.

8 Ōta Tōru is a producer for Fuji TV and has been responsible for the debut of many popular Japanese "trendy" dramas such as *Tokyo Love Story, The 101st Proposal*, and *All under One Roof.*

9 Benjamin Ng (2004) has recognized no fewer than twenty-four Hong Kong dramas broadcast between 1994 and 2004 that closely resemble Japanese dramas in terms of characters, themes, story lines, and length. They include

Broken Hearted Man (TVB), *Instinct* (TVB), *Detective Investigation Files* (TVB), *Food For Love* (TVB), *Our Far Elder Brother* (ATV), *A Recipe for the Heart* (TVB), *My Big Brother* (ATV), *Till When Do Us Part* (TVB), *The Disappearance* (TVB), *A Place of One's Own* (TVB), *A Kindred Spirit* (TVB), *Happy Ever After* (TVB), *A Matter of Business* (TVB), *Face to Face* (TVB), *Burning Flame* (TVB), *Return of the Cuckoo* (TVB), *A Taste of Love* (TVB), *Invisible Journey* (TVB), *In the Realm of Success* (TVB), *Healing Hands* (TVB), *File of Justice 3* (TVB), *Survivor's Law* (TVB), *Dreams of Color* (TVB).

10   *Friends* tells a romantic story of Jihoon (Korean idol Won Bin), a son to a conservative Korean family, and Tomoko (Kyoko Fukada), a Japanese girl, who together overcome all their differences and difficulties. *Sonagi, an Afternoon Showers* is a two-part romantic thriller starring Ryoko Yonekura and Ji Jinhee. *Star's Echo* features Noriko Nakagoshi and Cho Hyun-Jae and portrays the transnational love relations between a Japanese heroine and a Korean hero. For a contextual analysis of these dramas see Lee D.-H. 2004.

11   Tanaka Akira, interview with the author, Tokyo, September 17, 2010.

12   "Shinkan to Hannichi Sure Chigau Ishki" [Different Perceptions of Pro-Korea and Anti-Japan], *Yomiuri Shinbun,* June 10, 2005, 27. On the popularity of the South Korean television drama *Winter Sonata* and its star, Bae Yong Joon, *Newsweek,* May 3, 2004; "Korean star shows fans what they're missing," *Asahi Shinbun,* September 9, 2005, 30.

13   May Masangkay, "K-pop's girl idols striking gold in Japan," *The Japan Times Online,* January 21, 2011.

14   The term "Korean Wave" is a direct translation of the word *hallyu* (韓流) and first appeared in a sampler CD package offered by the Korean Ministry of Culture and Tourism for the international promotion of Korean popular music. See Shin 2010, 55.

15   A focus study by Kim Sowon (2011), comparing *shōjo* manga (manga marketed for female audience) in Japan and its Korean version, called *sunjeong manhwa,* has shown that the two share the same visual characteristics and qualities and differ only linguistically. Similar developments are also taking place in Taiwan and Hong Kong, where local artists may be using elements from Japanese manga as a platform for expressing their creative ideas and proposing alternatives to already available Japanese-made manga and animation (Hu 2010, 149).

16   Anonymous by request, interview with the author, Seoul, May 11, 2005.

17   Hong Jung-Ui, interview with the author, Seoul, May 16, 2006.

18   Anonymous by request, interview with the author, Seoul, April 12, 2005.

19   Music industry personnel, interviews with the author, Hong Kong (April–June 2004), Singapore (June 2004), and Bangkok (February 2005).

20 Keyman Luk, interview with the author, Forward Music, Hong Kong, June 14, 2004.

21 Liu Xia, interview with the author, Japan Creative Center, Singapore, October 11, 2011.

22 Tatiana Kampempool, interview with the author, Bangkok, January 17, 2005.

23 Josephine Lee, interview with the author, Hong Kong, June 12, 2004.

24 Kieven Yim, interview with the author, Hong Kong, June 21, 2005.

25 Hong Junh-Ui, global marketing manager, interview with the author, Seoul, May 16, 2006. The official himself has a technological background. Before assuming his job in the agency he worked as a researcher at a leading Korean electronics company and at Korea's second biggest Internet provider.

26 Other studies, beyond the context of East Asia, also emphasize the importance of the human aspect and not only the access to technology or capital. In his studies of alternative media productions (print, video, Internet), Chris Atton (2003) shows that grassroots alternative media projects that flourish tend to be the ones with a small, committed collective that is responsible for the day-to-day running and planning of the publication. In the same volume, Simon Cottle (2003) also advocates looking at workplace practices in the media industries to understand how producers successfully manage and mediate a complex of forces (economic, political, regulatory, technological, professional, cultural, and normative).

27 Lee Jon, interview with the author, Seoul, May 2006.

28 Manager at Channel 9, anonymous by request, interview with the author, Bangkok, January 17, 2005.

29 Varangkana Trivittayakhum, general manager, EMI Thailand, interview with the author, Bangkok, February 7, 2005.

30 Savasdi Navavorge, interview with the author, Bangkok, January 17, 2005.

31 Anonymous by request, interview with the author, Hong Kong, June 21, 2005.

32 In 2003, nearly fifty of the five hundred biggest global companies are Japanese (nearly half are American), as well as seven of the top one hundred global brands, while sixty-two are American. See Coggan 2003, 72–78.

33 Mitsukoshi has fourteen department stores in East Asia, seven in Europe, and two in the United States. Takashimaya has two branches in East Asia, one in Europe, and one in the United States. ISETAN has twelve branches in East Asia, two representatives in Europe, and one representative in the United States, http://www.takashimaya.co.jp; http://www.mitsukoshi.co.jp; http://www.isetan.co.jp.

34 *Foreign TV Networks Hungry for Japan Formats*, Asahi.com, December 2, 2008.

Chapter 6: Conclusion

1 Yamada Yasuhide, vice president of JETRO Bangkok, interview with the author, Bangkok, January 27, 2005.

2 As I discussed in chapter 3, although the effectiveness of its policies is subject to debate, it is generally agreed that the Japanese government was at least *involved* in actively looking for ways to encourage industrial exports. For a view that emphasizes the active role of the Japanese government, see Hatch and Yamamura 1996; Johnson 1986; and Tsuru 1993. A perspective that downplays the government's role in providing industrial guidance can be found in Beason and Weinstein 1996; Calder 1993; Dore 1986; and Uriu 1996.

3 One group of rocky islets is called Takeshima by Japan and Dokdo by South Korea; another group is called Senkaku by Japan and Diaoyu by China and Taiwan.

4 Matsushita Tadahiro, interview with the author, ION Orchard Building, Singapore, October 6, 2011.

5 Matsumoto Keisuke, secretary general of the Japanese Chamber of Commerce in Bangkok, interview, January 25, 2005.

6 Panadda Thanasatit, president of Kantana, and Wasin Buranahet, assistant managing director, interview, Bangkok, February 8, 2005.

7 Yamada Yasuhide, vice president of JETRO Bangkok, interview, Bangkok, January 27, 2005.

8 Ricky Fung, IFPI chief executive officer, interview, Hong Kong, June 4, 2004.

REFERENCES

////////////////////////////

Acharya, Amitav. 2000. *The Quest for Identity: International Relations of Southeast Asia.* Singapore: Oxford University Press.

———. 2010. "Asia Is Not One." *The Journal of Asian Studies* 69, no. 4:1001–1013.

Acharya, Amitav, and Ananda Rajah. 1999. "Introduction: Reconceptualizing Southeast Asia." *Southeast Asian Journal of Social Science* 27, no. 1:1–6.

Adorno, Theodor W. 1991. *Cultural Industry: Selected Essays on Mass Culture.* London: Routledge.

Adorno, Theodor W., and Max Horkheimer. 1973. *Dialectic of Enlightenment.* London: Lane.

Aggarwal, Vigod K. 1993. "Building International Institutions in Asia-Pacific." *Asian Survey* 33, no. 11:1029–1042.

Aksoy, Asu, and Kevin Robins. 1992. "Hollywood in the 21st Century: Global Competition for Critical Mass in Image Markets." *Cambridge Journal of Economics* 16, no. 1:1–22.

Alder, Emanuel, and Patricia Greve. 2009. "When Security Community Meets Balance-of-Power." *Review of International Studies* 35 (February). 1:59–84.

Allen, Matthew, and Rumi Sakamoto, eds. 2006. *Popular Culture, Globalization and Japan.* New York: Routledge.

Allison, Anne. 2006. *Millennial Monsters: Japanese Toys and the Global Imagination.* Berkeley and Los Angeles: University of California Press.

Aoki, Tamotsu. 2004. "Toward Multilayered Strength in the 'Cool' Culture." *Gaikō Fōramu* 4, no. 2:8–16.

Aoyagi, Hiroshi. 2000. "Pop Idols and the Asian Identity." In *Japan Pop! Inside the World of Japanese Popular Culture,* ed. Craig J. Timothy, 309–326. New York: M. E. Sharpe.

Appadurai, Arjun. 2000. "Grassroots Globalization and the Research Imagination." *Public Culture* 12, no. 1:1–19.

Asahi, Motofumi. 1989. *Nihon Gaikō: Hansei to Tenkai* [Japanese Diplomacy: Review and Change]. Japan: Iwananmishinsho.

Asai Sumiko. 2008a. "Factors Affecting Hits in Japanese Popular Music." *Journal of Media Economics* 21:97–113.

———. 2008b. "Firm Organization and Marketing Strategy in the Japanese Music Industry." *Popular Music* 27, no. 3:473–485.

Asia Pacific Music Forum. 2008. *Music Matters.* Hong Kong, June 3–5.

Asian Development Bank. 2008. *Emerging Asian Regionalism.* Manila: Asian
    Development Bank.

Association of Japanese Animations. 2005. Available at http://www.aja.gr.jp/.
    Accessed December 16, 2005.

Atton, Chris. 2003. "Organization and Production in Alternative Media." In
    Media Organization and Production, ed. Simon Cottle, 41–55. London: Sage
    Publications.

Azuma, Hiroki. 2009. *Otaku: Japan's Database Animals.* Translated by Jonathan
    E. Abel and Shion Kōno [English ed.]. Minneapolis: University of Minnesota
    Press.

Ba, Alice D. 2009. *(Re)Negotiating East and Southeast Asia: Region, Regionalism, and
    the Association of Southeast Asian Nations.* Studies in Asian Security. Stanford,
    Calif.: Stanford University Press.

Babe, Robert E. 2009. *Cultural Studies and Political Economy: Toward a New
    Integration.* Lanham, Md.: Lexington Books.

Baker, Sarah, and David Hesmondhalgh. 2010. *Creative Labour: Media Work in
    Three Cultural Industries.* London: Routledge.

Ball, Desmond. 1993. "Strategic Culture in the Asia-Pacific Region." *Security
    Studies* 3, no. 1:44–74.

Beason, Richard, and David E. Weinstein. 1996. "Growth, Economies of Scale,
    and Targeting in Japan (1955–1990)." *The Review of Economics and Statistics*
    78, no. 2:286–295.

Beck, Andrew, ed. 2003. *Cultural Work: Understanding the Cultural Industries.*
    Bodmin: Routledge.

Beeson, Mark. 2007. *Regionalism and Globalization in East Asia.* New York:
    Palgrave Macmillan.

Ben-Ari, Eyal. 2000. "Globalization, 'Folk Models' of the World Order and
    National Identity: Japanese Business Expatriates in Singapore." In *Japanese
    Influence and Presences in Asia,* ed. Marie Soderberg and Ian Reader, 51–77.
    London: Curzon.

Berger, Thomas, Mike M. Mochizuki, and Jitsuo Tsuchiyama, eds. 2007. *Japan in
    International Politics: The Foreign Politics of an Adaptive State.* Boulder, Colo.:
    Lynne Rienner Publishers.

Berkeley, Dina. 2003. "Creativity and Economic Transactions in Television
    Drama Production." In *Cultural Work: Understanding the Cultural Industries,*
    ed. Andrew Beck, 103–120. Bodmin: Routledge.

Berry, Chris, Nicola Liscutin, and Jonathan D. Mackintosh, eds. 2009. *Cultural
    Studies and Cultural Industries in Northeast Asia: What a Difference a Region
    Makes.* Hong Kong: University of Hong Kong Press.

Betts, Richard. 1994. "Wealth, Power, and Instability: East Asia and the United
    States after the Cold War." *International Security* 18, no. 4.

Bilton, C., and S. Cummings. 2010. *Creative Strategy: Reconnecting Business and Innovation.* Wiltshire: Wiley-Blackwell.

Blechinger, Verena, and Jochen Legewie. 2000. *Facing Asia-Japan's Role in the Political and Economic Dynamism of Regional Cooperation.* Munich: Iudicium.

Borrie, J. 2005. *Alternative Approaches to Multiculturalism.* Geneva: UNDIR.

Borrus, Michael, Dieter Ernst, and Stephan Haggard, eds. 2000. *International Production Networks in Asia: Rivalry or Riches.* London: Routledge.

Bose, Derek. 2006. *Brand Bollywood: A New Global Entertainment Order.* New Delhi: Sage Publications.

Breslin, Shaun, and Richard Higgot. 2002. *New Regionalisms in the Global Political Economy.* Warwick Studies in Globalisation. London and New York: Routledge.

Bunkachō [Agency for Cultural Affairs]. 2003. *Kongo no Kokusai Bunka Kōryū no Suishin ni tsuite* [About the Future of International Cultural Exchange]. Edited by Kokusai Bunka Kōryū Kondan Kai [International Cultural Exchange Committee]. Tokyo: Bunkachō.

Buzan, Barry. 1998. "The Asia-Pacific: What Sort of Region in What Sort of World?" In *Asia-Pacific in the New World Order,* ed. Anthony McGrew and Brook Christopher. London and New York: Routledge.

Calabrese, Andrew. 2004. "Toward a Political Economy of Culture." In *Toward a Political Economy of Culture: Capitalism and Communication in the Twenty-First Century,* ed. Andrew Calabrese and Colin Sparks, 1–12. Lanham, Md.: Rowman & Littlefield Publishers.

Calder, Kent E. 1993. *Strategic Capitalism: Private Business and Public Purpose in Japanese Industrial Finance.* Princeton, N.J.: Princeton University Press.

Calder, Kent E., and Francis Fukuyama, eds. 2008. *East Asian Multilateralism: Prospects for Regional Stability.* Baltimore: The Johns Hopkins University Press.

Caldwell, John. 2008. *Production Culture: Industrial Reflexivity and Critical Practice in Film and Television.* Durham, N.C.: Duke University Press.

Capel, David. 2004. "The Japanese and Music." *Japan Spotlight* (July–August): 46–47.

Castells, Manuel. 1996. *The Rise of the Network Society.* Cornwall: Blackwell Publishers.

———. 2000a. *End of Millennium.* 2nd ed. Cornwall: Blackwell Publishers.

———. 2000b. "Materials for an Exploratory Theory of the Network Society." *British Journal of Sociology* 1, no. 1:5–24.

Caves, Richard E. 2002. *Creative Industries: Contracts between Art and Commerce.* Cambridge, Mass.: Harvard University Press.

CESA (Computer Entertainment Supplier's Association). 2004. *Gēmu Hakusho* [Games White Paper]. Tokyo: CESA.

Chalaby, K. Jean. 2012. "At the Origin of a Global Industry: The TV Format Trade as an Anglo-American Invention." *Media, Culture & Society* 34, no. 1:36–52.

Chan Hau-Nung, Annie. 2000. "Middle-Class Formation and Consumption in Hong Kong." In *Consumption in Asia: Lifestyles and Identities,* ed. Beng-Huat Chua. London: Routledge.

Ching, Leo. 1996. "Imagining in the Empires of the Sun: Japanese Mass Culture in Asia." In *Contemporary Japan and Popular Culture,* ed. John Whittier Treat. London: Curzon.

Chirathivat, Suthiphand. 2003. "ASEAN's Strategy toward an Increasing Asian Integration." Paper presented at the JSPS-NRCT Workshop on Perspective of Roles of State, Market, Society, and Economic Cooperation in Asia, Kyoto University.

Choo, Kukhee. 2012. "Nationalizing 'Cool': Japan's Global Promotion of the Content Industry." In *Popular Culture and the State in East and Southeast Asia,* ed. Nissim Otmazgin and Eyal Ben-Ari, 85–105. London: Routledge.

Christopherson, Susan, and Danielle Van Jaarsveld. 2005. "New Media after the Dot.Com Bust." *International Journal of Cultural Policy* 11, no. 1:77–93.

Chua, Beng-Huat. 2000. "Consuming Asians: Ideas and Issues." In *Consumption in Asia: Lifestyles and Identities,* ed. Beng-Huat Chua, 1–34. London: Routledge.

———. 2003. *Life Is Not Complete without Shopping: Consumption Culture in Singapore.* Singapore: Singapore University Press.

———. 2004. "Conceptualizing an East Asian Popular Culture." *Inter-Asia Cultural Studies* 4, no. 1:117–125.

Chua, Beng-Huat, and Koichi Iwabuchi, eds. 2008. *East Asian Pop Culture: Analyzing the Korean Wave.* Hong Kong: University of Hong Kong Press.

Clements, Jonathan, and Tamamuro Motoko. 2003. "Introduction." In *The Dorama Encyclopedia: A Guide to Japanese TV Drama since 1953,* ed. Jonathan Clements and Tamamuro Motoko, x–xxix. Berkeley: Stone Bridge Press.

Coggan, Philip. 2003. "Uncle Sam Stands above the Rest." *Financial Times, FT Report- FT 500,* 3.

Condry, Ian. 2013. *The Soul of Anime: Collaborative Creativity and Japan's Media Success Story.* Durham, N.C.: Duke University Press.

Cottle, Simon. 2003. "Media Organization and Production: Mapping the Field." In *Media Organization and Production,* ed. Simon Cottle, 1–24. London: Sage Publications.

Cowhey, Peter F. 1993. "Domestic Institutions and the Credibility of International Commitments: Japan and the United States." *International Organization* 4 (Spring):299–326.

Craig, Timothy J., ed. 2000. *Japan Pop! Inside the World of Japanese Popular Culture.* New York: M. E. Sharpe.

Craig, Timothy J., and Richard King. 2002. *Global Goes Local: Popular Culture in Asia.* Vancouver: UBC Press.

Crone, Donald. 1993. "Does Hegemony Matter? The Reorganization of the Pacific Political Economy." *World Politics* 45:501–525.

Crothers, Lane, and Charles Lockhart. 2000. *Culture and Politics: A Reader.* New York: St. Martin's Press.

Curtin, Michael. 2007. *Playing to the World's Biggest Audience: The Globalization of Chinese Film and TV.* Berkeley: University of California Press.

Daliot-Bul, Michal. 2009. "Japan Brand Strategy: The Taming of 'Cool Japan' and the Challenges of Cultural Planning in a Postmodern Age." *Social Science Japan Journal* 12, no. 3:227–245.

Davoudi, Salamander. 2009. "Pirates on Parade." *Financial Times,* July 22.

Dentsū Communication Institute. 2005. *Jōhō Media Hakusho* [White Paper on Information and Media]. Tokyo: Daiyamondosha.

———. 2009. *Jōhō Media Hakusho* [White Paper on Information and Media]. Tokyo: Daiyamondosha.

Desser, David. 2003. "Consuming Asia: Chinese and Japanese Popular Culture and the American Imagery." In *Multiple Modernities: Cinemas and Popular Media in Transcultural East Asia,* ed. Jenny Kwok Wah Lau, 179–199. Philadelphia: Temple University Press.

Digital Content Association of Japan. 2005. *Dejitaru Kontentsu Hakusho* [Digital Content White Paper]. Tokyo: Japan Ministry of Economy, Trade and Industry.

———. 2009. *Dejitaru Kontentsu Hakusho* [Digital Content White Paper]. Tokyo: Japan Ministry of Economy, Trade and Industry.

Dimitrov, Martin K. 2009. *Piracy and the State: The Politics of Intellectual Property Rights in China.* New York: Cambridge University Press.

Dore, Ronald Philip. 1986. *Flexible Rigidities: Industrial Policy and Structural Adjustment in the Japanese Economy 1970–80.* Stanford, Calif.: Stanford University Press.

Dorfman, Ariel, and Armand Mattelart. 1984. *How to Read Donald Duck: Imperialist Ideology in the Disney Comic.* 2nd ed. New York: International General.

du Gay, Paul, and Michael Pryke, eds. 2002. *Cultural Economy: Cultural Analysis and Commercial Life.* London: Sage Publications.

Emmerson, Donald K. 2000. "Singapore and the 'Asian Values' Debate." In *Culture and Politics: A Reader,* ed. Lane Crothers and Charles Lockhart. New York: St. Martin's Press.

Ernst, Dieter. 2006. "Searching for a New Role in East Asian Regionalization: Japanese Production Networks in the Electronics Industry." In *Beyond Japan: The Dynamics of East Asian Regionalism,* ed. Peter Katzenstein and Takashi Shiraishi, 161–187. Ithaca, N.Y.: Cornell University Press.

Faiola, Anthony. 2003. "Japan's Empire of Cool." *Washington Post Foreign Service.*

Fajes, Fred. 1981. "Media Imperialism: An Assessment." *Media, Culture, and Society* 3, no. 3:281–289.

Fawcett, Louise, and Andrew Hurrell, eds. 1995. *Regionalism in World Politics — Regional Organizations and International Order.* Oxford and New York: Oxford University Press.

Film Industry of Hong Kong. 2006. Available at http://www.info.gov.hk/info/hkin/film.pdf. Accessed April 19, 2006.

Film Service Office Hong Kong. 2004. Available at http://www.fso-tela.gov.hk/index.html. Accessed November 12, 2004.

Frankel, Jeffrey A., and Miles Kahler. 1993. "Introduction." In *Regionalism and Rivalry: Japan and the United States in Pacific Asia,* ed. Jeffrey A. Frankel and Miles Kahler. Chicago: University of Chicago Press.

Frith, Simon. 1991. "Anglo-America and Its Discontents." *Cultural Studies* 5, no. 3:263–269.

———. 1997. "Consumer Culture." In *A Dictionary of Culture and Critical Theory,* ed. Michael Payne. Oxford: Blackwell Publishing.

Frost, Ellen L. 2008. *Asia's New Regionalism.* Boulder, Colo.: Lynne Rienner Publishers.

Fujie, Linda. 1989. "Popular Music." In *Handbook of Japanese Popular Culture,* ed. Richard Gid Powers and Hidetoshi Katō, 197–220. Westport, Conn.: Greenwood Press.

Funabashi, Yoichi. 1993. "The Asianization of Asia." *Foreign Affairs* 72, no. 5:75–85.

Fung, Anthony. 2005. "Marketing a Pop Artist in China: The Case Study of Jay Chow." In *Culture Industry and Cultural Capital Conference.* Hallym University, Seoul.

Gamble, Andrew, and Anthony Payne. 1996. "The New Regionalism." In *Regionalism and World Order,* ed. Andrew Gamble and Anthony Payne. London: Macmillan.

Garnham, Nicholas. 1995. "Political Economy and Cultural Studies: Reconciliation or Divorce?" *Critical Studies in Mass Communication* 12, no. 1:62–72.

———. 2005. "A Personal Intellectual Memoir." *Journal of Media, Culture and Society* 27, no. 4:469–493.

Garon, Sheldon. 2006. "The Transnational Promotion of Saving in Asia: 'Asian Values' or the 'Japanese Model'?" In *The Ambivalent Consumer: Questioning*

Consumption in East Asia and the West, ed. Sheldon Garon and Patricia L. Maclachlan, 163–187. Ithaca, N.Y.: Cornell University Press.

Gibb, Richard, and Wieslaw Michalak. 1994. *Continental Trading Blocs: The Growth of Regionalism in the World Economy*. Chichester; New York: J. Wiley.

Gilpin, Robert. 2001. *Global Political Economy: Understanding the International Economic Order*. Princeton, N.J.: Princeton University Press.

Golding, Peter, and Graham Murdock. 2000. "Culture, Communication and Political Economy." In *Mass Media and Society*, ed. James Curran and Michael Gurevitch. London: Oxford University Press.

Goodman, Grant K. 1991. "Introduction." In *Japanese Cultural Policies in Southeast Asian During World War 2*, ed. Grant K. Goodman, 1–6. London: Macmillan Press.

Gopal, Sangita, and Sujata Moorti. 2010. "Introduction: Travels of Hindi Song and Dance." In *Global Bollywood: Travels of Hindi Song and Dance*, ed. Sangita Gopal and Sujata Moorti. Noida: Orient Blackswan.

Graves, Christopher. 2011. "Cool Is Not Enough." In *Reimagining Japan: The Quest for a Future That Works*, ed. McKinsey & Company, 411–416. San Francisco: VIZ Media, LLC.

Green, Michael J. 2001. *Japan's Reluctant Realism: Foreign Policy Challenges in an Era of Uncertain Power*. 1st ed. New York: Palgrave.

Grieco, Joseph. 1997. "Systemic Sources of Variation in Regional Institutionalization in Western Europe, East Asia, and the Americas." In *The Political Economy of Regionalism*, ed. Edward D. Mansfield and Helen V. Milner. New York: Columbia University Press.

Gripsrud, Jostein. 1998. "High Culture Revisited." In *Cultural Theory and Popular Culture: A Reader*, ed. John Storey, 532–545. London: Prentice Hall.

Grossberg, Lawrence. 1995. "Cultural Studies vs. Political Economy: Is Anybody Else Bored with This Debate?" *Critical Studies in Mass Communication* 12, no. 1:72–95.

Haggard, Stephan. 1997. "The Political Economy of Regionalism in Asia and the Americas." In *The Political Economy of Regionalism*, ed. Edward D. Mansfield and Helen V. Milner. New York: Columbia University Press.

Hakuhōdō News. 2003. http://www.hakuhodo.co.jp. Accessed October 2005.

Hamamura, Hirokazu. 2005. "Trends and the Outlook for Japan's Game Market." *Japan Spotlight*, May–June.

Hamano, Yasuki. 2003. *Hyōgen no Bijinesu* [Business of Content]. Tokyo: Tokyo University Press.

———. 2005. "Current Conditions and Prospects for the Japanese Content Industry." *Japan Spotlight*.

Hamashita, Takeshi. 2008. *China, East Asia and the Global Economy: Regional and Historical Perspectives*. London and New York: Routledge.

Hamelink, Cees. 1983. *Cultural Autonomy in Global Communications*. New York: Longmans.

Haneda, Masashi. 2009. *Asian Port Cities, 1600–1800: Local and Foreign Cultural Interactions*. Honolulu: University of Hawai'i Press.

Hara, Yumiko. 2004. "Nihon Terebi Bangumi no Yushutsunyū Jyōkyō~2001–2nen Icfp Chōsa Kara~" [Import and Export of Japanese Television Programs: Icfp Survey in 2001–2]. In *Nihon wo Koeru Nihon no Terebi Dorama: Sono Toransu Nashonaru na Imi to Eikyō* [Japanese TV Dramas that Go Beyond 'Japan': Their Transnational Significance and Influence]. Tokyo: Japan Media Communication Center.

Hartley, John, ed. 2005. *Creative Industries*. Cornwall: Blackwell Publishing.

Harvie, Charles, Fukunari Kimura, and Hyun-Hoon Lee, eds. 2005. *New East Asian Regionalism: Causes, Progress and Country Perspectives*. Cornwall: Edward Elgar Publishing Limited.

Hass, Ernest. 1973. "The Study of Regional Integration: Reflecting on the Joy and Anguish of Pretheorizing." In *Regional Politics and World Order*, ed. Richard Falk and Saul Mendlovitz. San Francisco: W. H. Freeman and Company.

Hatch, Walter, and Kozo Yamamura. 1996. *Asia in Japan's Embrace: Building a Regional Production Alliance*. Hong Kong: Cambridge University Press.

Hattori, Tamio, Tsuruyo Funatsu, and Takashi Torii. 2002. *Ajia Chūkansō no Seisei to Tokushitsu* [The Emergence and Features of the Asian Middle Classes]. Tokyo: Ajia Keizai Kenkyū sho.

Hau, Caroline S., and Takashi Shiraishi. 2013. "Regional Contexts of Cooperation and Collaboration in Hong Kong Cinema." In *Popular Culture Co-Productions and Collaborations in East and Southeast Asia*, ed. Nissim Otmazgin and Eyal Ben-Ari, 68–96. Singapore: National University of Singapore Press and Kyoto University Press.

Havens, Thomas. 1987. "Government and the Arts in Contemporary Japan." In *The Patron State: Government and Arts in Europe, North America, and Japan*, ed. Milton C. Cummings, Jr., and Richard Katzenstein. New York: Oxford University Press.

Heng, Teow. 1999. *Japanese Cultural Policy toward China—1918–1931: A Comparative Approach*. Cambridge, Mass.: Harvard University Press Asia Center.

Herman, Edward S., and Robert Waterman McChesney. 1997. *The Global Media: The New Missionaries of Corporate Capitalism*. London; Washington, D.C.: Cassell.

Hesmondhalgh, David. 2002. *The Cultural Industries*. Wiltshire: Sage Publications.

Hettne, Björn. 2005. "Beyond 'New' Regionalism." *New Political Economy* 10, no. 4:543–571.

Hettne, Björn, Inotai András, and Shukle Osvaldo, eds. 1999. *Globalization and the New Regionalism*. Hampshire: Palgrave Macmillan Press.

Higgott, Richard. 1998. "The Pacific and Beyond: APEC, ASEM and Regional Economic Management." In *Economic Dynamism in the Asia Pacific: The Growth of Integration and Competitiveness*, ed. Grahame Thompson, 319–337. UK: Routledge.

Hjorth, Larissa. 2009. "Imaging Communities: Gendered Mobile Media in the Asia-Pacific." *The Asia-Pacific Journal* 9, no. 3.

Holt, Jennifer, and Alisa Perren, eds. 2009. *Media Industries: History, Theory, and Method*. Singapore: Wiley-Blackwell.

Hu, G. Tze-Yue. 2010. *Frames of Anime: Culture and Image-Building*. Hong Kong: University of Hong Kong Press.

Hu, Kelly. 2004. "Chinese Re-Makings of Pirated VCDs of Japanese TV Dramas." In *Feeling Asian Modernities: Transnational Consumption of Japanese TV Dramas*, ed. Koichi Iwabuchi, 205–226. Hong Kong: University of Hong Kong Press.

———. 2013. "Chinese Subtitle Groups and the Neoliberal Work Ethic." In *Popular Culture Co-productions and Collaborations in East and Southeast Asia*, ed. Nissim Otmazgin and Eyal Ben-Ari, 207–232. Singapore: National University of Singapore Press.

Huntington, Samuel P. 1993. "The Clash of Civilizations?" *Foreign Affairs* 72, no. 3:22–49.

Hurrell, Andrew. 1995. "Regionalism in Theoretical Perspective." In *Regionalism in World Politics—Regional Organizations and International Order*, ed. Louise Fawcett and Andrew Hurrell, 37–73. Oxford: Oxford University Press.

Industrial Reports. 2004. *Japan's Music Industry*. Tokyo: Japan External Trade Organization. http://www.jetro.go.jp/en/market/trend/industrial/pdf/jem0406-2e.pdf.

Inoguchi, Takashi. 2002. "Japan Goes Regional." In *Japan's Asian Policy*, ed. Takashi Inoguchi. New York: Palgrave Macmillan.

Inoue, Takako. 2010. *Ajia no Popyurā Ongaku: Gurōbaru to Rōkaru no Sōkoku* [Asia's Popular Music: Global and Local Conflict]. Tokyo: Keisō Shobō.

International Federation of Phonogram and Videogram Producers. 2000–2002. "The Recording Industry in Numbers: Statistics Yearbook.

———. 2002. "Music Piracy Report." http://www.ifpi.org.

Ishii, Ken'ichi. 2001. *Higashi Ajia no Nihon Taishū Bunka* [Japanese Mass Culture in East Asia]. Tokyo: Sōsōsha.

Itō, Kinko. 2008. "Manga in Japanese History." In *Japanese Visual Culture: Exploration in the World of Manga and Anime*, ed. Mark W. MacWilliams, 26–47. New York: M. E. Sharpe.

Iwabuchi, Kōichi. 1998. "Marketing 'Japan': Japanese Cultural Presence under a Global Gaze." *Japanese Studies* 18, no. 2:165–180.

———. 1999. "Returning to Asia?: Japan in Asian Audiovisual Markets." In *Consuming Ethnicity and Nationalism,* ed. Kōsaku Yoshino. London: Cruzon Press.

———. 2001. "Uses of Japanese Popular Culture: Trans/Nationalism and Postcolonial Desire for 'Asia.'" *Emergences* 11, no. 2:199–222.

———. 2002. *Recentering Globalization.* Durham, N.C.: Duke University Press.

———, ed. 2004. *Feeling Asian Modernities: Transnational Consumption of Japanese TV Dramas.* Hong Kong: University of Hong Kong Press.

Jamalunlaili, Abdulla. 2004. "Economic Growth, Migration and Suburbanization of Kuala Lumpur Metropolitan Area, Malaysia." Paper presented in the Core University Workshop on Middle Classes in East Asia, Kyoto University, October 6–8.

Japan Foundation. 2003. *Aratata na Jidai no Gaikō to Kokusai Kōryū no Aratatana Yakuwari* [Diplomacy in a New Era and a New Role for International Exchange]. Tokyo: International Exchange Research Group.

———. 2011. *Kaigai no Nihongo Kyōiku no Genjō: Nihongo Kyōiku Kikan Chōsa 2009* [Present Condition of Overseas Japanese-Language Education: Survey Report on Japanese-Language Education Abroad 2009]. Tokyo: The Japan Foundation.

Japan Media Communication Center (JAMCO). 2004. "*Nihon no Terebi Bangumi no Yushutsunyū jōtai ~2002*" [The Export and Import of Japanese Television Programs until 2002]. Available at http://www.Jamco.org.jp.

Japan Ministry of Finance, Custom Tariff Bureau. 1988–2004. "Trade and Statistics." Compiled by Nissim Otmazgin.

Japan Ministry of Foreign Affairs. 2002. *ASEAN ni Okeru Tai-Nichi Yoron Chōsa* [Public Opinion Polls in ASEAN Regarding Japan]. http://www.mofa.go.jp/mofaj/area/asean/yoron.html. Accessed August 14, 2002.

———. 2006a. *Heisei 17nendo Kaigai Zairyū Hōjin sū Toukei Chōsa* [2006 Statistics of the Number of Japanese Residents Abroad]. http://www.mofa.go.jp/mofaj/toko/tokei/hojin/index.html. Accessed August 14, 2006.

———. 2006b. *Kankoku Seifu ni yoru Nihon Bunka Kaihō Seisaku* [The South Korean Government's Openness toward Japanese Culture]. http://www.mofa.go.jp/mofaj/area/korea/bunka. Accessed May 6, 2006.

JETRO (Japan External Trade Organization). 2001. *Hakusho* [White Paper]. http://www.jetro.go.jp/en/.

———. 2002. *Hakusho* [White Paper].

———. 2003. "Conditions and Prospects of US-Anime Market." http://www.jetro.go.jp/en/. Accessed February 14, 2004.

———. 2004a. "Focus: Gross National Cool." http://www.jetro.go.jp/en/. Accessed February 14, 2004.

————. 2004b. "Japan's Music Industry." Industrial Reports. Available at http://www.jetro.go.jp/en/market/trend/industrial/pdf/jem0406–2e.pdf. Accessed February 9, 2005.

————. 2005. "Japanese Film Industry," Industrial Reports. Available at http://www.jetro.go.jp/en/market/trend/industrial/pdf/jem0505–2e.pdf. Accessed November 14, 2005.

————. 2006. *Hakusho* [White Paper].

————. 2007. "'Japan Cool' rises in Global Importance and Significance." *Focus Newsletter* (May) http://www.jetro.org/documents/focus/JETRO_Focus_May2007.pdf.

————. 2009. *Hakusho* [White Paper].

————. 2011. *Beikoku ni Okeru Kontentsu Shijō* [America's Content Market], Tokyo.

Jin, Yong Dal, and Dong-Hoo Lee. 2007. "The Birth of East Asia: Cultural Regionalization through Co-Production Strategies." *Spectator* 72, no. 2:31–45.

Johnson, Chalmers. 1982. *MITI and the Japanese Miracle: The Growth of Industrial Policy, 1925–1975*. Stanford, Calif.: Stanford University Press.

————. 1986. "The Institutional Foundation of Japanese Industrial Policy." In *The Politics of Industrial Policy*, ed. Claude E. Barfield and William A. Schambra, 187–205. Washington: American Enterprise Institute.

Johnston, Alastair Iain. 2003. "Socialization in International Institutions: The ASEAN Way and International Relations Theory." In *International Relations Theory and the Asia Pacific*, ed. John G. Ikenberry and Michael Mastanduno, 107–162. New York: Columbia University Press.

Jones, David Martin. 1997. *Political Development in Pacific Asia*. Cambridge, UK; Malden, Mass.: Polity Press; Blackwell.

Jones, David Martin, and Michael L. R. Smith. 2007. "Constructing Communities: The Curious Case of East Asian Regionalism." *Review of International Studies* 33, no. 1:165–186.

Jones, Mike. 2003. "The Music Industry as Workplace: An Approach to Analysis." In *Cultural Work: Understanding the Cultural Industries*, ed. Andrew Beck, 147–156. Bodmin: Routledge.

Kahler, Miles. 1995. *Institutions and the Political Economy of Integration*. Washington D.C.: Brookings Institution.

Kahn, B. Winston. 1999. "Changing Attitudes toward Cultural Interaction in Postwar Japan." *Asia-Pacific Review* 6, no. 2:65–77.

Kanno, Tomoko. 2000. *Suki Ni Natte ha Ikenai Kuni: Kankoku J-Pop Sedai ga Mita Nihon* [The Country That I Don't Like: Japan as Seen from Young Fans of J-Pop]. Tokyo: Nihon Bungei Shunjū.

Katzenstein, Peter J. 1997. "Introduction: Asian Regionalism in Comparative Perspective." In *Network Power: Japan and Asia*, ed. Peter Katzenstein and Takashi Shiraishi, 1–44. Ithaca, N.Y.: Cornell University Press.

———. 2002. "Variations of Asian Regionalism." In *Asian Regionalism*, ed. Peter J. Katzenstein et al. Ithaca, N.Y.: Cornell University East Asia Program.

———. 2005. *A World of Regions: Asia and Europe in the American Imperium.* Cornell Studies in Political Economy. Ithaca, N.Y.: Cornell University Press.

———. 2006. "East Asia—Beyond Japan." In *Beyond Japan: The Dynamics of East Asian Regionalism*, ed. Peter Katzenstein and Takashi Shiraishi, 1–33. Ithaca, N.Y.: Cornell University Press.

Katzenstein, Peter, and Takashi Shiraishi, eds. 1997. *Network Power: Japan and Asia.* Ithaca, N.Y.: Cornell University Press.

———. 2006. *Beyond Japan: The Dynamics of East Asian Regionalism.* Ithaca, N.Y.: Cornell University Press.

Kavalski, Emilian. 2009. "'Do as I Do': The Global Politics of China's Regionalization." In *China and the Global Politics of Regionalization*, ed. Emilian Kavalski, 1–16. Surrey, Burlington: Ashgate.

Keane, Michael. 2002. "Television Drama in China: Engineering Souls for the Market." In *Global Goes Local: Popular Culture in Asia*, ed. Timothy J. Craig and Richard King, 120–137. Canada: UBC Press.

———. 2006. "Once Were Peripheral: Creating Media Capacity in East Asia." *Media, Culture & Society* 26, no. 6:835–855.

———. 2007. *Created in China: The Great New Leap Forward. Media, Culture and Social Change in Asia.* London; New York: Routledge.

Kelts, Roland. 2007. *Japanamerica: How Japanese Pop Culture Has Invaded the U.S.* New York: Palgrave Macmillan.

Kim, Ho Jung. 2004. "The 'Asian Values' Debate and New East Asian Democratic Values." *Journal of Political Science and Sociology* 2:13–32.

Kim Hyun-Mee. 2004. "Kankoku ni okeru Nihon Taishū Bunka no Juyō to Fan-Ishiki no Keisei." [The Acceptance of Japanese Mass Culture in South Korean and the Construction of Fun's Consciousness]. In *Nisshiki Kanryū: 'Fuyu no Sonata' to Nikkan Taishū Bunka no Genzai* [Japanese Style, Korean Boom: 'Winter Sonata' and Current Japanese-Korean Mass Cultural Relations], ed. Mōri Yoshitaka. Tokyo: Serika Shobō.

Kim, Seung-kuk. 2000. "Changing Lifestyles and Consumption Patterns of the South Korean Middle Class and New Generations." In *Consumption in Asia: Lifestyles and Identities*, ed. Beng-Huat Chua. London: Routledge.

Kim Sowon. 2011. *Nikkan Shōjo Manga no Hikaku: Junjō Manga no Seiritsu to Tenkai o Chūshin ni* [A comparison of Japanese and Korean comics for girls with a special focus on the emergence and evolution of *sunjeong manhuwa*]. PhD thesis, Ritsumeikan University, Kyoto.

Kim, Yung Duk. 2005. "Kankoku ni okeru Nihon Hōsō Kontentsu no Ryūtsū to sono Ukeire" [Japanese Broadcasting Contents' Flow and Acceptance in South Korea]. Unpublished manuscript. Seoul: Korean Broadcasting Institute.

King, Victor T. 2008. "The Middle Class in Southeast Asia: Diversities, Identities, Comparisons and the Vietnamese Case." *International Journal of Asia Pacific Studies* 4, no. 2:75–112.

Kinniya, Yau Shuk-Ting. 2009. "The Early Development of East Asian Cinema in a Regional Context." *Asian Studies Review* 33 (June):161–173.

Kinsella, Sharon. 2000. *Adult Manga: Culture and Power in Contemporary Japanese Society.* Richmond, Surrey: Curzon Press.

Kishimoto, Shūhei. 2001. "Ajia Kinyū Senryaku no Tenkai: Shin-Miyazawa Kōsō wo Koeta Hōkatsu-teki Shien ha Jitsugen Surunoka" [Development of Asian Financial Strategy: Carry out Comprehension over the New Miyazawa Initiative?]. In *Ajia Seiji-Keizairon: Ajia no Naka no Nihon wo Mezashite* [Political-Economic Theory of Asia: Aiming for Japan within Asia], ed. Suehiro Akira and Yamakage Susumu. Tokyo: NTT.

Kohari, Susumu. 2005. "Kankoku ni okeru Tai-Nichi Rekishi Ninshiki Mondai," [Problems in the Historical Perception of Japan in South Korea]. *Kokusai Mondai* 549 (December):21–45.

Kozuka, Sōichirō. 2008. *Dejitaru Kontentsu Hō no Paradaimu* [The Paradigm of Digital Content Law]. Tokyo: IP Research Center.

Kumagai, Shin'ichirō. 2006. *Han-Nichi toha Nanika Chūgoku-jin Katsudōka ha Kataru* [What Is "Anti-Japanese": Talks with Chinese Activists]. Tokyo: Chūō Kōron Shinsha.

Kurian, George T. 2002. *Dictionary of World Politics.* Washington: CQ Press.

Lam, Peng Er. 2007. "Fukuda Dokutorin Sanju-Shūnen to Nihon ASEAN Kankei" [30th Anniversary of the Fukuda Doctrine and Japan-ASEAN Relations]. *Kokusai Mondai* [Issues of International Relations] 565 (October).

Lebra, Joyce C. 1975. *Japan's Greater East Asia Co-Prosperity Sphere in World War II: Selected Readings and Documents.* Kuala Lumpur: Oxford University Press.

Lee Dong-Hoo. 2004. "Cultural Contact with Japanese TV Dramas: Modes of Reception and Narrative Transparency." In *Feeling Asian Modernities: Transnational Consumption of Japanese Television Dramas,* ed. Kōichi Iwabuchi, 251–274. Hong Kong: University of Hong Kong Press.

———. 2008. "Popular Cultural Capital and Cultural Identity: Young Korean Women's Cultural Appropriation of Japanese TV Dramas." In *East Asian Pop Culture: Analyzing the Korean Wave,* ed. Beng-Huat Chua and Koichi Iwabuchi, 157–172. Hong Kong: University of Hong Kong Press.

Lee, Keehyeung. 2008. "Mapping out the Cultural Politics of the 'Korean Wave' in Contemporary South Korea." In *East Asian Pop Culture: Analyzing the*

Korean Wave, ed. Beng-Huat Chua and Iwabuchi Kōichi, 175–189. Hong Kong: University of Hong Kong Press.

Lee, Miji. 2010. "Kankoku Seifu ni yoru tai Tōnan Ajia [Kanryū] Shinkō Seisaku Tai, Betonamu no Terebi Dorama: Yūshitsu wo Chūshin ni" [Korean Wave (Haryū) Promotion Policies of the South Korean Government towards Southeast Asia: The Export of Korean Television Dramas to Vietnam and Thailand]. *Southeast Asian Studies* 48, no. 3:265–293.

Lee, Ming-tsung. 2004. "Traveling with Japanese TV Dramas: Cross-Cultural Orientation and Flowing Identification of Contemporary Taiwanese Youth." In *Feeling Asian Modernities: Transnational Consumption of Japanese TV Dramas*, ed. Kōichi Iwabuchi, 129–154. Hong Kong: University of Hong Kong Press.

Leheny, David. 2006. "A Narrow Place to Cross Swords: 'Soft Power' and the Politics of Japanese Popular Culture in East Asia." In *Beyond Japan: The Dynamics of East Asian Regionalism*, ed. Peter J. Katzenstein and Takashi Shiraishi. Ithaca, N.Y.: Cornell University Press.

Leung, Yuk-ming Lisa. 2004. "Ganbaru and its Transcultural Audience: Imaginary and Reality of Japanese TV Dramas in Hong Kong." In *Feeling Asian Modernities: Transnational Consumption of Japanese TV Dramas*, ed. Kōichi Iwabuchi, 89–105. Hong Kong: University of Hong Kong Press.

Lin, Angel, and Shin Dong Kim. 2005. "Transnational Flow of Korean Historical Dramas: Cultural Capital, Cultural Literacies and Transnational Cultural Imageries." In "Cultural Industry and Cultural Capital Conference." Unpublished manuscript. Seoul, Hallym University.

Lincoln, Edward J. 1993. "Japanese Trade and Investment Issues." In *Japan's Emerging Global Role*, ed. Danny Unger and Paul. J. Blackburn. Boulder, Colo.: Lynne Rienner.

———. 2004. *East Asian Economic Regionalism*. New York and Washington: Brookings Institution Press.

Linhart, Sepp. 2009. "Popular Leisure." Edited by Yoshio Sugimoto, 216–235. New York: Cambridge University Press.

Liu, Fu-kuo. 2003. "East Asian Regionalism: Theoretical Perspectives." In *Regionalization in East-Asia: Paradigm Shifting?*, ed. Liu Fu-kuo and Philippe Régnier, 3–29. London: Routledge Curzon.

Liu, Fu-kuo, and Philippe Régnier. 2003. "Prologue: Whither Regionalism in East Asia?" In *Regionalization in East-Asia: Paradigm Shifting?*, ed. Liu Fu-kuo and Philippe Régnier. London: Routledge Curzon.

Lo, Kwai-Cheung. 2012. "Manipulating Historical Tensions in East Asian Popular Culture." In *Popular Culture and the State in East and Southeast Asia*, ed. Nissim Otmazgin and Eyal Ben-Ari, 177–190. London: Routledge.

Low, Morris. 2009. "Technological Culture." In *The Cambridge Companion to Modern Japanese Culture*, ed. Yoshio Sugimoto, 130–146. New York: Cambridge University Press.

Mahbubani, Kishore. 1995. "The Pacific Way." *Foreign Affairs* 74:100–111.

Mansfield, Edward D., and Helen V. Milner. 1997. "The Political Economy of Regionalism: An Overview." In *The Political Economy of Regionalism*, ed. Edward D. Mansfield and Helen V. Milner, 1–19. New York: Columbia University Press.

Martinez, Dolores P., ed. 1998. *The Worlds of Japanese Popular Culture: Gender, Shifting Boundaries and Global Cultures*. Shanghai: Cambridge University Press.

Mayall, James. 1995. "National Identity and the Revival of Regionalism." In *Regionalism in World Politics—Regional Organizations and International Order*, ed. Louise Fawcett and Andrew Hurrell. Oxford: Oxford University Press.

Mayer, Vicky, Miranda J. Banks, and John T. Caldwell. 2009. *Production Studies: Cultural Studies of Media Industries*. London and New York: Routledge.

McChesney, Robert. 1999. *Rich Media, Poor Democracy*. Urbana and Chicago: University of Illinois Press.

McGray, Douglas. 2002. "Japan's Gross National Cool." *Foreign Policy* (May–June):44–54.

McQuail, Denis. 1994. *Mass Communication Theory: An Introduction*. 3rd ed. London: Sage.

Mehta, Suketu. 2005. "Welcome to Bollywood." *National Geographic* 207, no. 2:52–69.

Mertha, Andrew. 2005. *The Politics of Piracy: Intellectual Property in Contemporary China*. Ithaca, N.Y.: Cornell University Press.

METI (Japan Ministry of Economy, Trade and Industry). 1993. *Maruchi media hakusho* [Multimedia White Paper]. Tokyo.

———. 2002. *Kontentsu Sangyō no Jōtai to Kadai* [Challenges and Prospects for the Content Industrial Policy]. Edited by the Media and Content Industry Division, Commerce and Information Policy Bureau, Contents Distribution Promotion Committee.

———. 2003. *Chūkan Torimatome* [Mid-Term Report]. In International Strategy Study Group.

———. 2004. "Focus: Gross National Cool." Available from http://www.jetro.go.jp/en/. Accessed in February 14, 2004.

Milner, Helen V. 1998. "Regional Economic Cooperation, Global Markets and Domestic Politics: A Comparison of NAFTA and the Maastricht Treaty." In *Regional and Global Economic Integration*, ed. William Coleman and Geoffry Underhill. London: Routledge.

Mitani, Taichirō. 2004. "The Idea of a Regionalism: The Case of Modern Japan." *Review of Asian and Pacific Studies* 26:35–49.

Mitsui, Tōru, and Shūhei Hosokawa, eds. 1998. *Karaoke around the World: Global Technology, Local Singing.* London: Routledge.

Mittelman, James H. 1996. "Rethinking the 'New Regionalization' in the Context of Globalization." *Global Governance* 2:189–213.

Moeran, Brian. 2000. "Commodities, Culture and Japan's Corollanization of Asia." In *Japanese Influence and Presences in Asia,* ed. Marie Soderberg and Ian Reader, 25–50. London: Curzon.

Mohamad, Mahathir, and Shintarō Ishihara. 1995. *The New Voice of Asia: Two Leaders Discuss the Coming Century.* Tokyo and New York: Kōdansha International.

Moran, Albert. 2008. "Makeover on the Move: Global Television and Programme Formats." *Journal of Media & Cultural Studies* 22, no. 4:459–469.

Mōri, Yoshitaka, ed. 2004. *Nisshiki Kanryū: 'Fuyu no Sonata' to Nikkan Taishū Bunka no Genzai* [Japanese Style, Korean Boom: 'Winter Sonata' and Current Japanese-Korean Mass Cultural Relations]. Japan: Serika Shobō.

———. 2009. "J-Pop: From the Ideology of Creativity to DiY Music Culture." *Inter-Asia Cultural Studies* 10, no. 4:498–512.

Mosco, Vincent. 1996. *The Political Economy of Communication: Rethinking and Renewal.* London: Sage.

———. 1999. "New York.Com: A Political Economy of the 'Informational' City." *The Journal of Media Economics* 12, no. 2:103–116.

Motion Picture Producers Association of Japan. 2010. "Statistics of Film Industry in Japan 1955–1999." Available at http://www.eiren.org/statistics_e/index.html.

Mulcahy, Kevin V. 2006. "Cultural Policy: Definitions and Theoretical Approaches." *The Journal of Management, Law, and Society* 35, no. 4:319–330.

Munakata, Naoko. 2006. *Transforming East Asia: The Evolution of Regional Economic Integration.* Tokyo and Washington, D.C.: Brookings Institution Press.

Nabers, Dirk. 2003. "The Social Construction of International Institutions: The Case of ASEAN + 3." *International Relations of the Asia Pacific* 3:132–133.

Nakamura, Ichiya. 2003. "Japanese Pop Industry." In Stanford Japan Center Discussion Papers, November 22. http://www.stanford-jc.or.jp/research/publication/DP/pdf/DP2003_002_E.pdf. Accessed on July 10, 2005.

———. 2004. "Poppu Karuchā Seisaku Gairon" [Introduction to Pop Culture Policy]. In Stanford Japan Center Discussion Papers, February. http://www.ppp.am/p-project/english/paper/nakamura.pdf. Accessed on July 10, 2005.

Napoli, Philip M. 2009. "Media Economics and the Study of Media Industries." In *Media Industries: History, Theory, and Method,* ed. Jennifer Holt and Alisa Perren, 161–170. Singapore: Wiley-Blackwell.

Narine, Shaun. 2002. *Explaining ASEAN: Regionalism in Southeast Asia.* Boulder, Colo.: Lynne Rienner Publishers.

Negus, Keith. 1992. *Producing Pop: Culture and Conflict in the Popular Music Industry.* London: Edward Arnold.

Negus, Keith, and Michael Pickering. 2004. *Creativity, Communication and Cultural Value.* London: Sage.

Ng, Francis, and Alexander Yeats. 2003. "Major Trade Trends in East Asia: What Are Their Implications for Regional Cooperation and Growth?" In Policy Research Working Paper: The World Bank Development Research Group.

Ng, Wai-ming Benjamin. 2004. "The Impact of the Japanese TV Dramas on Hong Kong TV Dramas." In The 8th Asian Studies Conference. Tokyo: Sophia University.

Nihon Gakusei Shien Kikou [Japan's Student Services Organization]. 2011. *Ryūgakusei Ukeire no Gaikyō* [Prospect of Receiving Students]. http://www.jasso.go.jp. Accessed August 17, 2006.

Nomura Sōgō Kenkyū Sho [Nomura Research Institute]. 2005a. "Arata na Konsyūmā-tachi no Pawā: Otaku Shijō wo Saguru" [The New Power of Consumers: Visit the *Otaku* Market]. Tokyo: Nomura Sōgō Kenkyū Sho [Nomura Research Institute].

———. 2005b. "*Otaku Shijō no Kenkyū*" [Research on the *Otaku* Market]. Tokyo: Nomura Sōgō Kenkyū Sho [Nomura Research Institute].

Norris, Craig. 2009. "Manga, Anime and Visual Art Culture." In *The Cambridge Companion to Modern Japanese Culture,* ed. Yoshio Sugimoto, 236–260. New York: Cambridge University Press.

Nye, Joseph S. Jr. 1990. *Bound to Lead: The Changing Nature of American Power.* New York: Basic Books.

———. 2004a. *Soft Power: The Means to Success in World Politics.* New York: Public Affairs.

———. 2004b. "Nihon no Sofuto Pawā: Sono Genkai to Kanōsei" [Japan's Soft Power: Its Limits and Possibilities]. *Gaikō Fōramu* (June).

———. 2008. "Foreword." In *Soft Power Superpowers: Cultural and National Assets of Japan and the United States,* ed. Watanabe Yasushi and David L. McConnell. New York: M. E. Sharpe.

Ogura, Kazuo. 1999. "Creating a New Asia." *Japan Echo* 26, no. 3:12–16.

Okuno, Takuji. 2004. *Nihon-hatsu Itto Kakumei* [Japanese IT Revolution]. Tokyo: Iwanami.

Oman, Charles. 1994. *Globalization and Regionalisation: The Challenge for Developing Countries.* Development Centre Studies. Paris, France: Development Centre of the Organization for Economic Co-operation and Development.

Onouchi, Megumi. 2005. "The Impact of Digital Distribution on the Japanese Music Market." *Japan Spotlight.* May/June: 22–23.

Orr, Gordon, Brian Salsberg, and Naoyuki Iwatani. 2011. "Japan's Globalization Imperative." In *Reimagining Japan: The Quest for a Future That Works,* ed. McKinsey & Company, 150–160. San Francisco: VIZ Media, LLC.

Ōta Tōru. 2004. "Producing (Post-) Trendy Japanese TV Dramas." In *Feeling Asian Modernities: Transnational Consumption of Japanese TV Dramas,* ed. Kōichi Iwabuchi, 69–86. Hong Kong: University of Hong Kong Press.

Ōtake, Akiko, and Shūhei Hosokawa. 1998. "Karaoke in East Asia: Modernization, Japanization, or Asianization?" In *Karaoke around the World: Global Technology, Local Singing,* ed. Shūhei Hosokawa and Tōru Mitsui. London: Routledge.

Otmazgin, Nissim. 2005. "Cultural Commodities and Regionalization in East Asia." *Contemporary Southeast Asia* 27, no. 3:449–523.

———. 2008a. "Contesting Soft Power: Japanese Popular Culture in East and Southeast Asia." *International Relations of the Asia-Pacific* 8:73–101.

———. 2008b. "Japanese Popular Culture in East and Southeast Asia: A Time for a Regional Paradigm?" *The Asia Pacific Journal: Japan Focus,* February 8. http://japanfocus.org/-Nissim_Kadosh-Otmazgin/2660.

———. 2011a. "A Tail That Wags the Dog? Cultural Industry and Cultural Policy in Japan and South Korea." *Journal of Comparative Policy Analysis: Research and Practice* 13, no. 3:307–325.

———. 2011b. "Commodifying Asian-ness: Entrepreneurship and the Making of East Asian Popular Culture." *Media, Culture & Society* 33, no. 2:259–274.

Otmazgin, Nissim, and Eyal Ben-Ari. 2012. "Cultural Industries and the State in East and Southeast Asia." In *Popular Culture and the State in East and Southeast Asia,* ed. Nissim Otmazgin and Eyal Ben-Ari, 3–26. London: Routledge.

———. 2013. "Introduction: History and Theory in the Study of Cultural Collaborations." In *Popular Culture Co-productions and Collaborations in East and Southeast Asia,* ed. Nissim Otmazgin and Eyal Ben-Ari, 1–25. Singapore: National University of Singapore Press and Kyoto University Press.

Ozawa, Terutomo. 1979. *Multinationalism, Japanese Style: The Political Economy of Outward Dependency.* Princeton, N.J.: Princeton University Press.

Pack, Soyon. 2004. "Intānetto ni okeru Nihon Dorama Ryūtsū to Fan no Bunka Jissen" [The Flow of Japanese Dramas in the Internet and the Reciprocity of the Funs]. In *Nisshiki Kanryū: "Fuyu no Sonata" to Nikkan Taishū Bunka no Genzai* [Japanese Style, Korean Boom: "Winter Sonata" and Current

Japanese-Korean Mass Cultural Relations], ed. Mōri Yoshitaka, 203–229. Tokyo: Serika Shobō.

Pang, Laikwan. 2006. *Cultural Control and Globalization in Asia: Copyright, Piracy, and Cinema*. Abingdon: Routledge.

Patten, Fred. 2004. *Watching Anime, Reading Manga: 25 Years of Essays and Reviews*. Berkeley, Calif.: Stone Bridge Press.

Payne, Michael, ed. 1996. *A Dictionary of Cultural and Critical Theory*. Cornwall: Blackwell Publishing.

Peck, Janice. 2006. "Why We Should Not Be Bored with the Political Economy Versus Cultural Studies Debate." *Critical Studies* 64 (Fall):92–126.

Pempel, T. J. 2005. *Remapping East Asia: The Construction of a Region*. Edited by T. J. Pempel. Ithaca, N.Y.: Cornell University Press.

Petri, Peter A. 1993. "The East Asian Trading Bloc: An Analytical History." In *Regionalism and Rivalry: Japan and the United States in Pacific Asia*, ed. Jeffrey A. Frankel and Miles Kahler, 21–48. Chicago: University of Chicago Press.

Pettman, Ralph. 1999. "Globalism and Regionalism: The Cost of Dichotomy." In *Globalism and the New Regionalism*, ed. Björn Hettne, András Inotai, and Osvaldo Sunkel. London: Macmillan Press.

Pink, Daniel H. 2007. "Japan Ink: Inside the Manga Industrial Complex." *Wired*, no. 15 (November).

Poitras, Gilles. 2008. "Contemporary Anime in Japanese Pop Culture." In *Japanese Visual Culture: Exploration in the World of Manga and Anime*, ed. Mark W. MacWilliams, 48–67. New York: M. E. Sharpe.

Pope, Edgar. 2012. "Importing Others: American Influences and Exoticism in Japanese Interwar Popular Music." *Inter-Asia Cultural Studies* 13, no. 4:507–517.

Power, Dominic, and Allen J. Scott. 2004. "A Prelude to Cultural Industries and the Production of Culture." In *Cultural Industries and the Production of Culture*, ed. Dominic Power and Allen J. Scott, 3–15. London and New York: Routledge.

Prime Minister of Japan. 2008. *Official Website*. http://www.kantei.go.jp. Accessed August 14, 2008.

Purnendra, Jain. 2000. "Will the Sun Ever Shine in South Asia?" In *Japanese Influence and Presences in Asia*, ed. Marie Soderberg and Ian Reader. London: Curzon.

Pyle, Kenneth P. 2007. *Japan Rising: The Resurgence of Japanese Power and Purpose*. New York: Public Affairs.

Recording Industry Association of Japan. 2004. Available at http://www.riaj.or.jp/index.html.jp. Accessed November 10, 2004.

Research Institute for Publications. 2009. *Shuppan Shihyō Nenpō 2009* [Publication Index Yearly Report]. Tokyo: Zenkoku Shuppan Kyōkai. A summary report is available from http://www.ajpea.or.jp/statistics/statistics.html.

Richie, Donald. 2003. *The Image Factory: Fads and Fashions in Japan.* London: Reaktion.

Robertson, Ronald. 1991. "Social Theory, Cultural Relativity and the Problem of Globality." In *Cultural Globalization and World Systems,* ed. A. King. London: Macmillan.

Robson, Daniel. 2009. "J-Pop Prepares an Assault on the West in '09." *The Japan Times Online,* February 2.

Ross, Andrew. 2004. *No Collar: The Humane Workforce and Its Hidden Costs.* Philadelphia: Temple University Press.

Rotchild, Nadav. 2011. "From Cheap Comics to National Art: The Image of Manga in Modern Japan." Master Degree thesis, the Hebrew University of Jerusalem.

Roy, Denny. 2003. *Taiwan: A Political History.* Ithaca, N.Y.; London: Cornell University Press.

Ryan, Bill. 1992. *Making Capital from Culture: The Corporate Form of Capitalist Cultural Production.* De Gruyter Studies in Organization 35. Berlin; New York: Walter de Gruyter.

Samuels, Marwyn S. 2012. "Banned in China: The Vagaries of Censorship." In *Popular Culture and the State in East and Southeast Asia,* ed. Nissim Otmazgin and Eyal Ben-Ari, 162–176. London: Routledge.

Sanrio. 2012. Financial Report. Available at http://www.sanrio.co.jp/corporate/index.html. Accessed December 26, 2012.

Sassen, Saskia. 2000. *Cities in a World Economy.* 2nd ed. *Sociology for a New Century.* Thousand Oaks, Calif.: Pine Forge Press.

Satō, Kumiko. 2009. "From Hello Kitty to Cod Roe Kewpie: A Postwar Cultural History of Cuteness in Japan." *Education about Asia* 14, no. 2:38–42.

Schiller, Herbert I. 1976. *Communication and Cultural Domination.* New York: M. E. Sharpe.

Schlesinger, Jacob M. 1997. *Shadow Shoguns: The Rise and Fall of Japan's Postwar Political Machine.* New York: Simon & Schuster.

Scott, David Adam. 2008. "The Japan-Indonesia Economic Partnership: Agreement between Equals?" *The Asia Pacific Journal: Japan Focus,* July 13. http://japanfocus.org/-David_Adam-Stott/2818. Accessed June 22, 2009.

Sedgwick, Mitchell W. 2000. "Japanese Manufacturing in Thailand: An Anthropology Seeking 'Efficient, Standardized Production.' " In *Japanese Influence and Presences in Asia,* ed. Marie Soderberg and Ian Reader. London: Curzon.

Seki, Mitsuhiro. 1994. *Beyond the Full-Set Industrial Structure: Japanese Industry in the New Age of East Asia.* LTCB International Library Selection no. 2. Tokyo, Japan: LTCB International Library Foundation.

Shambauch, David, and Michael Yahuda, eds. 2008. *International Relations of Asia.* Lanham, Md.: Rowman & Littlefield Publishers, Inc.

Shibuichi, Daiki. 2005. "The Yasukuni Shrine Dispute and the Politics of Identity in Japan: Why All the Fuss?" *Asian Survey* 45, no. 2:197–215.

Shim, Doobo. 2008. "The Growth of Korean Cultural Industries and the Korean Wave." In *East Asian Pop Culture: Analyzing the Korean Wave,* ed. Beng-Huat Chua and Kōichi Iwabuchi, 15–31. Hong Kong: University of Hong Kong Press.

———. 2013. "Korean Cinema Industry and Cinema Regionalization in East Asia." In *Popular Culture Co-Productions and Collaborations in East and Southeast Asia,* ed. Nissim Otmazgin and Eyal Ben-Ari, 52–67. Singapore: National University of Singapore Press and Kyoto University Press.

Shimoku, Kio. 2008. *Genshiken Official Book.* New York: Del Rey.

Shin, Hyunjoon. 2007. "K-Pop (Music) in the Emerging Cultural Economy of Asian Pop." *Journal of Communication Arts* 29, no. 4:1–11.

———. 2010. "Kanryū Poppu no Genjō" [The Present Situation of Korean Pop Music]. In *Ajia no Popyurā Ongaku: Gurōbaru to Rōkaru no Sōkoku* [Asia's Popular Music: Global and Local Conflict], ed. Takako Inoue, 49–77. Tokyo: Keisō Shobō.

Shiraishi, Saya. 2000. "Doraemon Goes Abroad." In *Japan Pop! Inside the World of Japanese Popular Culture,* ed. Timothy J. Craig. New York: M. E. Sharpe.

Shiraishi, Takashi. 1997. "Japan and Southeast Asia." In *Network Power: Japan and Asia,* ed. Peter J. Katzenstein and Takashi Shiraishi. Ithaca, N.Y.: Cornell University Press.

———. 2000. *Umi no Teikoku: Ajia wo Dou Kangaeruka* [Sea Empire: Thoughts About Asia]. Tokyo: Chūkō Shinsho.

———. 2005. "East Asian 'Cultural' Market in the Making." *Japan Spotlight,* May–June.

———. 2006. "The Third Wave: Southeast Asia and Middle-Class Formation in the Making of a Region." In *Beyond Japan: The Dynamics of East Asian Regionalism,* ed. Peter Katzenstein and Takashi Shiraishi. Ithaca, N.Y.: Cornell University Press.

Shiraishi, Takashi, and Phongpaichit Pasuk. 2008. In *The Rise of Middle Classes in Southeast Asia.* Kyoto Area Studies on Asia, vol. 17. Melbourne: Kyoto University Press.

Shita, Eiji. 1995. *Nihon Hīrō ha Sekai wo Seisu* [Establishing Japanese Heroes around the World]. Tokyo: Kadokawa Shoten.

Sinclair, John, Elizabeth Jacka, and Stuart Cunningham, eds. 1996. *New Patterns in Global Television: Peripheral Vision.* Oxford: Oxford University Press.

Siriyuvasak, Ubonrat, and Hyunjoon Shin. 2007. "Asianizing K-pop: Production, Consumption and Identification Patterns among Thai Youth." *Inter-Asia Cultural Studies* 8, no. 1:109–136.

Slaymaker, Douglas. 2000. "Popular Culture in Japan: An Introduction." In *A Century of Popular Culture in Japan*, ed. Douglas Slaymaker, 1–16. Lewiston, N.Y.: The Edwin Mellen Press.

Smith, Anthony. 2004. "ASEAN Ninth Summit: Solidifying Regional Cohesion, Advancing External Links." *Contemporary Southeast Asia* 26.

Soderberg, Marie, and Ian Reader, eds. 2000. *Japanese Influence and Presences in Asia*. London: Curzon.

Solingen, Etel. 1996. "Democracy, Economic Reform and Regional Cooperation." *Journal of Theoretical Politics* 8, no. 1:79–114.

Stevens, Carolyn S., and Shūhei Hosokawa. 2001. "So Close and yet So Far: Humanizing Celebrity in Japanese Music Variety Shows, 1960s–1990s." In *Asian Media Productions*, ed. Brian Moeran, 223–245. Honolulu: University of Hawai'i Press.

Stocker, Joel F. 2001. "Yoshimoto Kōgyō and Manzai in Japan's Media Culture: Promoting the Intersection of Production and Consumption." In *Asian Media Productions*, ed. Brian Moeran, 247–269. Honolulu: University of Hawai'i Press.

Storper, Michael. 1994. "The Transition to Flexible Specialisation in the US Film Industry: External Economies, the Division of Labour and the Crossing of Industrial Divides." In *Post-Fordism: A Reader*, ed. Ash Amin, 195–226. Oxford: Blackwell.

Story, John. 1999. *Cultural Consumption and Everyday Life*. London: Curzon.

Sudō, Sueo. 2002. *The International Relations of Japan and Southeast Asia: Forging a New Regionalism*. London: Routledge.

Sugiura, Tsutomu. 2003. "Monetary Value of Japanese Arts and Cultural Products Based on Japan's Ministry of Finance Data." Marubeni Economic Research Institute.

———. 2004. "Japanese Culture on the World Stage." *Journal of Japanese Trade and Industry* (March–April):2.

———. 2008. "Japan's Creative Industries: Culture as a Source of Soft Power in the Industrial Sector." In *Soft Power Superpowers: Cultural and National Assets of Japan and the United States*, ed. Watanabe Yasushi and David L. McConnell, 128–153. New York: M. E. Sharpe.

Suzuki, Sadami. 2005. *Nihon no Bunka Nashonalizumu* [Japan's Cultural Nationalism]. Tokyo: Heibonsha.

Tolentino, Rolando B. 2013. "Niche Globality: Philippine Media Texts to the World." In *Popular Culture Co-Productions and Collaborations in East and*

Southeast Asia, ed. Nissim Otmazgin and Eyal Ben-Ari, 150–168. Singapore: National University of Singapore Press and Kyoto University Press.

Tomlinson, John. 1991. *Cultural Imperialism.* Baltimore: Johns Hopkins University Press.

———. 1997. "Cultural Globalization and Cultural Imperialism." In *International Communication and Globalization: A Critical Introduction,* ed. A. Mohammadi, 170–190. London: Sage.

Torii, Takashi. 2006. "Higashi Ajia Chūkansō no Mittsu no Yakuwari" [East Asia's Middle Class's Three Roles]. In *Higashi Ajia Kyōdōtai wo Sekkei Suru* [Planning an East Asian Community], ed. Eiichi Shindō and Hirakawa Hitoshi, 289–294. Tokyo: Nihon Keizai Hyōronsha.

Torrance, Richard. 2000. "Pre–World War Two Concepts of Popular Culture and Takeda Rintarō's 'Japan's Three Penny Opera.'" In *A Century of Popular Culture in Japan,* ed. Douglas Slaymaker, 17–43. Lewiston, N.Y.: The Edwin Mellen Press.

Treat, John W. 1996. *Contemporary Japan and Popular Culture.* London: Curzon.

Tsunoyama, Sakae. 1995. *Ajia Runessansu* [Asian Renaissance]. Tokyo: PHP Kenkyūsho.

Tsuru, Shigeto. 1993. *Japan's Capitalism: Creative Defeat and Beyond.* Cambridge Economic Policies and Institutions. New York: Cambridge University Press.

Tsutsui, William. 2010a. *Japanese Popular Culture and Globalization.* Ann Arbor, Mich.: Association for Asian Studies, Inc.

———. 2010b. "Japanese Popular Culture and Globalization: An Interview." *Education About Asia* 15, no. 2:53.

Ugaya, Hiromichi. 2005. *J-Poppu toha Nanika Kyodaika suru Ongaku Sangyō* [What Is J-Pop? The Expanding Music Industry]. Tokyo: Iwanami Shinsho.

Urata, Shūjirō. 2003. "The Emergence of New Regionalism in East Asia: A Shift from Market-led to Institution-led Regional Economic Integration in East Asia." Paper presented at the JSPS-NRCT Workshop on Perspective of Roles of State, Market, Society, and Economic Cooperation in Asia, Kyoto University.

Uriu, Robert M. 1996. *Troubled Industries: Confronting Economic Change in Japan.* Ithaca, N.Y.: Cornell University Press.

Vatikiotis, Michael R. J. 1999. "ASEAN 10: The Political and Cultural Dimensions of Southeast Asian Unity." *Southeast Asian Journal of Social Science* 1, no. 1:77–88.

Venturelli, Shalini. 2005. "Culture and the Creative Economy in the Information Age." In *Creative Industries,* ed. John Hartley, 391–398. Cornwall: Blackwell Publishing.

VGCharts. 2010. *Weekly Hardware Charts.* Available at http://www.vgchartz.com. Accessed January 10, 2011.

Watanabe, Yasushi, and David L. McConnell, eds. 2008. *Soft Power Superpowers: Cultural and National Assets of Japan and the United State*. New York: M. E. Sharp.

Weingast, Barry R., and Donald A. Wittman. 2006. "The Reach of Political Economy." In *The Oxford Handbook of Political Economy*, ed. Barry R. Weingast and Donald A. Wittman, 3–25. New York: Oxford University Press.

Wendt, Alexander. 1994. "Collective Identity Formation and the International State." *American Political Science Review* 88, no. 2:384–396.

Wyatt-Walter, Andrew. 1995. "Regionalism, Globalism and World Economic Order." In *Regionalism and World Politics: Regional Organization and International Order*, ed. Louise Fawcett and Andrew Hurrell, 74–121. Oxford: Oxford University Press.

Yamanaka Chie. 2010. "Manga Hyōgen Keishiki no Ekkyō: Kankoku ni okeru Mohō Kaizokuban Manga wo Jirei toshite" [Manga Expression Style over the Border: The Case of Manga Imitation in Korea]. In *Comonzu to Bunka: Bunka ha Dare no Monoka* [Commons and Culture: Culture Belongs to Who?], ed. Shōji Yamada. Tokyo: Tokyo dō.

Yano, Christine R. 2009. "Wink on Pink: Interpreting Japanese Cute as It Grabs the Global Headlines." *The Journal of Asian Studies* 68, no. 3:681–688.

Yim, Haksoon. 2002. "Cultural Identity and Cultural Policy in South Korea." *The International Journal of Cultural Policy* 8, no. 1:37–48.

———. 2003. *The Emergence and Change of Cultural Policy in South Korea*. Seoul: JinHan Books.

Yoda, Tasumi. 2005. "Content Development by a Cross-Industry Organization." *Japan Spotlight* (May–June):10–11.

Yomota, Inuhiko. 2006. *Kawaii Ron* [Theory of Kawaii]. Tokyo: Chikuma Shinsho.

Yoshikawa, Akitoshi. 1991. "Globalization and Restructuring the Japanese Economy." In *Japan, ASEAN and the United States*, ed. H. H. Kendall and Clara Joewono. Berkeley: University of California, Institute of East Asian Studies.

Yoshimatsu, Hidetaka. 2008. *The Political Economy of Regionalism in East Asia: Integrative Explanation for Dynamics and Challenges*. London: Palgrave Macmillan.

Zykas, Aurelijus. 2011. "The Discourses of Popular Culture in 21st Century Japan's Cultural Diplomacy Agenda." In *The Reception of Japanese and Korean Popular Culture in Europe*, ed. Takashi Kitamura, Kyoko Koma, and SanGum Li. Kaunas: Vytautus Magnus University.

INDEX

////////////